◉◉◉◉◉◉◉◉◉◉◉◉◉◉◉◉◉

SOLDIERS
IN THE SUN

◉◉◉◉◉◉◉◉◉◉◉◉◉◉◉◉◉

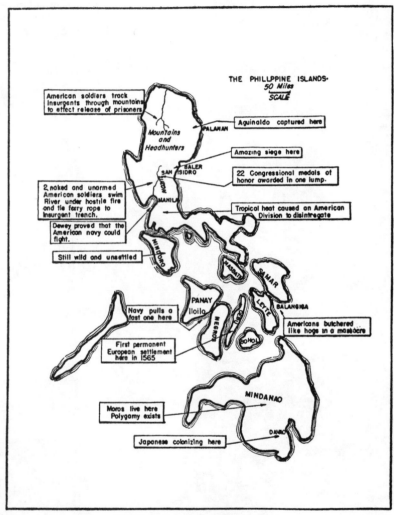

THE PHILIPPINE ISLANDS.
50 Miles
SCALE

American soldiers track insurgents through mountains to effect release of prisoners

Mountains and Headhunters

PALANAN

Aguinaldo captured here

BALER
SAN ISIDRO

Amazing siege here

LUZON

22 Congressional medals of honor awarded in one lump.

2 naked and unarmed American soldiers swim River under hostile fire and tie ferry rope to insurgent trench.

MANILA

Tropical heat caused an American Division to disintregate

Dewey proved that the American navy could fight.

MINDORO

Still wild and unsettled

MASBATE

SAMAR

Navy pulls a fast one here

PANAY
Iloilo

LEYTE
BALANGIGA

NEGROS

CEBU

BOHOL

Americans butchered like hogs in a massacre

First permanent European settlement here in 1565

MINDANAO

Moros live here Polygamy exists

DAVAO

Japanese colonizing here

THE PHILIPPINE ARCHIPELAGO

Contents

Preface

Any opinions expressed in this book are entirely those of the author, which have been reached as a result of his own research on this subject and *must* not be construed as reflecting in any way the thoughts of the Army as a whole or of the War Department in particular.

To My Daughter, Elaine Sexton

Who though only four years of age, loved to sit and watch her daddy "play map." God needed an angel and took her away.

First Published 1939
Reprinted 1971

INTERNATIONAL STANDARD BOOK NUMBER:
0-8369-5638-9

LIBRARY OF CONGRESS CATALOG CARD NUMBER:
70-146872

PRINTED IN THE UNITED STATES OF AMERICA

Soldiers In The Sun

An Adventure in Imperialism

by

William Thaddeus Sexton

BOOKS FOR LIBRARIES PRESS
FREEPORT, NEW YORK

List of Illustrations

INTRODUCTION

THE PURPOSE of this book is twofold: First, it is intended to close a gap which exists in American (and Filipino) history. Many people know that a war was fought in the Philippines nearly forty years ago, but heretofore no one has been able to go to a bookstore or library and obtain a book which would acquaint him with what actually happened. Magazine articles, memoirs and regimental histories have covered many phases of the Insurrection, but nowhere has the subject been covered from beginning to end. In 1916, James Leroy commenced an admirable work on the Philippines which was intended to cover the Insurrection and the early years of American rule, but the completion of the work was cut short by his death. Since that time the writing of a history of the Insurrection has not been attempted despite the laments of numerous participants.

The second purpose of the book is to describe some of the problems incident to the conduct of extended military operations in the tropics—a situation unique in the annals of American history. In 1898 we defeated Spain in war and received as spoils of victory her most prized colonial possession, the Philippine Islands. As a result of the treaty of Paris we blithely accepted sovereignty over ten million human beings living 7000 miles from our shores. We attempted to impose on these people who were of different race, language and social background, our American ideas and principles of government. Then when this normally law abiding race refused to be bought, sold and otherwise disposed of as chattels and opposed by force the assumption of our sovereignty, we found ourselves facing a new and distinct problem. We were compelled to call on the army to take by force what we had intended to gain by mere diplomatic procedure.

As usual and through no fault of its own, the army was caught unprepared. Never before had American troops left the continent of North America, let alone conduct military operations 7000 miles from the United States. Never before had the American army campaigned next the Equator. Never before had it attempted to quell an inspired insurrection of a people who were fighting for their independence.* Never before had an army officer been given supreme dictatorial authority over some 120,000 square miles of American owned territory. Never before had American sovereignty been

---

*With the possible exception of the American Indians.

extended over the polygamous Mohammedans. It was indeed a novel and interesting problem which was put up to the army for solution.

Officers and others who were present in the Philippines at the time and read this book may mentally remark to themselves that the writer has not scratched the surface. Probably they are correct. The justification which this writer can offer for what may be considered culpable omissions of hikes, skirmishes or captures is that if every march, contact, or incident which occurred throughout the Philippine Insurrection were assembled in one volume, no one would read it. Some readers who participated in the Philippine Insurrection or have heard incidents of that unusual war related in vivid detail over the campfire may question the accuracy of some of the material presented herein. To this form of criticism he defends himself on the premise that he has used the best evidence available, namely the Official Reports. These reports were made by the *best authorities on the ground at the time*. Hypercritical participants should also remind themselves that a long lapse of time often plays peculiar tricks on the memory. Of the 125,000 American soldiers who journeyed to the Philippines during the course of the Insurrection, the names of few are mentioned in this book. Such procedure is simply in keeping with the nature of the war. Grand strategy and tactics found little space in looking for a solution to the quelling of the Insurrection. It was the work of enterprising and courageous lieutenants who finally gave the answer. It has often been said that England's wars are won on the playing fields of Eton. If such is true, then the World War was won on the battlefields of the Philippines. A roster of the high command in the American Army during the World War is a roster of the lieutenants who served in the Philippines at the turn of the century. The only practical military experience which the American high command in the World War gained prior to that time was obtained in the Philippine Insurrection. The occupation of the Rhineland in 1919 by the American Army was accomplished with astonishing efficiency. Perhaps the answer lay in the experience which the higher officers had obtained in taking over the civil administration of the Philippine Islands back in 1898. Therefore, the subject is a matter of importance and many lessons can be learned from it.

The idea of this book came to the writer while he was serving a tour of duty in the Philippine Islands in 1931. Numerous monuments scattered throughout the Island of Luzon aroused a curiosity concerning the Insurrection which could not be satisfied in any library. He went over the battlegrounds and interviewed what few insurgent leaders he was able to find, and then using the Official Reports as source material, sat down to write the story purely from the standpoint of one who enjoys reading history and entirely for his own satisfaction. Pressure of normal military duties delayed its completion for nearly nine years, but finally, what started out to be a brief survey, has evolved into the present volume. If it adds to the richness of American history and gives anyone any pleasure in reading, its purpose has been served.

W. T. S.

Fort Leavenworth, Kansas,
Sept. 5, 1939.

Chapter I

BLACK WITH headlines, newspapers April 24, 1898, screamed: *"Congress Declares War," "Landing Made in Cuba," "Dewey to Leave for Manila Bay."* The declaration of war did not come as a surprise. For three years Americans had been conscious of the fact that the Cubans were in revolution against Spain. During the course of that revolt, the dissemination of pro-Cuban propaganda throughout the United States, memories of our own up-hill fight to gain independence, and reports of ruthless methods being used by the Spanish to suppress the revolt, had made the rebellion front page news. In addition, some American statesmen felt that the bloody squabble in which a European power was involved, going on at our back door only eighty miles from Florida, invited American intervention and that the continuation of Spanish sovereignty over Cuba was a definite barrier to American aspirations for turning the Caribbean Sea into an American lake. Further, American "Interests" had some fifty million dollars of American capital invested in the Cuban sugar industry; revolutions which devastated cane fields jeopardized these investments. The American press seized an opportunity for a national crusade, played up "Cuban atrocities," and nourished a growing feeling among the American people that Spain must get out of Cuba.

On February 15, 1898 the battleship *Maine*, having been sent to Cuba on a "friendly" visit, was, while anchored in Havana Harbor, destroyed by a mysterious explosion which cost the lives of 266 Americans. When a month later an investigating board reached the conclusion that the sinking of the *Maine* was the result of an external mine explosion, the anti-Spanish feeling in the United States reached its height. On April 21st, President William McKinley approved a congressional resolution demanding the withdrawal of Spain from Cuba. Spain responded by handing the American minister at Madrid his passports. On the 22d, Cuban ports were declared blockaded, and on the 24th, Spain declared war. The United States replied with a formal declaration on the following day, stating that war had existed since the 21st. The bulk of the American Navy assembled on the Atlantic coast, President McKinley issued a call for 125,000 volunteers, and preparations were made to invade Cuba and eject the Spaniards.

The first battle of the war, however, was not to be fought in Cuba, but in the Far East. Since 1784, when an American sailing ship from Boston had established trade with Chinese merchants at Canton, China, the United States has possessed an ever-increasing commercial stake in the Orient. However, despite a paternal non-aggrandizing policy in regard to the Far East, the United States has maintained an "Asiatic Naval Squadron" there for the protection of her interests and the lives of her citizens.

Spain in 1898 held sovereignty over the Philippine Islands, a rich colony situated some six hundred miles south of Hong Kong, China, and maintained a naval squadron there for its protection. Upon the declaration of war, John D. Long, the Secretary of the Navy, dispatched the following telegram to Commodore George Dewey, in command of the American Asiatic squadron then at Hong Kong, China: [1]

> "War has commenced between the United States and Spain. Proceed at once to the Philippine Islands. Commence operations, particularly against the Spanish fleet. You must capture vessels or destroy. Use utmost endeavor."

How Dewey carried out these instructions is a well-known episode of American history. The Spanish squadron was destroyed May 1, 1898 in the battle of Manila Bay, and the Spanish Naval Base at Cavite occupied by American bluejackets. Brilliant as had been Dewey's victory over the Spanish, he was impotent, however, to carry his success further. His nearest base was on the Pacific coast and, had he been forced to fight another naval engagement, his position would have been precarious.

The city of Manila, resting on the edge of Manila Bay, was occupied by 15,000 Spanish soldiers and contained modern defensive artillery weapons. Even though he might bombard the city and reduce it to a shambles, he could not claim possession until American armed forces actually occupied it. Since he did not have these forces, he had to anchor his squadron and telegraph the Secretary of the Navy that 5000 troops would be necessary to take and hold the city. The occupation and control of the Philippine Islands was henceforth to be essentially an army job.

Obviously the best navy in the world is absolutely useless unless it has bases within its cruising radius. Dewey had won a battle, but

---

[1] Many readers do not care to have their trend of thought interrupted by constant reference to footnotes. At the end of each chapter will be found complete documentation.

had he needed more ammunition or repairs to his ships, the 7000 mile voyage back to the United States would have been his only alternative.

News of Dewey's victory created a wave of enthusiasm in the United States. Although the majority of American citizens and many high in governmental circles were obliged to dig out their atlases and geographies to ascertain just where the Philippine Islands were, a quick decision was made to occupy the Islands as a diversion to the attack on the Spanish troops in Cuba. Also, many "imperialists," who had been disappointed at the aloofness of the United States for not participating in the then impending partition of China, felt that acquisition of the Philippines would compensate for the lack of an aggrandizing policy on the Asiatic mainland. Major General Nelson A. Miles, senior officer in the Army, was called upon for recommendations as to an expeditionary force to the Philippines, and on May 3 recommended that three regiments of volunteers and two battalions of regular infantry, two batteries of volunteer artillery and two troops of regular American cavalry [2] be sent, a total of about 5000 troops, of which approximately four-fifths were to be volunteers. The War Department tentatively accepted General Miles' estimate of the troops necessary, but overrode his suggestion that General Thomas M. Anderson be placed in command and detailed Major General Wesley Merritt, number two ranking officer in the Army.

General Merritt, then in command of the Department of the East (which comprised eastern United States), with Headquarters at Governor's Island, New York, was on May 12 directed to repair to San Francisco and organize the expeditionary troops which were assembling there. A few days later Merritt received from President McKinley a letter of instructions which was in substance as follows: [3]

> "Go to the Philippines, cooperate with the Navy, defeat the Spanish armed forces there, establish order and the sovereignty of the United States. Advise the Filipinos that the United States aims to protect, not fight them; follow existing laws as far as possible; take over public property, the collection of taxes and customs; open the ports to commerce."

Thus was born an enterprise which was to see within the next four years the movement of 126,468 [4] American soldiers and officers to a distant land over 7000 miles from their homes, the death of 4234 [4] while there, the wounding of 2818, [4] armed engagements with an enemy on 2811 occasions, [4] the death of some 16,000 Filipino soldiers

19

in battle, [5] the extinction of some 100,000 Filipino civilians from famine and pestilence, [5] and a cost to the United States of some 600 million dollars. [6] Although the casualties were insignificant when compared with World War figures, the venture marked for the United States its only departure from a policy continuously in existence for over one hundred and twenty-three years.

The leader of the expedition, General Wesley Merritt, was 62 years of age and was held in high regard by the military and civilians alike. With Custer, Sheridan, and McPherson he had been one of the "boy generals" of the Civil War. Graduating from West Point in 1860 he had been brevetted six times for gallantry during the war and by 1865 had risen to the rank of Brevet Major General of Volunteers. During the 1870's he had been one of the Army's leading "Indian Fighters." Although fairly old, his ability was proved and his large fund of experience in all types of warfare, made him an admirable choice for the command of an operation which was bound to be replete with difficulties.

The ignorance of the American people at this time, including those high in the War Department, concerning the Philippine Islands was remarkable. Many Americans had never heard of the Islands until after the battle of Manila Bay. The expedition which went out in '98 was little better off, as is indicated by the statement of Major General Arthur MacArthur, one of the Brigade Commanders, in testifying before a Senate Committee on his return. He said: [7]

> "Aside from high spirits and feelings of self-confidence which actuated all concerned, the distinctive characteristic of the command was absolute ignorance of the Philippine Archipelago in respect to geography, climate, people and the general aspects of nature. There was little or no literature aboard from which instructive information could be obtained. One writer to whom we had access advised all travelers to carry coffins, as few returned alive from Manila."

Command of an expedition which was to move by water some 7000 miles and then invade a strange country garrisoned by hostile troops, placed a heavy responsibility on General Merritt. Apparently he and General Miles were not particularly good friends and despite the obvious difficulties of his mission, he received little response from Miles to his suggestion that the strength of the expeditionary force be increased to 14,400 troops, of which approximately 40% would consist of regular army personnel. Miles considered the expedition to Cuba to be of prime importance. Although he finally increased the Philippine allotment to 12,500, the proportion of regulars to volunteers still remained at his original ratio of about five to one. Finally on May 17, Merritt complained directly to the War Department as follows: [8]

> "I consider the composition of the force outlined by the Major General commanding the Army as unsuited to the ends to be accomplished and insufficient in efficiency for the expedition to the Philippines. Two regiments of regular infantry is a very small proportion of the 42 regular regiments in the army when the work to be done consists of conquering a territory 7000 miles from our base, defended by a regularly trained and acclimated army of from 10,000 to 25,000 men and inhabited by 14 millions of people, the majority of whom will regard us with the intense hatred born of race and religion."

As is usual in the military service, when two officers disagree, the senior prevails. When the expedition finally got under way Merritt's command contained less than one half of the regular troops he had requested.

Worry over the paucity of information concerning the situation in the Philippines also actuated Merritt to write directly to President McKinley [9] urging him to expedite information from Dewey in regard to the Spanish strength in the Philippines and what supplies it would be necessary for the Americans to bring from San Francisco. The information finally received from Dewey indicated that there were 35,000 Spanish soldiers in the Islands, of whom some 15,000 were in Manila; that all supplies must be brought from the United States; that Cavite was in his possession and could be used as a base; that the rainy season would soon start and make military operations difficult; that the Spanish morale was low. With this as a basis Merritt organized his expedition.

On April 1, 1898, the regular army of the United States consisted of 28,183 officers and men. [10] When war was declared three weeks later, the President issued a call for 125,000 volunteers with another call for 75,000 more the following month. Congress also authorized the increase of the regular army to a strength of 61,000. By August of 1898 recruitments had brought the regular army strength up to 56,365, and 207,244 volunteers were under arms.

This quick expansion after 33 years of peace threw a heavy burden on the War Department, required suddenly to arm, feed, clothe and equip more than a quarter of a million men. Prohibited by law from expending funds or letting contracts until the money was actually appropriated by Congress, the Quartermaster General found his hands tied until within six weeks of the declaration of war. A heavily over-balanced demand for clothing and equipment suitable for use in the tropics added to the confusion. There was a shortage of experienced officers. Government-owned arsenals had limited facilities. The result was that recruits and volunteers poured into hurriedly constructed mobilization camps and were issued unwholesome food and defective equipment and were not given adequate medical attention. The death of some 2500 volunteers from disease brought complaints to congressmen and a thorough investigation following the war. The investigation placed the blame in general not on individuals, but on the system and eventually resulted in the establishment of the General Staff.

The expansion of the pitifully small regular army into an organization capable of fighting a foreign war presented other problems. Following the first call for volunteers, Congress authorized the President to muster into federal service, members of State Militia units who would enlist for two years or until the conclusion of the war. The Civil War had taught the War Department lessons on raising volunteer troops. Mustering in state units in toto had often meant over-officered, under-manned, skeletonized regiments of little value. Consequently, the quotas in 1898 allotted to states were for a certain number of full strength regiments and not for a certain number of volunteers. New York State's quota was twelve regiments of infantry and two troops of cavalry. Later when the war with Spain was over and volunteers were still needed to quench the ambitions of the Filipinos for independence, Congress authorized the organization of ten volunteer regiments to be recruited at large throughout the United States.

Expediency dictated that the volunteer regiments assigned to the Philippine expedition come from the western states and that their assembly point be San Francisco. [11] Camp Merritt, one of the mobilization camps, was pitched on sand dunes in a bleak area on the edge of Golden Gate park, unprotected from the winds of the Pacific Ocean. Cold breezes, damp fog and wet sand caused an epidemic of pneumonia and bronchial diseases. Improper construction and an insufficient number of latrines encouraged defecation on the ground. This residue was blown into the kitchens which had been injudiciously located nearby and brought on numerous cases of typhoid fever. The Tennessee and Oregon regiments arriving at the camp brought measles with them. Well-intentioned San Francisco ladies' auxiliaries flooded the camp with pies, cakes, and candies and thus encouraged gormandizing, which resulted in diarrhea, dysentery and other stomach disorders. Prostitutes, as usual, brought with them venereal diseases. Conditions became so bad that a board of medical officers conducted an investigation and caused the camp to be moved in September to the Presidio of San Francisco.

As the volunteer units trickled into San Francisco during the latter part of May, it became apparent that the United States was not a prepared nation. Nondescript in appearance and training, they hailed from California, Oregon, Nebraska, Colorado, Wyoming, Minnesota, Idaho, Kansas, Utah, South Dakota and Montana; a congressman from Pennsylvania had managed to have a regiment from that state assigned to the expedition. The regular army furnished the 23rd Infantry, parts of the 14th and some artillery.

All settled down to the serious business of preparing for a 7000 mile ocean voyage and fighting a war. Willing but untrained, the inexperienced volunteer officers added to the confusion. Scarcely one knew how to make out a requisition with which to obtain supplies for his troops. Some could not be relied upon to render a return showing the number and condition of their men. [12] General Merritt wired the War Department [13] that the Kansas regiment which had been there for some time, had made itself prominent by its want of capacity so far as its officers were concerned; that the Tennessee regiment arrived at San Francisco completely destitute of equipment of any kind, and wanting in drill. Although all regiments were expected to have reported fully uniformed, often the uniforms were badly torn or worn out and some men were dressed in civilian clothes. Entire units had to be re-armed, because of the defective condition or obsolescence of their equipment. A slip in the War Department had permitted the moderate quantity of military supplies, usually kept on the Pacific Coast, to be shipped East for the Cuban expeditions so that there resulted a frenzied mass buying from the San Francisco market. Food, clothing, equipment, in fact nearly everything needed to equip an army was scarce and it is surprising that the expedition sailed as quickly as it did.

Hoping to have the first expedition depart for Manila by May 21, the authorities made feverish efforts to supply and equip the 1st California volunteers, who had been among the early arrivals at the assembly point and had been assigned to the first expedition, but all exertions were rendered purposeless by the lack of transportation. Owning no transports, the Army was forced to charter commercial vessels and modify them to facilitate the conveyance of large bodies of troops and to permit the operation of army messes. Slowness in signing contracts and demands of shipowners for various guarantees, exasperated the military commanders to such an extent that General Otis, who was charged with getting them ready, threatened to impress commercial vessels into government service, if they were not released by the time the troops were ready to leave. [14]

On May 23 Brigadier General Thomas Anderson arrived at San Francisco and was assigned to command the first expedition consisting of the 1st California, the Oregon volunteers, and five companies of the 14th regular Infantry. He was a veteran of the Civil War, in which he had been brevetted for bravery. Arriving in San Francisco during the confusion in preparation for the departure of the first increment, he was given no control over, nor any opportunity to inspect his command until it was on the transports ready to sail on May 25.

Never noteworthy for comfort, the army transports in this case proved to be no exception, but were as satisfactory as could be expected. Lack of messing facilities reduced the number of meals served to two a day. Water for bathing was limited. Sea-sick men in cramped quarters occasioned nausea in others. "Greybacks" invaded the straw stuffed mattress ticks. When steam delousers destroyed underwear as well as lice, it was discovered that a large proportion of the men had no change; they were forced to go without underclothes. The Oregon regiment which had been issued only one pair of shoes, had brought civilian shoes along.

Convoyed by the Navy cruiser, *Charleston,* the expedition stopped at Hawaii, and then continued its journey to the Spanish owned Island of Guam. Anchoring off shore, the Charleston fired a few shots, an action that brought an unexpected apology from the Spanish commander, who did not know that war had been declared. He was sorry that shortage of ammunition prevented a return of the American "salute." Explanations followed; surrender was obtained in short order; and the expedition continued to Manila, arriving there thirty-seven days after its departure from San Francisco.

Leaving Anderson for a moment and casting a glance at the situation in the United States, we see that in San Francisco lack of transports worried Merritt, who complained to the War Department, urging that charters be expedited, until he was able finally to embark the second expedition on June 15. Comprising the Colorado, the 10th Pennsylvania, and the Nebraska volunteers, two battalions of regular infantry and two batteries of Utah Volunteers, this expedition was placed under the command of Brigadier General Francis V. Greene. A West Point graduate in the class of 1870,

Greene had been a military observer in the Russo-Turkish War of 1877-78 and had seen war at its worst. Having resigned from the Regular Army in 1886, he had become the Colonel of the 71st New York Volunteers. After accompanying that regiment to Tampa, Florida, he had been promoted to Brigadier General of Volunteers and shunted to the Philippine expedition as a brigade commander.

With General Merritt personally in command, the third expedition sailed from San Francisco on June 27. Largest yet to leave, it consisted of volunteer regiments from Idaho, Wyoming, Minnesota, and twelve companies of regulars. Along also was the Astor Battery, mountain artillery privately equipped by John Jacob Astor and manned principally by college students. The expedition was unconvoyed; hence rumors of a Spanish fleet in the Pacific caused some apprehension for the safety of the defenseless transports. No Spanish ships being seen, however, the expedition arrived safely off Manila July 31 at the height of the rainy season, ready to unfold a new page in American history.

NOTES ON CHAPTER I

1 cf Dewey, George, Autobiography, New York, 1913. p. 195

2 cf For full text see Senate Document No. 221 of the 1st session of the 56th Congress, Vol. 18 page 1191. Hereafter Senate Document references will be abbreviated as follows: SD 221 56th 1st Vol. 18 p. 1232 ff

3 cf Ibid p. 1232 et. seq.

4 cf Document of the House of Representatives, number 2 of the 2nd session of the 57th Congress, Volume 4, page 291. Hereafter House Document references will be abbreviated as follows: HD 57th 2nd No. 2 Vol. 4 p. 291

5 cf Blount, James H. "American Occupation of the Philippines"

6 cf Molinari, Gustave, "The Society of Tomorrow," New York, 1904 p. 214

7 cf Hearings before the Committee on the Philippines, United States Senate, 1902 Part II page 862. Hereafter references from these hearings will be abbreviated as follows: Hearings II p. 862

8 cf SD 221 56th 1st Vol. 18 p. 1204

9 cf Ibid p. 1201

10 cf SD 221 56th 1st Vol. 17 p. 113

11 cf SD 221 56th 1st Vol. 24 p. 165 et. seq.

12 cf Ibid p. 178

13 cf SD 221 56th 1st Vol. 18 p. 1263

14 cf Ibid p. 1228

Chapter II

BEFORE FOLLOWING the fortunes of Merritt and his little band of American soldiers, it might be well to become acquainted with the scene of his endeavors. It is beside the purpose of this volume to go into the early history of the Philippine Islands. That information can be obtained from many other sources. [1] The Philippine Islands were discovered March 16, 1521 by Ferdinand Magellan in the first circumnavigation of the globe. The first permanent settlement was set up on the Island of Cebu in 1565, and Manila was settled in 1572. With Spanish colonization came religious orders which not only introduced Christianity to the heathen Filipinos, but sought wealth through exploitation of the Island's rich resources. Continuous exploitation combined with the abuses usual to Spanish rule caused intermittent outbreaks among the Filipinos through the next three hundred years. One of these rebellions, which occurred in 1896, was to have a profound significance on our story.

The leader was a 27 year old youth from the Province of Cavite by the name of Emilio Aguinaldo y Famy. Born in 1869 into an impecunious middle class family, his education had been restricted to a brief attendance at a Manila secondary school. However, although unlettered, he possessed high intelligence and, besides being elected mayor of his native *barrio* of Cavite Viejo, had become a recognized leader of the Katipunan, a Filipino secret, nationalist organization. Fighting with some success against the organized Spanish soldiery throughout 1896, he saw his poorly equipped native insurrectos being pushed back during the next year into the mountains of Bulacan Province. Finally brought to bay in a mountain stronghold known as Biak-Na-Bato, he turned to make a last stand. His position was so strong, however, that the Spanish themselves, weary of extended field service in the tropics, and realizing that the rebellion was costing Spain large sums of money, proposed an armistice which Aguinaldo gladly accepted, and which eventually materialized into the so-called pact of Biak-Na-Bato.

The terms of this pact, which it appears were never put into writing, are obscure. Spaniards and Filipinos disagree substantially as to what they actually were. The Filipino version is given here principally because it indicates the aims of the Insurgent leaders. According to them, the Spanish agreed to: [2]

1. Expel religious orders.
2. Give Filipinos representation in the Spanish Cortes.
3. Afford equal treatment to Filipinos and Spaniards in the application of justice.
4. Employ Filipinos in the high posts of Government service.
5. Grant freedom of the press and the right to form associations.
6. To pay an indemnity of eight hundred thousand pesos to the leaders of the rebellion who were to leave the Islands. The indemnity was theoretically to indemnify widows and orphans and to recompense those who had lost property during the rebellion.

In return for these considerations, the Insurgents were to lay down their arms and return peaceably into the fold of the Spanish Government.

Regardless of what the verbal terms of the pact may have been, Aguinaldo and about forty of his followers did go to Hong Kong, China, following the settlement, where they cashed a draft for 400,000 pesos. Except for a few minor outbreaks the Islands again became quiet. Aguinaldo and his followers took up residence in Hong Kong and formed a Filipino Junta there. To Aguinaldo's credit, it must be said that he steadfastly refused to split the indemnity among his adherents and kept it in a Hong Kong bank for the purpose (he said) of buying arms and financing another rebellion in case the Spanish did not institute the promised reforms.

The tranquility of the Junta in Hong Kong was disturbed in April of 1898 when one Isabelo Artacho, a member of the group, entered a suit in a Hong Kong court for part of the indemnity which he claimed was due him as back salary as "secretary of the Interior" of the now defunct revolutionary insurgent government. At a council of war among the loyal members it was decided that Aguinaldo, the custodian of the fund, would depart sub rosa for Singapore and thus avoid the possibility of a court action which might tie up the funds for an indefinite time.

The Americans at that point entered the picture. When Aguinaldo landed at Singapore on April 21, war between the United States and Spain was imminent. The American Consul General at Singapore, Mr. E. Spencer Pratt, an enterprising but as it turned out, näive diplomat, conceived the idea of sending Aguinaldo back to the Philippines as an agent provocateur for the United States. Without authority from the State Department, it appears that Mr. Pratt held interviews with Aguinaldo and, according to the latter's reiterated statements, promised in effect that if Aguinaldo went to the Philippines and fomented another rebellion against the Spanish, the United States would grant the Filipinos independence. The Pratt-Aguinaldo conversations have been the subject of much controversy; [3] and, although Mr. Pratt strongly disclaimed having made any promises to Aguinaldo, he was reprimanded by the State Department and in comparatively short time, eased out of the consular service. At any rate, Pratt wired Dewey, who was in Hong Kong making final preparations for the Manila expedition, concerning his plan. Dewey wired back for Aguinaldo to come to Hong Kong as soon as possible. Aguinaldo left on the next boat for Hong Kong, but did not arrive there soon enough to see Dewey before he left for Manila.

Nominally at least allied with the United States, Aguinaldo, having settled the Artacho case out of court for $5000, busied himself with the purchase of arms and ammunition, using the indemnity for funds. He also sent a proclamation to the Philippine Islands urging the Filipinos to rise against the Spanish and to regard the Americans as friends. Two weeks after the battle of Manila Bay, the U. S. Revenue Cutter *Hugh McCullogh* arrived at Hong Kong and when it left on its journey to Manila, Aguinaldo was a passenger.

Arriving off Manila on May 19, Aguinaldo conferred with Admiral Dewey and then went ashore. Controversy also exists as to the Dewey-Aguinaldo conversations at this time, Aguinaldo claiming that Dewey reiterated Pratt's promises. However, the weight of evidence indicates that Dewey was much more circumspect than Pratt, and gave Aguinaldo no real reason for believing that the United States would grant independence to the Filipinos. Dewey did assist Aguinaldo, however, in the donation of some sixty-two captured Spanish rifles and several thousand rounds of ammunition. According to Dewey, Aguinaldo returned to the *Olympia* after his first day ashore, discouraged and desirous of leaving for Japan. Dewey patted him on the back and encouraged him to continue his efforts, which shortly thereafter became effective.

Aguinaldo's methods of organizing a revolt were quite conventional. First he issued a series of proclamations, then gathering a few followers, he looted the surrounding countryside and extracted money from the natives at the threat of death. [4] Soon he had assembled a sizable army.

On May 24 he proclaimed a dictatorial government with himself as Dictator and promised a constitution when the Islands had passed into his control. Four days later his undrilled but enthusiastic army defeated and captured a small Spanish column which had been sent

from Manila to disperse his force and capture his equipment. Shortly thereafter rebellion against the Spanish spread throughout central
Luzon. Spanish garrisons throughout the Islands were attacked
and overthrown, and control of the Island outside of Manila passed
into the hands of the Filipinos. Dewey adopted a benevolent attitude
towards Aguinaldo, in fact, expedited the landing of Insurgent
munitions shipments.

On June 23 Aguinaldo issued a proclamation establishing a revolutionary government, which was in effect a declaration of independence from Spain. [5] The government provided for a president, a
cabinet, and a unicameral legislative body, a committee of which
was to serve as a sort of supreme court. By the end of June Manila
was surrounded, besieged, and some 4000 Spaniards were prisoners
in the hands of the Insurgents; Spanish troops were demoralized.
Aguinaldo had received and turned down a tempting offer from the
Spanish for his allegiance. He had also gathered around himself a
clique of radical Filipino patriots, many of whom were educated men
well versed in the intricacies of international politics. One of them,
Apolinario Mabini, a paralytic cripple, was to exercise an ever increasing influence on the revolutionary government.

Dewey began to realize that in permitting this revolutionary government to develop he had possibly created a Frankenstein. However, Mr. E. Spencer Pratt could say that, apparently at least, his
plan had been a success. Aguinaldo had facilitated greatly the occupation of the Philippines by the United States. The only job left
to the American troops when they arrived was to capture Manila.

NOTES ON CHAPTER II

[1] An exhaustive survey of early Philippine history may be obtained from
Blair and Robertsons "The Philippine Islands" Cleveland 1898, 55 Vols.
[2] cf Forbes, Cameron, "The Philippine Islands" Vol. 1 p. 53
[3] For a full discussion of each version of this controversy see Blount, op. cit.
and Worcester, Dean "The Philippines Past and Present," New York, 1914
[4] cf Hearings, part III p. 2965
[5] cf Ibid p. 2950

Chapter III

THE WORLD WAR enhanced realization on the part of many American people of the difficulties involved in the successful accomplishment of an overseas troop movement. The nation responded quickly, however, and after expanding our Army from 200,000 to 4,000,000 men we managed to transport 1,500,000 to France and have some basis to the much mooted claim that "we won the war." It was evident, however, that the problem was considerably lessened by the scientific achievements of civilized nations during the early part of the 20th century. In 1917 cable messages could be transmitted between the two continents in a few hours. The journey between Europe and the United States could be made in less than ten days. Docking facilities existed at all European ports. On arrival in Europe our troops were given shelter in French villages. We possessed potent allies who were ready and willing to pass on to us the benefits of the experience gained after three years of devastating modern warfare. Despite these facts, however, much confusion resulted both in Europe and in the United States. However, when General Anderson and his little expedition set out for the Philippines in 1898, no such advantages existed for them. The journey to the Philippine Islands took over a month. No cable communication existed between Manila and the United States. No member of the expedition possessed even a modicum of knowledge concerning the country, on the shores of which he was to land and fight a war. The diplomatic status of the Insurgent government, which purported to be an ally, was indefinite. Military commanders were faced with the necessity of making decisions on political matters in which they were not well versed and which involved a departure from traditional American foreign policy.

Manila is exactly 6929 miles from San Francisco, via Honolulu and Guam. When General Anderson sailed into Manila Bay on June 30, 1898 with 2500 troops loaded into three transports, he was glad to see Dewey's squadron placidly anchored in the Bay and the American flag flying over the Arsenal at Cavite. Anderson's instructions, while authorizing him to use his judgment in case unforeseen contingencies arose, also directed that he confer with Dewey upon his arrival and that he keep his troops under the protection of Dewey's guns. Consequently he boarded the *Olympia* immediately upon his arrival and in a conference there with Dewey oriented himself on the situation, and made plans for the disembarkation of his command.

From the conversation, Anderson decided that the only logical place at which to land his troops was at Cavite, the erstwhile Spanish Naval Base. Then under Dewey's control, this narrow peninsula contained a small dock accessible to the shallow-draught native cascos, which constituted the only marine transportation available for hauling men and supplies ashore. Accordingly towed by navy launches, Anderson's command was brought ashore on July 1.

The American soldiers had heard that the Orient was full of "smells." Their belief was confirmed in an unanticipated manner. Quartered in the Spanish barracks and government buildings at Cavite, the putrescent odor of decaying human flesh constantly permeated the area. The source of the smell was easily ascertainable. Not far off shore in comparatively shallow water, still remained the sunken hulks of Montojo's unhappy squadron, with its complement of 150 odd Spanish sailors, who had gone down with their ships. Nature works quickly in the tropics and "bubbles" rising to the surface told the story. A decided nuisance, nobody had been able to do anything about it. Many a recruit paused and wondered if that was the glory of war.

Anderson set his command to work collecting transportation, constructing scaling ladders, practicing marksmanship and otherwise conditioning themselves for an attack on Manila.

Shortly after his arrival, while aboard the *Olympia,* he had remarked in a conversation with Dewey that in the United States there was talk of retaining the Philippine Islands. Dewey replied: "If the United States intends to hold the Philippine Islands, it will make things awkward, because just a week ago Aguinaldo proclaimed the Independence of the Philippine Islands from Spain and seems intent on establishing his own government." [1] The next afternoon, the two American commanders made a formal call on Aguinaldo, who had established his headquarters at Cavite. Before they left the *Olympia,* Dewey said: "We'll make this call just as unofficial as possible, no sidearms, no ceremony, give no indication to Aguinaldo that we take his government seriously." [1] Arriving at Insurgent Headquarters, Anderson found Aguinaldo rather suspicious and unfriendly. During the course of the conversation Aguinaldo posed Anderson by suddenly asking, "Had (or would) the United States recognize his government?" Taken back, Anderson replied that he was acting only in a military capacity and had no authority to recognize any government. [1]

A few days later Aguinaldo ceremoniously returned the call, bringing his cabinet, staff, and a band. With him he also brought an open letter written by a group of Filipinos in Manila, proposing a scheme for autonomous government under the Spanish. The writers stated that the Spanish would willingly grant autonomy to the Philippines, if Aguinaldo would give up the independence idea and place his Insurgent army under their flag. Stating that he had no intention of joining the Spanish, Aguinaldo again embarrassed Anderson by bluntly asking, "Does the United States intend to hold the Philippine Islands as dependencies?" Somewhat prepared this time, Anderson replied, "I cannot answer that, but in 122 years we have established no colonies." [1] Aguinaldo then thoughtfully replied, "I have studied attentively the Constitution of the United States and in it I find no authority for colonies, and I have no fear." The conversation drifted to other channels.

Two weeks after landing and establishing his camp at Cavite, Anderson apprehended that he was separated from the Spanish lines in Manila by some seventeen miles of practically impassable roads and some 10,000 armed Filipino Insurgents. So in order to be closer to the scenes of military activity, he moved part of his command across the Bay to Tambo, a small hamlet on the eastern shore, and established "Camp Dewey" a mile and a half south of the insurgent line of entrenchments.

Two days after this change had been made, General Greene's expedition, 3586 strong, arrived off Manila and was landed at the same place. The difficulties of debarking these troops at Tambo were great. Manila Bay, about twenty-five miles in breadth, furnishes a wide sweep for the southwest monsoon which was prevalent at that time of the year. Unprotected by a breakwater, the beach at Tambo received the full force of the sea and roared continually from the pounding of eight-foot breakers. The landing of troops and supplies, or in fact anything, on a beach which is pounded by breakers is no easy matter under the best of conditions. At Tambo this mission was given to the Quartermaster, who possessed absolutely no facilities of his own. Lieutenant Colonel Pope, the Chief Quartermaster, in desperate need of marine motive power finally managed to hire one launch from Filipinos and borrowed two more from the Navy. Then a few cascos, loaded with supplies or troops, were hauled to a minimum safe depth for the launches and cut loose. Dropping anchors, the crews of the cascos then slowly paid out the anchor lines and drifted onto the beach with the surf. Subjected to the vagaries of the wind sweeping across the bay, the cascos were frequently swamped,

Headquarters Dept. of the Pacific and 8th Army Corps, Manila.
Standing, left to right: Capt. C. H. Murray, Lieut. Fred. W. Sladen, Lieut. Louis P. Sanders. Sitting left to right: Gen. R. P. Hughes, Gen. E. S. Otis, Lieut. Col. T. H. Barry.

Insurgent Regiment Preparing to Leave Manila.

equipment lost, supplies damaged and soldiers drenched. When General Merritt came ashore he rode on the back of a native boat-man for the last few yards with his feet dangling in the water.

The use of navy boats for army purposes often caused complications in the chain of command. On one occasion, Colonel Pope pulled alongside the *Rapido,* a navy launch engaged in hauling cascos and had the following conversation with the *Rapido's* skipper: [2]

Col. Pope: "I want you to anchor the cascos and use the *Rapido* to transport some sick men to Cavite."

Skipper: "Who in the devil are you anyway?"

Col. Pope: "I'm Colonel Pope, the Chief Quartermaster."

Skipper: "To hell with the Pope; I take my orders from Commodore Dewey; Get out of my way or I'll swamp you."

And the *Rapido* proceeded on its original mission.

After several cascos had been swamped at Tambo, the inefficacy of the system became apparent and another landing place was sought. Searching along the beach the quartermaster discovered a small river at Paranaque, one mile south of the proposed camp site for the troops. Supplies were then hauled up the river at high tide and unloaded there in comparative safety. A native carabao-and-pony train was organized to haul supplies to the camp.

As in any military operation, the matter of land transportation was one of primary importance. As yet the Americans had brought over no animals and were forced to depend on what animals and vehicles they could purchase from the quasi-friendly natives. The matter was complicated, not only in the purchase of animals but in the matter of carts, firewood, and lumber, by the adoption of a form of passive resistance on the part of the natives. Aguinaldo had inventoried all transportation in the neighborhood and had issued orders that none would be sold without his express authority. Very few natives desired to run the risk of having a bolo hacked through their skulls in order to receive a few pesos. Anderson made representations to Aguinaldo in the matter and after pointing out (theoretically at least) the unity of their purposes, threatened to seize what he needed if not offered for sale immediately. Aguinaldo gave in on the matter, but shortly thereafter demonstrated the hostile demeanor his attitude was taking by advising Anderson in return that even though the United States had not recognized his revolutionary government, the Americans would, if they desired to avoid trouble, notify him before they landed any more troops on his sovereign soil. However, the following day when General Merritt arrived off Manila he landed his troops without delay, completely ignoring Aguinaldo or his government. Though angered, Aguinaldo simply nursed the slight to his assumed dignity and committed no overt hostile act towards the Americans.

Established on what had been a peanut farm, Camp Dewey was decidedly uncomfortable, but had its merits. Proximity to the beach facilitated bathing and the washing of clothes; the rainy season being in full swing, sleeping on the ground was out of the question. The soldiers set to and built double decker beds of bamboo, the bottom one being raised some eighteen inches above the ground. Then covered with small shelter tents, which were part of each soldier's field equipment, they furnished some protection except in heavy rains. Drinking water was a problem because of the known contamination of unboiled water in the tropics. Shallow surface wells were dug, from which the water had to be boiled for at least fifteen minutes before it was deemed potable by the medical authorities. Cooking was another problem, because of the scarcity of dry wood. The difficulty increased as more troops arrived, demanding more fires and more boiled water. The rain, which poured incessantly on 24 successive days made the ground a boggy morass, and clothes virtually impossible to dry. As a result, men wore some articles of damp clothing almost continuously. Leather mildewed and became stiff. The hazardous journey between ship and shore made the landing of food supplies erratic and uncertain. The only refrigerating system for keeping meat was on an Australian refrigerator ship which Dewey had purchased. The Admiral was loath to open its doors except at stated intervals.

In the midst of these uncomfortable conditions, army regulations asserted their prerogative by stating that rations became the responsibility of troop organizations at shipside. This meant if a ration casco capsized enroute to shore, the organization for which the supplies were intended, received no more rations until a board of officers could act. [3] In some cases regiments went hungry while waiting for the board to meet. The coffee as issued was green and the current lack of firewood made roasting such a problem that the soldiers often went without a potable issue of their greatest boon in the field. Despite these handicaps, however, morale was good and the men were cheerful and willing.

Little more than a week after his arrival, Anderson, anticipating trouble with Aguinaldo and the Insurgents, reported to the War Department: [4]

"He (Aguinaldo) has declared himself dictator and president and is trying to take Manila without our assistance. This is not probable, but if he can effect his purpose, he will I apprehend antagonize any attempt on our part to establish a provisional government."

Merritt who arrived July 25 came armed with instructions from the President of the United States to "establish supreme political control over the inhabitants of the Philippine Islands." [5] This premise was bound to clash with the pretensions of the independent Filipino government. Merritt solved the rather touchy matter of diplomatic courtesies between the two "governments" by establishing his headquarters aboard ship and ignoring the existence of Aguinaldo and his government. In return, Aguinaldo ignored Merritt and dispensed with even the formality of a call. On July 26th, Dewey cabled to the Navy Department in Washington: [6] "Merritt's most difficult problem will be how to deal with the Insurgents under Aguinaldo, who has become aggressive and even threatening towards our army."

Making an estimate of the situation before attempting to take any steps pointing towards the capture of Manila, Merritt found himself in an embarrassing situation. The Insurgents with whom he was disinclined to come to any kind of an agreement, held entrenchments completely surrounding the city. The Americans possessed no terrain over which they could advance on Manila without first riding roughshod over Filipino trenches and soldiers. It was absolutely necessary that a portion of the Insurgent line be obtained before any kind of an attack could be made.

The problem was solved by a diplomatic play, Merritt to Aguinaldo via Anderson and Noriel. General Noriel commanded the Insurgent troops in front of Camp Dewey and was on friendly terms with General Anderson. A request by Anderson that the Filipinos move over and permit the Americans to occupy that portion of the line in front of Camp Dewey in order that the modern American artillery weapons could be trained on the Spanish lines was favorably received by Noriel, who took the matter up with Aguinaldo. Aguinaldo gave a rather grudging permission, stating that he was still relying on promises which Dewey had made him regarding independence and the intentions of the United States. So on July 29, Noriel moved a portion of his brigade to the east so that a portion of Greene's brigade went into the line and faced the Spanish, some 800 yards away.

The Spanish army now showed its hand. Shortly before midnight some two days after the Americans had moved into the trenches, the Spaniards opened fire on the American line with a heavy rifle fire and a barrage from some 3.2 inch guns which they had mounted in their trenches. The two battalions of the 10th Pennsylvania Volunteers and one battery of the 3d Regular Artillery returned the fire with vim. The sound of bullets passing through bamboo thickets being mistaken for the crack of a rifle close by, the Americans believed that a general assault by the Spanish was in progress.

One volunteer regiment, under fire for the first time, became excited and began firing wildly into the darkness. Several men left cover and straggled to the rear. A courier, sent to General Greene asking for reinforcements, greeted him with the message:[7] "General send reinforcements, send every man, send every company, we're whipped, we're whipped. The — Battery is wiped off the earth. We're out of ammunition. Send help." The general call to arms was sounded and an artillery regiment which was acting as infantry, was sent forward, taking with them ammunition for the volunteer regiment reported "whipped." A battalion of another volunteer regiment, also moving to the front, mistook an abandoned Insurgent trench for the American front lines and hearing firing in their front, fired three volleys into the backs of the regiment first demoralized.[8] The arrival of the artillery regiment, firing steady volleys, settled the nerves of the front line troops. After a discharge of 60,000 rounds of rifle and 160 rounds of artillery ammunition in an hour and a half, the front became quiet.

The panicked volunteer regiment had been without adequate cover, and the reinforcing troops marching up from Camp Dewey received the full force of the Spanish shots, which were aimed too high. These two groups suffered the bulk of the casualties, which consisted of ten men killed and forty-three wounded. Daylight indicated that the Spanish had never left their trenches, but were merely indulging in the Spanish-Filipino form of "attack" in which the attacker remains in his trenches and sends a fusillade of bullets towards the enemy. Nightly fusillades of this nature continued during the following week and caused such an expenditure and wastage of ammunition that orders were issued prohibiting the return of Spanish fire, unless it was certain that the Spanish had actually left their trenches and were making an assault.

Life in the trenches during this period was not pleasant for the American soldier. They contained some two feet of water. After standing in the muck for twenty-four hours at a stretch, recruits had ample opportunity for philosophizing on the discomforts of war. The mud was so deep that many of the men ruined their shoes and were forced to go barefoot.[9] Any head poked above the parapet was sure to draw a Spanish bullet.

Nearly two years later, these series of "attacks" by the Spanish had their repercussion in the United States. The Springfield, Massachusetts *Republican* carried an excerpt from a book written by Aguinaldo which he had designated as the "True Version of the Philippine Revolution." In it was the following statement:[10]

> "After the Americans occupied the trenches, their outposts were surprised by the Spaniards who made a night attack . . . (The outposts) abandoned their rifles and six field guns in their precipitate retreat. Our (The Filipino) troops immediately rushed to their assistance, repulsed the Spanish, and recaptured rifles and field guns. Alleging that they did not belong to the Americans since Filipino troops had captured them from the Spanish, General Noriel opposed the restitution of the arms which I ordered returned to the Americans as a token of our good will and friendship."

Since the newspapers or army reports had carried no mention of this "precipitate retreat and abandonment of their arms" by Greene's troops, the American public thought it had been hoodwinked as to some of the exploits of the Army in the Philippines. A question was asked on the floor of the United States Senate concerning the matter and an investigation was conducted under the direction of the President. Depositions were sent to all parts of the United States in order to obtain evidence from officers and men who had been present during the attacks, but had been since discharged and returned to their various civil pursuits. The substance of the depositions was an imposing list of indignant denials from Anderson, Greene, and the regimental and battalion commanders.[11]

On August 4th, another American brigade under the command of Brigadier General Arthur MacArthur arrived at Manila, bringing the total strength of the American forces in the Philippines up to 10,907 officers and men.[12] General MacArthur, who was later to be a most prominent figure in the quelling of the insurrection and eventually the Military Governor of the Islands, was another product of the Civil War. Entering the army in 1862 as a lieutenant in the 24th Wisconsin Infantry, he had risen to the grade of Colonel by 1865. During the war he had been twice brevetted for bravery during action and had in addition been decorated with the Congressional Medal of Honor for "seizing the colors of his regiment at a critical moment and planting them on the captured works on the crest of Missionary Ridge." Having won his spurs under fire, thirty years of peacetime army training had developed him into a most capable and competent officer.

With the arrival of MacArthur's brigade, Merritt felt strong enough to undertake an attack on Manila and organized his troops into a division, designating Anderson as division commander, Greene and MacArthur each in command of a brigade.

Meanwhile, Dewey, who had been informally negotiating with the Spanish, believed that if the Americans actually threatened to bombard and attack the city that General Fermin Jaudenes, the Spanish Governor General, would not fight. Merritt was skeptical but agreed that any arrangement with the Spanish which would save American lives was desirable.

Jaudenes' position was indeed quite hopeless. Counting Insurgent and American troops, who must both be listed as enemies, he was outnumbered. He was surrounded by an entrenched force and could not feasibly even attempt an escape into the provinces. He was encumbered by numerous sick and wounded, both soldiers and civilians. Since the Insurgents had surrounded the city, the municipal water supply had been shut off; food was so short that many of the inhabitants had been glad to subsist on horse meat, dogs and cats. There was not the slightest possibility of a relieving force being sent from Spain to his assistance.

Early in August Jaudenes intimated informally to Dewey through the Belgian consul that:[13] If attacked, he would not use the powerful artillery defenses located in the walled city unless Manila was shelled; and if the Americans would promise to prevent the entry of Insurgent troops into the city, his resistance would be only of sufficient strength to satisfy the demands of "Spanish Honor." After a consultation, Merritt and Dewey in reply "intimated" that if such was the case, the city proper would not be bombarded and that after they had captured Manila the generosity of their terms would vary directly with the brevity of the Spanish resistance.

That the age old custom of the transmission of courtly communications between opposing military commanders still existed is indicated by the official correspondence preceding the attack.[14]

Headquarters United States Land and
Naval Forces, Manila Bay, P. I.
August 7, 1898

The General in Chief
Commanding Spanish Forces in Manila.
Sir: We have the honor to notify your excellency that op-
erations of the land and naval forces of the United States
against the defenses of Manila may begin at any time after the
expiration of forty-eight hours from the hour of receipt by you
of this communication or sooner if made necessary by an attack
on your part.
This notice is given in order to afford you an opportunity
to remove all noncombatants from the city.
Very respectfully,
Wesley Merritt,
Major General, United States Army,
Commanding Land Forces of the United States.

George Dewey,
Rear Admiral, United States Navy,
Commanding United States Naval Forces on Asiatic Station.

The Governor General and Captain General of the Philippines to the Major General of the Army and the Rear Admiral
of the Navy Commanding respectively the Military and Naval
forces of the United States.
Gentlemen:
I have the honor to inform your excellencies that at half
past twelve today I received your notice with which you favor
me that after forty-eight hours have elapsed, you may begin
operations against this fortified city or at an earlier time if the
forces under your command are attacked by mine.
As your notice is sent for the purpose of providing for the
safety of noncombatants, I give thanks to your excellencies for
the humane sentiments you have shown and state that finding
myself surrounded by insurrectionary forces, I am without place
of refuge for the increased numbers of wounded, sick, women
and children who are now lodged within the walls.
Very Respectfully and Kissing the hands of your Excellencies,
Fermin Jaudenes,
Governor General and Captain General of the Philippines.

Headquarters United States Land and Naval Forces,
Manila Bay, P. I., August 9, 1898.

To the Governor General and Captain General of the Philippines:
Sir: The inevitable suffering in store for the wounded, sick,
women and children in the event that it becomes our duty to
reduce the defenses of the walled town in which they are gath-

ered, will we feel assured appeal successfully to the sympathies of a general capable of making the determined and prolonged resistance which your excellency has exhibited after the loss of your Naval forces and without hope of succor.

We therefore submit, without prejudice to the high sentiments of honor and duty which your excellency entertains, that surrounded on every side as you are by a constantly increasing force, with a powerful fleet in your front and deprived of all prospect of reinforcement and assistance, a most useless sacrifice of life would result in the event of attack and therefore every consideration of humanity makes it imperative that you should not subject your city to the horrors of a bombardment. Accordingly we demand the surrender of the city of Manila and the Spanish forces under your command.

W. Merritt,
Major General, U. S. Army.
George Dewey,
Rear Admiral, U. S. Navy.

The Governor General and Captain General of the Philippines
Manila, August 9, 1898.

The Major General of the Army and the Rear Admiral of the Navy, Commanding respectively the Military and Naval Forces of the United States.
Gentlemen:

Having received an intimation from your excellencies that in obedience to the sentiments of humanity to which you appeal and which I share, I should surrender this city and the forces under my orders, I have assembled the council of defense which declares that your request cannot be granted. But taking account of the most exceptional circumstances, existing in this city which your excellencies recite, and which unfortunately I have to admit, I would consult my government, if your excellencies will grant the time strictly necessary for this communication by way of Hong Kong.

Very respectfully,

Fermin Jaudenes,
Governor General and Captain General of the Philippines.

Headquarters United States Land and Naval Forces,
Manila Bay, August 10, 1898.

The Governor General and Captain General of the Philippine Islands.

Sir: We have the honor to acknowledge the communication of your excellency of the 8th instant, in which you suggest your desire to consult your government in regard to the exceptional circumstances in your city, provided the time to do so can be granted by us.

In reply we respectfully inform your excellency that we decline to grant the time requested.

Very respectfully,

W. Merritt,
Major General, U. S. Army.

George Dewey,
Rear Admiral, U. S. Navy.

Two days previous, swashing through the mud at Pasay, MacArthur and Greene had drawn up a plan of attack and submitted it to Merritt for his approval. Opposing the Americans was the Spanish line of entrenchments, flanked on the beach side by the Stone Fort San Antonio Abad and on the other side, nearly a mile east, by a heavy wood and concrete blockhouse. Although bold reconnaissance had indicated that all streams between the two lines were fordable, and that some firm ground existed, the dense bamboo thickets, multitudinous estuaries, and swampy areas, made a deployed advance difficult. The only feasible route of advance was along the beach or on the two roads running between the Spanish-American lines of entrenchments. Such an advance would of course be difficult for the attacker, did he encounter determined resistance. However as a result of the unofficial negotiations, the Americans were counting on little opposition and planned their attack on that basis.

The American plan can perhaps best be explained by citing a memorandum which General Merritt sent to all general officers on the day preceding the attack:

Memorandum for General Officers in Camp regarding the possible action of Saturday, August 13th.

"The Navy under Rear Admiral Dewey is to sail at 9:00 in the morning, August 13th, moving up to the different positions assigned to warships and open fire about 10 o'clock. The troops are to hold themselves in readiness as already agreed upon, to advance on the enemy in front, occupying the trenches after they are so shaken as to make the advance practicable without a serious disadvantage to our troops. In case the navy is delayed in dismounting the enemy's guns, and leveling the works, no advance is to be made by the army unless ordered from these headquarters. In the event of a white flag being displayed by the enemy on the angle of the walled city, or prominently anywhere else in sight, coupled with a cessation of firing on our part, it will mean surrender as the Admiral proposes after having fired a satisfactory number of shots, to move up toward the walled city and display the international signal "surrender." If a white flag is displayed, this will be an answer to his demand

and the troops will advance in good order and quietly.

These headquarters will be on board the *Zafiro,* which has been placed at the disposal of the Commanding General by the Admiral. Six companies of the Second Oregon Regiment, now quartered at Cavite will accompany these headquarters, to be used in occupying and keeping order in the walled city in event of necessity. If the white flag is displayed, the Admiral will send his Flag-Lieutenant ashore, accompanied by a staff officer from these Headquarters, who will bring word as to the proposition made by the enemy. The troops in the meantime will advance and entering the enemy's works by our left flank move in such positions as may be assigned them from these headquarters. This is not intended to interdict the entrance if possible by the first brigade or part of the troops over the enemy's works on the right. It is intended that these results shall be accomplished without the loss of life; and while firing continues from the enemy with their heavy guns, or if there is an important fire from their intrenched lines, the troops will not attempt an advance unless ordered from these headquarters.

In the event of unfavorable weather for the service of guns on board ship, the action will be delayed until further orders.

Memorandum of the positions to be occupied by the troops after entering the enemy's defenses will be carried by the Chief of Staff, General Babcock, and will be complied with as far as is practicable."[15]

More detailed instructions, issued later, directed that "General MacArthur's Brigade, in the event that it can pass the enemy line on the road leading to Singalon, will leave a force in the Spanish trenches at this point of crossing with instructions to permit no armed bodies other than American troops to cross the trenches in the direction of Manila." In other words, when the Americans advanced, they were not going to permit the Insurgents to follow.

The actual attack on Manila, carefully planned and supervised, went for the most part strictly according to schedule. At 9:35 a. m. August 13th, four ships of Dewey's squadron, and portions of the Utah artillery mounted in the American trenches, opened fire on Fort San Antonio Abad and the Spanish front lines. No reply was received from the enemy. Forty-five minutes later, each man carrying field equipment, 200 rounds of ammunition, two days' rations and entrenching tools, Greene's brigade with some three hundred members barefooted, moved forward. It was essential that Dewey's ships lift their fire at the proper time, hence the front line of the 1st Colorado Volunteers who were on the left of the brigade, and wading along the beach, was marked with large flags. Without opposition the Colorado regiment walked into Fort San Antonio Abad a few minutes later and hoisted the American flag. At the same time Dewey displayed from the *Olympia* the international flag code DWHB meaning "Demand surrender." Pausing until the 18th regular Infantry and the 1st Nebraska Volunteers, who had advanced along the road, arrived at the Fort, Greene's brigade continued its advance, receiving from the second line of Spanish trenches a straggling fire which killed one man. The half-hearted and intermittent fire was ineffective, however; and Greene's troops advanced without difficulty through the suburbs of Malate and Ermita towards Manila. On arriving at the clearing in front of the walled city they found a white flag displayed on one of its bastions and six or seven thousand armed Spanish soldiers on the walls.

MacArthur's brigade, which was to the east of Greene, encountered more opposition. The Insurgents, who were on the right of this brigade, commenced at daybreak and continued until the attack was launched, an indiscriminate fire on the Spanish lines. In retaliation the Spanish replied, and much to the discomfiture of the Americans, showered their lines with bullets. However, when the attack moved forward about 10:30 a. m., Spanish blockhouse No. 14, directly in front of the American lines, was silenced with a few shots from the 3.2 inch guns of the Utah Artillery, and the first line of Spanish trenches was occupied without difficulty. Dropping off two battalions to prevent the Insurgent "allies" from following the attack, the brigade then moved forward towards the village of Singalon. On approaching this barrio it was subjected to a hot fire and forced to halt and advance slowly. The nature of the ground precluded deployment so that it was not until 1:35 and the Astor Battery was put into the fight, that the brigade was able to enter Singalon. But that time the white flag had been run up on the walled city and the battle was over to all intents and purposes. The brigade then marched into Manila through the Paco district, having left detachments at bridges and street intersections for the purpose of blocking the entrance of any Insurgent groups which might have sifted through.

Greene reached the walled city shortly after the arrival of the leading elements of his brigade. His original orders had been to march around the wall and occupy the bridges over the Pasig River to the north in order to prevent Insurgents from entering from that direction. Although the white flag was displayed, the walls were lined with armed Spanish soldiers; firing could still be heard from the front of MacArthur's brigade, and Greene hesitated to leave while this large force of armed Spaniards was in his rear. His brigade moved up to the walled city, a few feet under the guns of the Spaniards on the wall, and halted. The gates into the city were closed and barred. At this time the situation was further complicated by the arrival of a column of Spanish troops, retreating from in front of MacArthur's brigade. Closely pursuing them was a battalion of Insurgents which had slipped around MacArthur's right flank. As the Spanish column approached, it was evident that it was trying to reach the walled city and that it was being fired upon by the Insurgents. Seeing their retreating comrades being peppered with shots by the Insurgents, the Spanish troops on the wall opened fire. The American troops were between the two, and white flag or not, anything might have happened with Americans, Spaniards and Insurgents intermingling, all excited and fingering or shooting their rifles. After a hasty conference between Greene, the commander of the Spanish column, and a Spanish officer on the wall, the gates of the city opened and the Spanish marched in. The 1st California Volunteers and the 18th Infantry physically blocked further advance to the Insurgents. In the confusion two American soldiers had been killed. At this time Greene received a message from the walled city that negotiations were being pursued inside for the surrender of Manila. He assembled his brigade and leaving a guard to keep the Insurgents away from the wall, crossed the Pasig River and sent patrols into the districts of San Sebastion, Sampaloc, Santa Cruz, Quiapo and San Miguel. The Spanish being definitely eliminated as a hostile factor, his mission now was to keep the Insurgents from entering the city from the north. His brigade spent the night patrolling the streets and on the following morning established a line running through Calle Azcarraga, a broad thoroughfare which cut across the north part of the city.

The white flag flying on the bastion of the walled city had been noticed by Dewey and Merritt at about 11:20 a. m. The representatives which they immediately sent ashore secured a nominal surrender. A short time later Merritt, with his staff and two battalions of the Oregon Volunteers, disembarked and entered the city from the Pasig River side. There Merritt met Jaudenes and the two went into conference regarding the terms of capitulation.

Although an epochal event in American history, the actual surrender was unimpressive, but was a study in contrast.[16] Clad in grey linen, Merritt, who was a foot taller than Jaudenes, met the ostentatious formality of the red-besashed Spanish aristocrat with midwestern democracy. However, he was inclined to be liberal. By five o'clock in the evening an agreement had been reached and a rough draft of the articles of capitulation drawn.

The substance of the capitulation which gave the United States sovereignty over Manila—its city, harbor, and bay, was as follows:[17] The Spanish surrendered Manila and all of its defenses with all "Honors of War"; officers excepted, all arms in the hands of Spanish troops were to be placed in the custody of the Americans pending the conclusion of peace between Spain and the United States. Although their official status was that of "prisoners of war," the Spanish troops were to remain at liberty, under the orders of their own officers; the Americans were to furnish the Spaniards with rations and necessary medical aid. All public property and funds were to be turned over to the American authorities. The protocol ended with the statement that "The city, inhabitants, churches and private property will be placed under the safeguard of the faith and honor of the American army." The material gain was, in addition to the public buildings, nearly 900,000 pesos in cash, 22,000 arms, 10 million rounds of ammunition and 13,000 prisoners.[18] The total American casualties for the day were six killed and forty-four wounded. Actual facts as to the number of Spanish casualties were not ascertainable, but it has been estimated that between August 1st and 13th the list amounted to forty killed and one hundred wounded.

As a matter of fact, the battle of Manila never needed to have been fought. On August 12th, the day before the attack took place, the following telegram was dispatched to Merritt from Washington:[19]

> "The President directs that all military operations against the enemy be suspended. Peace negotiations are nearing completion, a protocol just having been signed by representatives of the two countries. You will inform the Commander of the Spanish forces in the Philippines of these instructions; Further orders will follow. Acknowledge receipt."

Thus was ended the Spanish-American War; a conflict in which not an Ameircan defeat was met and not a color or gun captured by the enemy.

The cable connection between Manila and Hong Kong having been cut, however, Merritt did not receive the message until August 16th, four days later. It would have, had it been received in time, saved the lives of the six American soldiers who were killed in the attack.

Let us return to the Filipino Insurgents who had been forestalled in every attempt to enter the walled city. Having as Aguinaldo said, "besieged Manila for two and a half months, sacrificing thousands of lives and millions in material interests," their exclusion from entry into Manila and participation in the surrender proceedings came as a bitter disappointment. The night before the attack they had been notified by Merritt that they must not enter the city in the event of its capture by the Americans. However, they made their own preparations for an attack and when dawn broke at 4:00 a. m. on the 13th, they began firing on the Spanish trenches. Later, as the Spanish withdrew under the pressure of the American bombardment, the Insurgents swept forward in the lee of the American attack and actually occupied the suburbs of Paco and Malate. One group, moving to the east of MacArthur's brigade, had managed to evade the detachments he left behind to guard avenues of approach, and had reached the walled city, where, as mentioned, they had been blocked by Greene's brigade. One company which insisted on pushing forward had been disarmed by American troops. On the north side of the city they attacked also, but the Spanish line after withdrawing slightly held firm until it was relieved by American troops. To the Filipinos it appeared as though the Spanish and Americans, though erstwhile enemies, were uniting to thwart their ambition to occupy and (possibly) loot the city.

By seven o'clock on the evening of the 13th some 4000 angry Filipino Insurgents had massed in Malate and were deporting themselves in a manner that boded ill for the American detachments who blocked their further movement to the north. The attitude of the Americans was not friendly. They were certain that the constant sniping which had occurred throughout the day and had caused American casualties had been the work of Insurgents. Feeling that the situation was becoming critical, Merritt directed General Anderson, the division commander, to remove the Insurgents from Paco and Malate. Anderson, realizing the responsibility of keeping his eye on 13,000 Spanish "prisoners of war" and faced with the possibility of a fight with the entire Insurgent army, hesitated to use force. He compromised by sending the following telegram to Aguinaldo who was at Bacoor, some 11 miles away:[20]

> "Serious trouble threatening between our forces. Try and prevent it. Your forces should not try to force themselves into the city until we have received the full surrender. Then we will negotiate with you."

By this telegram, Anderson intimated that when the full surrender had been received, the Insurgents would be permitted to enter. And it was true that at this time only a rough draft of the articles of capitulation had been signed. However equivocal, the telegram was discreet under the circumstances. Four hours later he received the following answer from Aguinaldo:[21]

"I received a telegram. My interpreter is in Cavite. In consequence of this I have not answered until now. My troops are forced by yours by means of threats of violence to retire from positions taken. It is necessary to avoid a conflict which I should lament that you order your troops that they avoid difficulty with mine, as up to now they have conducted themselves like brothers to take Manila. I have given strict orders to my chiefs that they preserve strict respect to American forces and aid them if attacked by a common enemy. I do not doubt that the good relations and friendship which unite us will be continued if your soldiers correspond to the conduct imposed upon mine."

Stalemated, Anderson waited until the following morning, having been further advised that Aguinaldo was sending a commission to confer on the matter.

The commission which arrived the next morning consisted of Gregorio Araneta, Felipe Buencamino, and Benito Lagarda, three wealthy and educated Filipinos who had joined the Insurgent government. Representing Aguinaldo, they voiced no objection to the withdrawal of the Insurgent forces, if the Americans would promise to reinstate them in their present positions upon the probable resumption of Spanish sovereignty in the Islands following the peace negotiations between the United States and Spain. Having received instructions from Washington that there must be no dual occupation of the city, Merritt felt unable to make any pledges of this nature. He advised the commission to trust America and read to them a proclamation which he was issuing to the pepole of the Philippine Islands, announcing the establishment of military government and asking for the cooperation of the people in return for the protection which the United States would give them. Disgruntled, the commission retired to confer with Aguinaldo and returned the next day with a list of conditions which they stated must be fulfilled before they would withdraw from the suburbs. In brief these conditions were as follows:[22]

1. American jurisdiction to be confined to Manila proper and the suburbs immediately adjacent thereto.
2. The Insurgents were to retain control of the Manila water works which were located four miles outside the city. (These water works had been under the control of the Insurgents since

the beginning of the siege.) The Americans were to pay the cost of operating and maintaining the system.

3. Insurgent troops were to have free access to the city and their officers permitted to bear sidearms therein.

4. Filipino products entering the city were to be admitted duty free.

5. The monies and arms taken in the capitulation of Manila were to be divided between the Insurgents and the Americans.

6. Filipino Insurgents were to be given preference in the filling of municipal offices not held by Americans.

7. American troops were to be prohibited from passing through the Insurgent lines without authority from the Insurgent government.

Although excessive in most respects, Merritt was inclined to give the demands consideration. For one thing, he was extremely anxious to have the Manila water supply turned on. In addition, he was busy organizing the administration of the citiy and desired if possible to avoid the necessity of forcibly ejecting the Insurgents at the point of a bayonet. So with the exception of forbidding the wearing of arms by Insurgents while in the city, refusing to share any of the "spoils of war" and insisting that Americans be permitted to pass through the Insurgent lines, he agreed to the remainder and stated that if and when the Americans left the Philippines, he would leave Aguinaldo "in as good condition as when he found him."[23] Aguinaldo then agreed to withdraw his troops.

Ten days went by without any move on the part of the Insurgents towards withdrawing. Merritt wrote a sharp letter to Aguinaldo concerning the matter. The reply received three days later stated that "the price of withdrawal is a promise to restore these suburbs if and when the United States forces leave." Apparently the promise to "leave him in as good condition as when he found him" had been discussed in Insurgent councils and found to be unsatisfactory. Further negotiations on the withdrawal of the Insurgents was delayed by the departure of General Merritt from the Philippine Islands. The Spanish-American Peace Conference at Paris was now in session and the Commander of the American forces in the Philippines had been directed to appear before it and give his views on the Islands.

The negotiations were turned over to Merritt's successor, Major General Ewell S. Otis, who had arrived in the Philippines a week before. Otis was to find them a knotty problem and it would be some time before he would be able to force the Insurgents to withdraw.

The final disposition of the Islands being contingent on the

Battalion of Filipino Insurgents.

Gen. MacArthur's Private Car.

treaty of peace with Spain, the American forces sat down to weeks and possibly months of waiting. The troops were moved into quarters and the officers busied themselves with the unfamiliar job of taking over the administration of a large foreign city.

NOTES ON CHAPTER III

1 cf Article by General Anderson in the North American Review, February 1900, p. 275
2 cf Millett "The expedition to the Philippines," New York, 1899, p. 71, et. seq.
3 cf S.D. 221, 56th 1st, vol. 19, p. 106
4 cf S.D. 221, 56th 1st, vol. 18, p. 1334
5 cf S.D. 221, 56th 1st, vol. 18, p. 1233
6 cf Dewey's report, Navy Dept. 1898 p. 58
7 cf Davis, Oscar King, Our Conquests in the Pacific, New York 1899, p. 177
8 cf Ibid. p. 178. This incident is not mentioned in official reports.
9 cf S.D. 221, 56th 1st, vol. 19, p. 105
10 cf Aguinaldo, Emilio, The True Version of the Philippine Revolution, Tarlac (P. I.) 1899, p. 37
11 cf S.D. 208, 56th 1st, part 5, p. 1, et. seq.
12 cf H.D. 2, vol. 5, 56th 1st, p. 3
13 cf Dewey, op. cit. p. 27, et. seq.
14 cf H.D. No. 2, vol. 3, 55th 3rd, p. 46, et. seq.
15 cf Ibid. p. 82
16 cf Millett, op. cit. p. 159
17 cf For full text see H.D. No. 2, vol. 3, 55th 3rd, p. 48
18 cf H.D. vol. 3, 55th 3rd, p. 44
19 cf S.D. 221, vol. 18, 56th 1st, p. 1306
20 cf S.D. 208, 56th 1st, Part. 1, p. 17
21 cf Ibid.
22 cf Ibid. p. 19, et. seq.
23 cf Ibid. p. 22

Chapter IV

THE SIEGE had left Manila in a demoralized condition. The water supply had been shut off for two months and until the service was resumed the only water obtainable came from a few surface wells or what could be caught in rain barrels. The food supply had been so nearly exhausted that most of the horses and small animals in the city had been killed and used for meat. Such garbage and refuse collection system as existed had been permitted to lapse completely as had most of the other public utilities. Business was at a standstill.

However, except for comparatively minor friction with the Insurgent troops who desired to enter the city after the capitulation, the occupation of Manila by American troops was accomplished without difficulty. By late afternoon of the 13th the Spanish troops had surrendered their arms and had been housed in their own barracks. Within 24 hours General Merritt and staff were quartered in the "Malacanan," the palace of the erstwhile Spanish Governor General. Within a week practically all stores in Manila had been reopened, horse cars were running, and banks were functioning. Except for numerous American soldiers seen on the streets, the city appeared to be resuming its normal aspect.

In the capture of the city, however, Merritt had carried out only the first part of his mission. There was still left to be accomplished, the "establishment of American sovereignty in the Islands, the assumption of customs, and tax collections, the transfer of Spanish civil administration to control by the Americans and the opening of the ports to trade." The fulfillment of these purposes was complicated, as we shall see, by many unexpected factors.

In the first place, the protocol of peace signed August 12th between the United States and Spain had in its wording been ambiguous in regard to the status of the Philippine Islands. The protocol stated that the United States would retain control of "Manila, Harbor, and Bay," while the remainder of the Islands would remain in status quo until the Peace Commission had determined their final disposition. Since the protocol had been signed on August 12th, the day before the city was captured, the Spanish Governor General advanced the theory that "status quo" should be interpreted to mean the status of the city on August 12th; in other words, under Spanish sovereignty and that the articles of capitulation should be abrogated. Receiving an unsympathetic reaction to that interpretation, the idea was then advanced that American control was to be essentially local and confined to matters pertinent only to the city and harbor of Manila while the Spanish should retain colonial buildings, funds, and administration. If a strictly literal interpretation of the protocol were taken, the second argument contained a germ of reason, but was in effect academic because outside of Manila practically every province in Luzon and many of the provinces on the neighboring islands of the archipelago were under the control of the Insurgents. Merritt was loath to engage in any sort of dual administration with the Spanish, not only because of its impracticability but because recognition of this status would mean the retention by the Spanish of the large sums of colonial funds which had been surrendered under the terms of the capitulation. He therefore directed his activities on the premise that control of "Manila city, Harbor and Bay" meant control of all governmental agencies located in that area, and proceeded to take over the administration of Manila on that basis.

The result was opposition both active and passive to every change the Americans proposed. In practically all cases, Spanish officials refused to surrender the keys to their offices until an American officer had signed a statement that the change had been made by the exercise of force. In many cases the erstwhile incumbent took with him when he left, all experienced members of the office staff and in numerous other cases all office records which would have been of any value to his successor. Keys to office safes which were known to contain funds were often so difficult to locate that only after the new custodian had threatened to blow up the safe would the keys be produced. The Spanish adopted the attitude that the laborious transfer upon which the Americans insisted was purely temporary and a retransfer would take place as soon as the peace treaty was signed.

Another feature which complicated the transfer of authority was the nature and composition of the population of Manila. In 1898 Manila contained some 240,000 souls. Of these 181,000 were Filipinos of varying degree of racial purity, some 50,000 were Chinese, and some 10,000 European and American. Although Tagalog was the Filipino dialect most usually spoken by the majority of the natives who lived in Manila, many of the eighty-six other recognized Filipino dialects were often heard. The Chinese of course conversed in their native dialects whenever possible. The official language was Spanish. French, German, Japanese, and Dutch merchants spoke their language whenever convenient. The average American officer or soldier spoke only English. Hence in most cases where official intercourse took place between the Americans and the natives or Spanish, an interpreter who might or might not be honest and loyal was necessary. The language situation was a major problem to the officers charged with taking over the city administration.

A third feature which complicated the smooth establishment of American sovereignty was the attitude and assumed authority of Aguinaldo's Insurgents who were encamped in large numbers at all entrances to the city. Following the capitulation, the Insurgent government claimed the right to levy an "export tax" on all foodstuffs brought into Manila from the interior. Having control of the provinces, the "tax" was comparatively easy to collect and caused the price of food brought into the city to rise to a scandalously high level. Meat rose to a dollar a pound, eggs over a dollar a dozen. It was later found that Insurgent "tax collectors" were actually entering the city and by means of ill-concealed threats collecting money sub rosa from city merchants. Aguinaldo also showed his hand by influencing the Filipino laboring classes to strike for higher wages under the new administration and even in some cases to refuse to accept proffered jobs. However, despite these handicaps, the Army set to with a will and in a short time had the wheels of the new government machinery running in a surprisingly smooth manner.

Merritt's first official act following the capitulation of the city was to issue a proclamation to the people of the Philippines in which he stated in part:[1]

> "The commander of the United States forces has instructions from his government to assure the people of the Philippine Islands that he has not come to wage war on them, but to protect them in their homes, in their employments, and in their personal and religious rights . . . The government established among you by the United States is a government of military occupation; and for the present it is ordered that the municipal laws, such as affect private rights of persons and property, regulate local institutions, and provide for the punishment of crime shall be considered as continuing in force and that they be administered through the ordinary tribunals substantially as before occupation . . . The Port of Manila and other ports and places in the Philippines which may be in the actual possession of our land and naval forces will be open while our military occupation may continue, to the commerce of all neutral nations . . . The Commanding General in entering upon his

duty as military governor, desires to assure the people that so long as they preserve the peace and perform their duties towards the representatives of the United States, they will not be disturbed in their persons and property."

The proclamation was printed in English, Spanish, and Tagalog and published in all Manila newspapers. Other copies were circulated among the natives. Having announced his intentions, Merritt could proceed with the initiation of the new regime.

Obviously the reestablishment of firm municipal law and order was of prime importance. On the day following the capitulation, General MacArthur was appointed Provost Marshal General of the city and assigned three regiments of infantry with which to maintain order. Within a week these troops had replaced the Spanish municipal police guard and were performing the duties of civil policemen. The judges in the various Manila courts were replaced by army officers who, using Spanish and native interpreters, held court in open session, following in principle the existing laws. The Manila city council was dissolved and all matters normally within its jurisdiction were referred to MacArthur's headquarters. City employees who were members of the Fire Department, Waterworks Bureau, and sanitation squad were retained. The actual transfer of the municipal authority from Spanish to American regime was accomplished with little difficulty.

The transfer of the financial phase of the administration was much more complex, principally because insular and municipal affairs were closely intertwined. General Greene was appointed "Intendente General de Hacienda" and charged with the inventory and transfer of Spanish state funds. Greene appointed a board headed by Lieutenant Colonel Charles L. Potter, which despite obstructionist tactics on the part of the Spanish, methodically counted all government funds in the city. The colonial treasury divulged $795,517.71 (mex); the Spanish mint $62,856.08; the office of the civil governor and city council (ayuntamiento), $3,624.82; the office of internal revenue $24,527.60. Credits in the Spanish Philippine Bank, stocks, bonds, and cash funds in various safes brought the total amount to $938,878.92 of which $890,186.99 was in cash. [2] It was ascertained that the Spanish-Philippine Bank was in a precarious position, principally because of loans made to the Spanish government. Hence checks and drafts drawn on it which were found among the seized funds were withheld in an effort to bolster the tottering institution. An examination of the treasury books indicated a shortage of some

$300,000 in the treasurer's accounts. Apparently this was nothing unusual to the Spanish officials, one of whom remarked that Weyler, a former Governor General, had made away with three million. [8] Apparently the municipal government of Manila, which had been run more or less jointly with the insular government, was penniless. It is small wonder that the Spanish desired to confine the activities of the Americans to the municipal government. The seized funds were turned over to Major Charles Whipple of the Paymasters (Finance) Department, who henceforth administered them as a sort of colonial treasurer.

The occupation by the United States caused an influx of American currency into the Islands and some anomalous situations. American money, which was based on gold, was established as legal tender. The current price of gold being 2.08 (in terms of silver) the value of an American dollar, was therefore theoretically more than doubled when used to purchase articles at current prices in the Philippines. However, it was often difficult for an American shopper who tendered United States currency to convince a Chinese or Filipino shopkeeper that the American dime should buy as much as the Spanish peseta which was nearly twice its size and of the same metal. After confidence in American currency had been established, however, American soldiers, who were paid in gold dollars, became in a measure, affluent citizens. An Oregon Volunteer, for instance, desiring to purchase a dollar hat, paid one dollar in American money, received the hat and in change a Mexican dollar which actually contained more silver than the one he had tendered. The American Eagle on his dollar had more than doubled its intrinsic value.

The assumption by the Americans of the collection of internal revenue involved several problems. Major R. C. B. Bement who was charged with this important duty encountered a formidable obstacle the first day he assumed his new duties. Intending to continue in force temporarily at least the system of collections used by the Spanish, he found that the disgruntled Spanish official whom he replaced had removed from the office all copies of the current regulations and decrees then in force. After a tedious search he was able to locate duplicate copies which were after more tedious hours of work translated into English. One of the taxes imposed during the Spanish regime had been an industrial tax which was levied on all industries, trades, and professions. The majority of the Chinese merchants in the city took advantage of the current confusion and American unfamiliarity with the city to endeavor to evade this tax by changing their names, the location of their shops, or the designation of their trade. Months elapsed before the Americans were able satisfactorily to adjust themselves to the situation. The Spanish method of collecting the "Urbana" or rent tax was so confusing that even army officers, experienced in red tape, were bewildered. The system of collection was changed, and the tax reduced from 5% to 3%. Strange to say, even though the amount of the tax was reduced, the collections under the new system were greater than the Spanish had been able to obtain. The "cedula" or head tax was reduced and continued in force with free registrations temporarily to the Chinese, in an effort to identify as many of the self-effacing orientals as possible. Despite the free registration, it was later ascertained that about 50% of the celestials had failed to register.

Issuance of licenses to various trades and businesses was the principal source of income to the municipal government of Manila. The list of trades required to hold a license was formidable, including besides the usual hotels, bars, and places of amusement such trades as cobblers, tinkers, and "speculators." Also licensed were the three thousand odd native vendors who assembled with their wares at the various Manila market places. The Americans refused to license cockfights. This sport was the nearest approach to a Filipino national pastime, and lack of licenses in no way stopped sub rosa gatherings. The net effect of the prohibition was merely loss of revenue which would have been derived from the issuance of licenses. The Americans also discontinued the national lottery which had been a prolific source of income to the Spanish.

The collections of the Customs of the Port of Manila was placed under the direction of a naval officer entitled "Captain of the Port." The tariff rates in effect under the Spanish regime were continued in force as were the Spanish methods of collection. Modifications in the system were applied, however, following instructions from Washington shortly after the occupation. Later, government revenue experts were sent to the Philippines and reestablished the system along American lines. The Captain of the Port had, in addition to the collection of customs duties, the function of quarantine, emigration, harbor improvement, marine licenses, and salvage operations. The naval staff and its soldier assistants performed their duties so assiduously that customs receipts increased nearly 20% under the American administration.

When Major Frank S. Bourns of the Army Medical Corps attempted to take over his duties as President of the Manila Board of Health, he found that no sanitary service worthy of the name appeared to have been maintained under the Spanish regime. [4] The one public hospital in Manila was limited to the care of lepers. Leprosy was said to have been introduced into the Philippines from Japan in 1633, and had claimed by 1898 over 30,000 Filipinos as victims. Some 400 of these were housed in the San Lazaro Leper Hospital under the care of Franciscan Friars. In an effort positively to identify all lepers in Manila, a careful house to house inspection was later made under the supervision of the Army Medical Corps. Some one hundred more were found concealed in out-of-the-way localities throughout the city. [5]

In municipal sanitation Manila was reminiscent of many European cities in the 15th century. Within the walled city a purported drainage system handled in an inadequate fashion the sewage disposal problem; in the suburbs the network of tidal estuaries, which criss-crossed the area, theoretically served the same purpose. No underground sewage system existed. If a surface drain or estero was not conveniently located nearby, many natives did not bother to move refuse away from their houses. However, the 200,000 odd people who did use the small streams and drains for that purpose, had turned them into rank, stinking, open air cesspools, which were flushed only on the occasion of a heavy rain. Surrounding the walled city was a swampy morass which had originally been a moat, but had from neglect deteriorated into a wallowing ground for carabaos and a breeding place for mosquitoes. The better homes contained a form of indoor privy, the vault of which was cleaned and emptied only when the odor became distinctly unpleasant. During the Spanish regime, the garbage removal probem was solved in those parts of the city which received the service by hauling it to the edge of town where it was dumped and left to rot. The Americans were handicapped at the outset, for they found that the majority of the animals which had been used to haul this refuse had been eaten during the siege. Limited as they were in the matter of transportation, they improved on the system by loading garbage into cascos, which were hauled into the bay to a point where the current was off shore and there emptied. Eventually municipal incinerators were installed. In the disposal of human wastes the new regime introduced the Chinese "dry earth" or "night soil" system which, though not entirely satisfactory, was better than no system at all. Indoor toilets were required to be cleaned weekly and gradually conditions improved. Today, of course, Manila has a modern sewage system.

In 1898 an epidemic of smallpox and later the bubonic plague swept Manila. Its spread to the American troops caused the Army Medical Corps to view the general health and living conditions of the civil population of Manila as being pertinent to the well-being of the American command. A vaccine farm was established and some 80,000 natives vaccinated; rat poison was distributed to natives living in the congested areas of the city. Later a thorough census of the city was taken during which practically every native abode was visited by medical personnel. This census brought to light several interesting facts concerning the native population of the city. Among other things it was found that whereas 350 cubic feet per person was considered minimum healthful space for sleeping rooms, few native homes within the city approached this figure, many containing as little as 25 cubic feet. It was found that the actual number of Chinese living in the city exceeded the current tabulations by some 10,000. It was found that of the 180,000 citizens who were carried on cedula records as "Filipino," more than one-third had Chinese fathers. Of the 60,000 Chinese living in the city only 350 were women. Of the 200 odd Japanese living in the city, 119 were women, practically all prostitutes. The information obtained in this census enabled the Army Medical Corps to make rapid strides in improving the living and sanitary conditions in the city. Its pioneer work was later carried on by the United States Public Health Service, so that today, Manila is one of the cleanest and most healthful cities in the orient.

From the standpoint of the military authorities, the paramount health problem was the prevalence of venereal diseases. Following the occupation of the Philippines by the United States Army, swarms of dissolute Japanese, European, and American women followed in its wake. These foreign prostitutes, ably assisted by hundreds of their native sisters in trade, soon boosted the venereal rate among the American soldiers to the point where 25% of the cases on sick report were of venereal origin. In no respect condoning prostitution, but realizing that efforts to stop it entirely were Utopian, the military authorities attempted to protect the soldiers by rigid control of the traffic. Loose women were registered, segregated and examined weekly. If found infected with a venereal disease, they were hospitalized at their own expense, treated, and visited by social workers who sought to interest and train them in moral occupations. Later subjected to criticism by various "white ribbon" societies in the United States for sponsoring "licensed prostitution" in the Philippines, the American authorities found the system the most satisfactory solution to a most difficult problem. It reduced the venereal rate to a level comparable with that in the United States.

Much has been written concerning the effect that the climate of the Philippines has or had on the health of American soldiers. Compilation by the Surgeon General of the Army of sickness rates as opposed to casualties, during the Spanish-American War and the Insurrection immediately following, presents an interesting light on this matter. The climate in the Philippine Islands is essentially different from that in the United States. The year is roughly divided into three seasons: the "cool" season which usually extends from October to March, during which the temperature approximates that of early fall in the United States; the "hot dry season" from March to June, during which the sun beats down with great intensity and exposed vegetation usually withers and dies; and the "rainy" season from June to October, during which it rains nearly every day, rivers frequently reach flood stage, leather mildews, and nearly everything is constantly damp. However, despite these three "seasons", the daily temperature never varies more than thirty degrees from the annual mean temperature of 80 degrees Fahrenheit. It is the extreme humidity of the air which makes the climate debilitating to Americans and necessitates occasional vacations to more temperate climates.

The Surgeon General's statistics on death rates from sickness indicate that during the period from May 1898 to June 1899, the death rate per thousand men in the United States Army was, [6] for the Philippines, 17.20; for Porto Rico, 38.15; for Cuba 45.14; for the United States 23.81. Those figures might be interpreted to mean that during the Spanish-American War, the safest place in which a soldier could serve was the Philippine Islands. These figures become more interesting when compared to the death rate among the civilian population of some of our large cities for the same year. [7] Washington with 20.74 deaths per thousand of population, Boston with 20.09, San Francisco with 19.41 and New York with 19.28, all exceeded the Philippine death rate. However, these figures show the deaths and not the non-fatal sickness rate; that is, the data on malaria, dysentery and diarrhea, which, though not fatal, often permanently incapacitated an individual and were apt to recur throughout the remainder of his life. As one Army Medical officer said: [8]

> "All sickness in the tropics, produces an effect on the general economy that does not follow similar sickness in the temperate regions, in that it saps vital forces which are not restored by natural processes. The effect of illness in the tropics is therefore cumulative, each illness great or small adding to the total until the patient becomes permanently disabled."

And experience proved that years after the war was over, many veterans of the Philippine Insurrection, suffered recrudescenses of malaria and dysentery which they had contracted in the Islands.

Of paramount importance to any city is its water supply. Like most cities the source of Manila's drinking water was not within the narrow confines of the city itself but some distance away. A pumping station on the Mariquina River, eight miles east of the city, pumped the water to reservoirs located four miles distant, from which it was piped into the city. The Insurgents controlled both the pumping station and the reservoirs and had cut off the city supply at the beginning of the siege. One of the demands made by Aguinaldo as the price of his withdrawal from the suburbs of Manila had been that the Americans were to bear the cost of maintaining the water works, which were also to be operated under American supervision. However the worn out condition of the plant, coupled with the hostile attitude evinced by Insurgent troops every time any Americans approached their lines, made the reestablishment of the water supply system in the city a matter of protracted delay. On one occasion Lieutenant William D. Connor, [9] an engineer officer who had been placed in charge of the plant and had visited the pumping station in the normal discharge of his duties, was marched back to the American lines at the point of rifles. Although 97% of the population of Manila used the city water, drawing it from public hydrants installed on various streets, it was found that two-thirds of these hydrants had been permitted to lapse into an unserviceable condition during the last days of the Spanish regime. As the Insurgents and American forces drifted apart during the fall of 1898, it became evident that the continuance of the city's water supply was becoming increasingly precarious. When actual hostilities broke out in February of 1899, one of the first moves made by the Americans was to capture the reservoir and pumping station. From that time on it was held under American control. Later, distilling plants were shipped from the United States and effectively supplemented the city system.

Captain Lea Febiger, who was placed in charge of the department of streets, parks, fire, and sanitation, encountered two difficult problems. In the first place he found it difficult to hire native labor because of pressure being exerted by the Insurgent groups. Secondly, the large piles of refuse which had been permitted to accumulate during the siege were difficult to move because of shortage of transportation. As mentioned before, the problem was temporarily solved by hauling the refuse into the bay and dumping it there. However, accumulations occasioned when stormy weather prevented the scows from being hauled into the bay and the unusual conditions of crowding in the city because of the large number of troops, both Spanish and American being quartered there, made the matter of city sanitation a subject of slow improvement. It took patience and time to educate natives to the standards of sanitation prevalent in the United States. Even today this standard has not been reached.

The Manila Fire Department, which consisted of some 92 professional firemen, assisted at times by some 240 laborers who also worked in the department of sanitation, was continued on its normal duties. Although the majority of the buildings within the walled city were of stone construction, the houses and shops in the suburbs which clustered nearby were universally constructed of flimsy tinder-like wood and bamboo and constituted an extreme fire hazard. When the Americans took over the city administration, the Fire Department's equipment consisted of two steam and five hand engines, all of which were unserviceable. Yankee ingenuity contrived to fabricate the seven useless into one serviceable vehicle, which became Manila's only fire protection until new equipment, including American horses, could be imported from the United States.

Carried on under the tutelage of the various religious orders, the Manila schools were continued status quo with minor modifications. Chaplain W. D. McKinnon who was placed in charge of their administration introduced one English instructor into each school. The practice of requiring instruction in religious subjects was discontinued. Later public schools were established using American soldiers as instructors. Eventually subsidized by the insular government, the number of schools and teachers and the amount of equipment grew until the Filipino educational system developed to a point where it was comparable to that in the United States.

An institution known as the Carcel de Bilibid had, during the Spanish regime, performed the combined functions of insular penitentiary and municipal jail. Using American soldiers as guards and turnkeys, the prison was taken over from the Spanish authorities and continued in use. On the transfer of records, three of the Spanish officers concerned with the prison administration were found to have embezzled the funds of the institution. They were tried by an American court martial, two of them were found guilty and both sentenced to incarceration in the seat of their former endeavors. Of the 2000 odd prisoners found confined, all who had been imprisoned for political offenses were released. The remainder were put to work manufacturing bamboo cots for the quartermaster.

Although army officers are not as a rule versed in the many intricacies of civil administration, their military training tends to make them able executives. The administration by the army of the civil government of the Philippines during the early days of '98 proved that industry and honesty are sufficient requisites for efficient civil administration. These officers and men entered a strange land, encountered strange languages and incipient hostility from both Insurgents and Spanish; they combatted a lackadaisical disinterestedness on the part of the native citizenry; and they found public utilities in a run-down or useless condition. They were forced to ferret out the acme of oriental guile in attempts at graft and tax evasion; but despite these handicaps they were able by working, many of them twelve hours a day, to keep the financial status of the government "in the black." Disregarding seized funds, they were able to show a balance at the end of this trying first nine months' period of $738,959.02. [10] The largest single item of income was the collection of customs, which was easily susceptible to graft or losses due to inefficiency. Compared with the year of 1897 under the Spanish, the customs receipts jumped nearly a million dollars the first year and six million the second. [11] The amount of money which had been embezzled by Spanish officials during their regime will probably never be known.

With the city captured and gradually assuming on the surface at least its normal tropical equanimity, and with the war with Spain concluded, the American volunteer soldiers in Manila began to think of home and became bored and undisciplined. An eyewitness who was present in Manila [12] reports that a typical posture of sentinels while on post was to be seated on the ground smoking a cigar, his back against a tree, and his rifle on the ground beside him. The common uniform on or off duty was a pair of ragged slacks, a blue flannel shirt with sleeves cut off at the shoulders and the felt hat cut full of fantastic holes. However, though he did not realize it, the American soldier was soon to find that his Philippine service would involve a much more arduous occupation than indolent guard duty. He would cross many mucky swamps, wade many swollen streams, and sleep in many sunbaked rice paddies before he would see his home again.

NOTES ON CHAPTER IV

1 For full text see H.D. No. 2, Vol. 3, 55th 3rd p. 49 *et. seq.*
2 *cf* HD No. 2. Vol. 5, 56th 1st p. 280
3 *cf* Millett *op. cit.* p. 178
4 *cf* HD No. 2 Vol. 8, 57th 1st p. 89

5 *cf* Ibid
6 *cf* HD No. 2 Vol. 2, 56th 1st p. 23
7 *cf* Ibid
8 *cf* HD No. 2 Vol. 6, 56th 2nd p. 119
9 Later Major General U. S. Army, Superintendent, U. S. M. A. at West Point
10 *cf* HD No. 2 Vol. 5, 56th 1st p. 290
11 *cf* HD No. 2, Vol. 11, 56th 2nd p. 8
12 *cf* Millett *op. cit.* p. 208

Chapter V

Assuming command of the American troops a week after his arrival in the Philippine Islands, Major General Ewell S. Otis inherited the incipient quarrel between the Americans and Insurgents over the joint occupation of Manila. His lack of knowledge concerning the Islands was as profound as that of any of the other officers and his arrival in the midst of the transference of the civil administration forced him into the awkward position of being dependent upon the advice of his subordinates. He was to find that regardless of the professed intentions on the part of Aguinaldo to evacuate the suburbs of the city, the actual withdrawal was to be a matter of protracted delay. It would result in weeks of diplomatic negotiation, finally culminating in the threat of removal by force. He was also to see the shift of Filipino-American relations from the status of allies to the point where a rift developed into an armed insurrection and war between the two peoples.

General Otis had graduated from the Harvard Law School with the class of 1861. In 1862 he had joined the Union Army as a Captain of Volunteers. During the war he was twice cited for gallantry and by 1865 had been promoted to the rank of Brevet Brigadier General of Volunteers. At the conclusion of the war he had been offered a commission as Lieutenant Colonel in the Regular Army which he had accepted and by 1897 had risen to the grade of Brigadier General. Upon the declaration of war with Spain, he had been temporarily commissioned as Major General of Volunteers.

Above average height, soft spoken, a wearer of old fashioned sideburns, his administration of the Philippine Islands during 1898 and 1899 has been both highly eulogized and bitterly censured. His critics maintained that he was puerile, that his perspective was microscopic, and that his careful attention to minute details and his insistence that all decisions, whether made in Manila or in the field, be referred to him, curbed initiative among his subordinates. His admirers pointed out that despite the difficulties involved in the administration of ten million foreign people, living some 7000 miles from the United States, he strove desperately to maintain peace and when the revolt did occur, he broke its backbone within a comparatively short time.

Since he was sixty-one years of age at the time, and an old Civil

War wound had rendered him the victim of insomnia, he spent many sleepless hours working at his desk at American Headquarters. He usually arrived at his office at 7:30 a. m. carrying in his pocket a sandwich for lunch so that he could remain until 5:00 p. m. Then after taking a short drive on the Luneta followed by dinner at his quarters, he was back at his office by 8:00 p. m., busy until midnight. He stayed close to his desk and refused to delegate his authority to subordinates regardless of their rank. He personally examined all papers requiring his nominal approval whether or not of any great importance. It is related that on one occasion a company requisition for cutlery, which involved an expenditure of $6.00, reached his desk after having received the favorable indorsement of intermediate commanders. Noting a technical flaw in the paper, he sent it back to all concerned with a stinging reprimand in his own handwriting.

By reason of his minute attention to detail, he was able without reference to a map or chart quickly and from memory to recite the names of all towns or sectors held by the American forces, the units occupying them and in many cases even the names and capabilities of the commanders of the units, to include those in company grade. During hostilities, he meticulously directed all movements of the American forces from his headquarters in Manila and in most cases refused to listen to the importunities of the commanders in the field. It has been said that the only time he left Manila during his two-year stay was when he made a railroad trip to Angeles, sixty miles away, for the purpose of seeing that the proper valuation was placed on a dead quartermaster mule. By his own admission, he took only one day of vacation during his entire tour of duty in the Philippines. His legal training asserts itself unmistakably in all his reports, communications and orders. It enabled him to face with equanimity the prolific verbal barrage with which Aguinaldo's European educated advisors were soon to shower him.

Otis had brought with him from the United States additional troops in the form of volunteer regiments from South Dakota and Montana, five companies of the 14th Infantry, six troops of the 4th Cavalry, and two batteries of the 6th Artillery. These additions brought the strength of the American forces in the Philippines up to 15,559 officers and men. [1]

On taking over his duties as Commanding General and Military Governor of the Philippines, Otis found that the prime unsolved problem was the matter of the Insurgents still encamped at the doorstep of the walled city. Merritt had turned over to him the still unanswered letter from Aguinaldo which had quoted the price of

Insurgent withdrawal to be the promise by the Americans that the Insurgent troops would be restored to the advantageous location they then held, in the event of the resumption of Spanish sovereignty in the Islands.

Otis pondered over the matter for ten days and on September 8 addressed a voluminous (3 thousand words), judicially phrased ultimatum to Aguinaldo, demanding his withdrawal within a week. A few brief excerpts of this communication give the tone which the relations between the Americans and Insurgents were taking at this time. In substance Otis said: [2]

> "The United States appreciates the services of the Insurgents in fighting a common enemy, the Spaniards. However, bear in mind that the United States has swept the Spanish flag from the seas, kept Spanish troops from being sent to the Philippines for the purpose of putting down your rebellion and has had Manila at its mercy since May 1st . . . Spain, the recognized owner, has capitulated Manila and its suburbs to the United States; there can be no legal question as to the propriety of full American sovereignty . . . Joint occupation of the suburbs is impossible; irresponsible members of either army, careless or impertinent actions, might incite grave disturbances . . . I have no authority and am powerless to make any promises in regard to the restoration of your troops to certain lines, contingent on the Americans leaving the Philippines . . . I deplore any conflict between our forces, but find it necessary to give you notice that if your troops are not withdrawn beyond the line of city defenses, within one week, I will force you to move and my government shall hold you responsible."

Aguinaldo's reaction to the letter was one of anger, coupled with the intent to oppose force with force. The day following receipt of Otis' letter, a reconnaissance by some American troops into Sampaloc, a suburb in the north part of the city, resulted in a minor clash between the Insurgents and Americans. Aguinaldo immediately enjoined General Pantaleon Garcia, who was in command at Sampaloc as follows: [3]

> "I gave an order long ago not to permit our line to be passed and to say frankly it was by my order. To be prepared to defend our rights, you are ordered to place troops in front of the American position at Sampaloc and to tell them plainly to leave, to warn the Sandatahan [4] and get everything ready. You must warn the Commanders of the zone about Manila. Do not forget whenever in doubt."

However, conditions in the Insurgent army as evidenced by a telegram which Aguinaldo received two days later from General Cailles, an Insurgent Brigadier General in command of troops on the south side of the city, may have determined his subsequent action. On September 13, Cailles, who did not mince words, wired Aguinaldo as follows: [5]

> "I inform your excellency that we have no Mauser cartridges; I hear there are many in Batangas. Americans pay a good price for empty cartridges and shells. I ask your excellency to order General Noriel to send us shells: the General has a factory at Paranaque. I am sorry for our soldiers. I see that the more they work and the more they expose their lives, the less they receive. Since your excellency has charged me with these operations, no one has given me a cent to meet the expenses of the Headquarters at Pineda. More than ten superior and other officers eat here at my wife's expense. She has no more. We do not smoke. I am perplexed. Patience I suffer everything for my most beloved and unforgettable President."

The same day that Aguinaldo received the above telegram from Cailles, he sent a commission to Otis. The purpose of the commission was to explain that, desirous as the Filipino leaders might be to evacuate the city, the Insurgent soldiers were belligerent, restless, and might not obey an order to withdraw were it given. If the American Commander would change his "demand" for a withdrawal to a "request," the Insurgent leaders could use the modification as an American olive branch and wave it before their undisciplined troops, who would probably withdraw quietly and save the faces of all concerned. A practical man, Otis readily agreed to the change and sent the commission back to Aguinaldo armed with a letter full of felicitations and "requesting" the withdrawal of Insurgent troops from Manila.

Two days later with bands playing and passing through cheering crowds, the Insurgents marched out of the city. The event is best described by quoting another telegram from General Cailles who in his näive way reported to Aguinaldo: [6]

> "The outgoing force was grand. I am at the head of a column of 1800 men almost all uniformed, three bands of music. As we came to the Luneta from Calle Real, Ermita, Americans and natives fell in behind yelling "Viva Filipinos," "Viva Emilio Aguinaldo." We answered "Viva America," "Viva la libertad." The Americans presented arms and at command my battalion came to a port."

Not evacuated however were the suburbs of Paco and Pandacan

which were occupied by Insurgents under the command of General Pio Del Pilar. According to Aguinaldo, Pilar refused to comply with instructions from the Insurgent Government to withdraw. Aguinaldo sent a note to Otis explaining that as soon as he was able, he would force Pilar to evacuate. As the days lapsed into weeks and Pilar did not move with his small brigade, Otis rightly suspected that Aguinaldo was exerting no pressure on Pilar to move. Further correspondence on the matter elicited the argument from Aguinaldo that since these two particular suburbs had not been mentioned in the terms of the capitulation of Manila (as had certain other suburbs from which the Insurgents had withdrawn) there was no legal basis for requiring them to withdraw. Aguinaldo was correct, and Otis, hesitating to use force, permitted them to remain. Pilar took advantage of the situation to fortify the districts which were separated from the rest of the city by the Pasig River and the large Estero de Paco. The Insurgent lines in Pandacan were just across the river from the Malacanan, Otis' quarters, and the undisciplined Filipino soldiers used their proximity to the city as means of provoking the Americans at every opportunity. Pilar's troops entered the American lines at night, engaged in highway robbery, kidnapped Filipinos unfavorable to their cause, and in some cases created disturbances within a block of Otis' quarters. Having wired the War Department that 5000 more American troops should be sent to the Philippines, Otis was enjoined to avoid hostilities with the Insurgents, if possible. Two years later while testifying before a Senate Committee, Otis made the statement: [6a]

"I not only had the right but it was my duty to make them remove beyond the city and its defenses; and I had a right, a perfect right, to drive them farther away from the city. And there is no nation except the United States in the world which would have allowed those people to have hemmed you in that city the way they did."

Prime provocation from Pilar's troops came early in October when General Anderson, the Division Commander, was arrested by an Insurgent guard and not permitted to pass through the Insurgent lines. General Anderson was so incensed that the next day he wrote the following letter to Otis: [7]

The Adjutant General, Department of the Pacific and 8th Army Corps, Manila, P. I.

Sir: I have the honor to report, that yesterday, while proceeding up the Pasig River in the steam launch "Canacao" with three officers of my staff, the American flag flying over the boat,

I was stopped by an armed Filipino guard and informed that we could go no further. Explaining that we were an unarmed party of American officers out upon an excursion, we were informed that by orders given two days before, no Americans, armed or unarmed, were allowed to pass up the Pasig River without a special permit from President Aguinaldo.

I demanded to see the written order and it was brought and shown to me. It was an official letter signed by Pio Del Pilar, Division General, written in Tagalog and stamped with what appeared to be an official seal. It purported to be issued by the authority of the President of the Revolutionary Government and forbade Americans, either armed or unarmed, from passing up the Pasig River. It was signed by Pilar himself.

As this is a distinctly hostile act I beg leave to ask how far we are to submit to this kind of interference.

It is respectfully submitted that whether this act of Pilar was authorized or not by the assumed Insurgent government, it should in any event be resented.

Very Respectively,

THOMAS H. ANDERSON,
Major General, USV Commanding Division.

Meanwhile the evacuation of the remainder of the Insurgents on September 15 had not been entirely satisfactory. Otis had intended them to withdraw beyond the line of Spanish blockhouses which surrounded the city. Aguinaldo maintained that American authority under the capitulation was confined to the city itself and that these blockhouses were outside the city limits. It appeared that no definite city boundary line had been surveyed during the Spanish regime. Consequently Otis, after searching through dusty Manila municipal records, assembled sufficient data to permit survey of the original city limits. He sent a blue print to Aguinaldo and said in effect "This map shows the official boundary line of the city of Manila. You must withdraw beyond the line." Divided in their counsels as to whether they should withdraw or fight, the Insurgents finally decided to withdraw and did so on October 25, first gaining permission from Otis, however, to occupy some of the Spanish blockhouses as shelter for their troops. It had taken the Americans two and a half months to get their erstwhile "allies" out of the city.

Except for Manila, Aguinaldo's government had extended its authority to such an extent that it now held complete sway over the Island of Luzon. As the rebellion spread through the provinces the numerous Spanish friars, priests, nuns, and civil officials isolated therein, found themselves defenseless and victims of Filipino resentment which had been restrained for generations. Thousands of these unfortunate Spaniards were imprisoned and subjected to numerous indignities. Highly colored rumors reached Manila and permeated to Europe and the United States that these unfortunate Spaniards were being starved, that nuns were being violated and that the conditions under which they were imprisoned were conducive to a lingering death. The Spanish government was aware of the situation but was helpless to remedy it.

Motivated by pressure from the Vatican and American Catholics, the War Department directed Otis to take the matter up with Aguinaldo and obtain if possible the release of those prisoners who were civilians. On November 2, Otis addressed a letter to Aguinaldo in which he pointed out that stories of the condition of these prisoners was causing "a great deal of severe criticism of the Filipino people in the United States and throughout Europe" and that in no civilized country are ecclesiastics and civil officials normally held as "prisoners of war." [8] Otis further offered to meet any expenses involved in transporting the Spanish to Manila and agreed to care for them while those who desired to return to Spain awaited transportation. Aguinaldo replied quickly and emphatically. In substance he said:[9] "I am holding civil officials because on numerous occasions they have been formed into armed volunteer corps and have borne arms against my troops. In regard to the ecclesiastics, since the Vatican refuses to recognize the Filipino clergy, in holding these priests I have an effective weapon with which to secure that recognition. Furthermore, numerous Filipinos have been deported for political offenses and are rotting in Spanish prisons. I hold these Spanish civilians as a medium of exchange." Otis transmitted the information to Washington and let the matter drop, but reorganized his troops into two divisions, placing MacArthur in command of the new division and assigning it to the front on the north of the city. Anderson retained command of the 1st division in the southern sector.

However bold as were his replies to Otis, Aguinaldo, who had moved his government to the town of Malolos, about twenty miles north of Manila, was encountering difficulties in his own government. In the area south of Manila, troops were deserting from the Insurgent army, supplies and funds were exhausted, and hunger was prevalent.

From Calamba Tayabas, General Lucban, who was later on the Island of Samar to become an anathema to American authority, wired to Aguinaldo on November 12: [10]

"Provincial Battalion of Tayabas suffers from hunger causing many desertions: local and provincial funds exhausted. Forward supplies and what you consider necessary. Urge quantity
to solve difficulty at once."

In Tarlac Province to the north, an incipient rebellion against
Aguinaldo's government broke out under the leadership of an ex-
sergeant in the Spanish civil guard. The revolt overthrew Aguinaldo's authority in the comparatively large town of Tarlac and was
a source of alarm and disturbance to the Insurgent government
until its leader was treacherously murdered two months later.
Throughout the Island numerous bands of Tulisanes, armed rob-
bers, roamed the countryside, recognizing the authority of no government. Such Insurgent troops as were armed and under control
were undisciplined and spoiling for a fight with the Americans.

By December, ensconced fairly comfortably in Manila, Otis noted
that the sick rate of his troops was decreasing and that total
American deaths in the Philippines to date had been 161, of which
eighty had been due to typhoid fever, dysentery, and smallpox.
Annoyed by seditious articles in a Manila newspaper, he brought
the editor to trial before a military commission and fined him $500.
The arrival of more transports from the United States brought
volunteers from Washington, Kansas, Tennessee and Iowa, detachments of the 18th and 23rd regular Infantry and increased his
strength on December 6 to 22,312 officers and men. [11]

On December 10, the news was flashed to Manila that the peace
treaty with Spain had been signed in Paris, and that the United
States had "purchased" the Philippine Islands from Spain for
$20,000,000. The announcement had a profound effect on both
Americans and Filipinos. In Paris Felipe Agoncillo, who had unsuccessfully attempted to state a case for Philippine Independence
before the peace commission, announced: "The Filipinos will not
permit themselves or their homes to be bought and sold like merchandise." In Manila, Otis was flooded with applications from
homesick volunteers for discharge and return to the United States.
Among the natives, resentment at the failure of their aspirations
to independence matured into open hostility towards the Americans. Otis refused all applications for discharge on the ground
that until the United States Senate had ratified the treaty the war
was not officially ended and completed his preparation for the
defense of the city if and when an attack by the Insurgents took
place.

An interesting but troublesome interlude now imposed itself upon the American Commander. Early in December he received a visit from a committee of native business men residing in Iloilo on the Island of Panay. Iloilo was the second port of the Philippine Islands and was about 300 miles south of Manila. Presenting Otis with a petition the committee in effect said: "We represent the business interests of Iloilo. The Spanish garrison there has been attacked by Filipino Insurgents and is preparing to evacuate the Island. We fear that as soon as the Spanish leave, a form of Insurgent anarchy will prevail. The Spanish commanding officer there states that if the Americans send troops to Iloilo he will be glad to turn the city and its defenses over to them before he leaves. Will you not send American troops there to protect the banks and business houses of the second largest port in the Archipelago?" Favoring immediate action Otis conferred with Dewey regarding a navy convoy. Dewey counseled a delay until authority from Washington was received. Uncertain, Otis vacillated and then on December 14th sent the following telegram to the War Department: [12]

> "Bankers and merchants with business houses at Iloilo petition American protection at Iloilo. Spanish authorities still holding out but will receive United States troops. Insurgents reported favorable to American annexation. Can send troops. Shall any action be taken?"

Ten days later, Otis received the reply: [13]

> "Answering your message December 14, the President directs that you send necessary troops to Iloilo to preserve the peace and protect life and property. It is most important that there should be no conflict with the Insurgents. Be conciliatory but firm."

The Island of Panay, an area about the size of the State of Connecticut, was progressive and enjoyed a prosperous trade in sugar, tobacco and rice. On the southern coast near the mouth of a river of the same name sat Iloilo, the provincial capital, a city of some 13,000 inhabitants. The Island was populated by Visayans, a native tribe who differed from the Tagalogs of Luzon both in language and racial characteristics.

The 51st Iowa Volunteers had arrived off Manila on December 6 and, pending the proposed expedition to Iloilo, had remained on the transport. On December 25 the personnel of the expedition was completed by adding the 18th (regular) Infantry and Battery G of the 6th Field Artillery. In command was placed Brigadier General

71

Marcus P. Miller, a West Point graduate who had seen forty-one years of active service in the Regular Army, but who was strictly limited in the scope of his actions by detailed instructions which he received from Otis prior to his departure. The substance of these instructions were as follows: [14]

> "If upon arrival at Iloilo you find the Spanish still there, take over from them and establish a government of military occupation similar to that now existing in Manila. If the Spanish troops have left and the Insurgent troops are found to be in possession, advise them that the United States has succeeded to all the rights of Spain in the Islands, and acquaint them with the benevolent aims of the Americans. Under no circumstance engage in a conflict with the Insurgents. Should they oppose the landing of American troops, stay on the transports and await instructions from Manila."

Then accompanied by the petitioning committee and some 200 Visayan Spanish prisoners of war, who were to be liberated on Panay as an evidence of American good intentions, and convoyed by the *Baltimore* and the captured Spanish gunboat *Callao*, Miller's expedition left Manila December 26 and arrived off Iloilo two days later.

The delay occasioned by the necessity of awaiting tardy instructions from Washington proved costly to the pacific accomplishment of Miller's purposes. Upon arrival at Iloilo, it was found that the Spanish had given up hope that the Americans were coming and had evacuated the city thirty-six hours previously; in possession of the place were some 3000 Insurgents. To the American emissaries who were sent ashore Martin Delgado, the Insurgent leader, politely but steadfastly refused to deliver the city over to the Americans without authority from Aguinaldo and hinted at armed resistance to any attempt of the Americans to obtain control by force. Sensing a shift in the political breeze, the petitioning committee indicated their allegiance to the Insurgents and begged Miller not to attack the city.

Hampered as he was by his orders, Miller could do nothing but remain on the transports and advise Otis of the situation, telling him at the same time that if permitted he could capture the city with little trouble. While telegrams were exchanged between Washington and Manila, Miller was forced to sit idly by in the harbor and watch the Insurgents fortify the city, take over the collection of customs duties in the prosperous port, and augment their strength until it amounted to some 12,000 men. The War Department was emphatic in its insistence to Otis that the Americans must not be the first to commence hostilities in the Islands.

With ships anchored in Iloilo Harbor the watchful waiting policy continued until January, when the sanitary conditions among the Iowa Volunteers, who had been continuously cooped up on the crowded transport *Pennsylvania* for nearly three months, became so bad that their debarkation became imperative. The *Pennsylvania* was returned to Manila and the Iowans put ashore. The remainder of the expedition remained at Iloilo but did not obtain possession of the city until it was attacked and captured in February after the rebellion had broken out in Luzon.

Nearly four years later in speaking of the incident Otis remarked: [15]

> "I should have never asked instructions from Washington. I should have gone there at once (before the Spanish evacuated) and by so doing I would have saved two million dollars worth of property."

Shortly after the treaty of peace with Spain was signed, President McKinley sent to Otis a proclamation announcing the assumption by the United States of sovereignty over the Philippine Islands and directed that it be published and circulated among the Filipino people. An orthodox, formally written type of document, the wording of the proclamation gave Otis food for thought. He knew that the Malolos government had just split on the question of a friendly or belligerent attitude towards the assumption of sovereignty by the Americans. Mabini's "war group" had won out, and a new cabinet composed of anti-Americanistas was formed with Mabini at its head. Although still President and nominally head of the government, Aguinaldo was being pushed into the position of a figurehead. Years of Spanish absolutism in government had given such expressions used in the proclamations as "sovereignty," "control," "supreme authority" an ominous meaning in the minds of many Filipinos.

Cognizant of the growing tension and acting on the advice of a few prominent Filipinos who had disavowed Aguinaldo's government, Otis made a move which was, for any army officer who values his commission rash in the extreme; he altered the President's proclamation and rewrote it in his own words. In the revised document, he eliminated all words or expressions which he believed might be misunderstood or misconstrued. Terms such as "supreme control" "authority must reign supreme" were eliminated. "Temperate administration of affairs" was changed to "temporary administration of affairs." The net effect of the changes was to soften the tenor of the document until it did not convey a distinct suggestion of an absolute control and domination of the United States. After he returned to the United States Otis was called to account for the changes he made in the President's proclamation. He explained his purpose by stating: [16]

"I was fighting hard for peace and I struck out words which I thought Mabini might use to excite the people."

His explanation was accepted and his action in this case deemed proper.

Modified or not, the proclamation which was issued on January 4, 1899, was seized upon by the Malolos Insurgent government as an excuse for the issuance of two vituperant protests against American assumption of authority in the Archipelago. Signed by Aguinaldo, these Filipino counter proclamations reviewed the cooperation between Americans and Filipinos which culminated in the overthrow of Spanish power in the Islands; mentioned "promises" of independence which Consul Pratt made to Aguinaldo in Singapore; and referred to the Americans as "intruders." They reviewed the situation in the Philippines from the standpoint of the Filipino and accused the Americans of duplicity and ingratitude. The first proclamation, which was withdrawn shortly after it had been concluded, closed with the following poignant statement. [17]

"My government cannot remain indifferent in view of such a violent and aggressive seizure of a portion of its territory by a nation which has arrogated to itself the title champion of oppressed nations. Thus it is that my government is disposed to open hostilities if the American troops attempt to take forcible possession of the Visaya Islands (meaning Iloilo). I denounce these (the various) acts (of the Americans) before the world in order that the conscience of mankind may pronounce its infallible verdict as to who are the oppressors of nations and the tormentors of mankind."

The more practical reaction of the Filipinos to the proclamations was evidenced in the exodus from Manila of some 40,000 natives with their household goods, the discovery that the Chinese metal workers of Manila were doing a booming business in the sub rosa manufacture of bolos, and in the interception of letters from Aguinaldo to prominent citizens in Manila, advising them to come to Malolos where they would be safe.

On his part, Otis was subjected to constant pressure from Washington enjoining him to try to convince the Filipinos that American intentions were benevolent and to stave off hostilities until time should weaken the unstable Insurgent government.

Aguinaldo's attitude at this time is indicated by a captured document issued under his signature on January 9. The missive was addressed to the "Brave soldiers of the Sandatahan of Manila" and appears to be a form of field order for an attack on Manila from within, combined with a training manual for these proletarian groups which he had organized into a sort of Insurrecto Militia. Interesting excerpts from the document are as follows: [18]

> "All Filipinos should observe our fellow countrymen in order to see whether they are American sympathizers. Whenever they are assured of the loyalty of the convert, they shall instruct them to continue in the character of an American sympathizer in order that they may receive good pay but without prejudicing the cause of our country.
>
> "All of the chiefs and Filipinos brothers should be ready and courageous for the combat and should take advantage of the opportunity to study well the situation of the American outposts and Headquarters . . .
>
> "The chief of those who go to attack the barracks should send in first four men with a good present for the American commander. They should not prior to the attack look at the Americans in a threatening manner. To the contrary the attack on the barracks by the Sandatahan should be a complete surprise and with decision and courage. In order to deceive the sentinel, one should dress as a woman and take care that the sentinel is not able to discharge his piece.
>
> "At the moment of attack, the Sandatahan should not attempt to secure rifles from their dead enemies, but shall pursue slashing right and left with bolos until the Americans surrender"
>
> "The Officers shall take care that on the tops of houses along the streets where the American forces shall pass there will be placed four to six men who shall be prepared with stones, timbers, red hot iron, heavy furniture, as well as boiling water, oil, and molasses, rags soaked in coal oil ready to be lighted and thrown down on passing American troops.
>
> "In place of bolos or daggers, if they do not possess the same, the Sandatahan can provide themselves with lances and arrows. These should be so made that in the withdrawal of the body, the head will remain in the flesh.
>
> "Experience has taught me, my dear brothers, that when the Sandatahan make their attack with courage and decision, taking advantage of the confusion in the ranks of the army, the victory is sure and in that case the triumph is ours.
>
> "Last, if as I expect the result shall favor us in the taking of

75

Manila and the conquering of the enemy, the chiefs are charged with seeing that the officers and soldiers respect the consulates, banks and commercial houses. I expect that you will respect the persons and goods of private persons of all nationalities, that you will treat well the prisoners and grant life to those of the enemy who surrender."

It was indeed fortunate for the little American Army which was isolated 7000 miles from home that the Sandatahan was unable to carry out these bloodthirsty instructions.

The Insurgent Army was in the meanwhile becoming more and more belligerent. On January 10 General Cailles, who at "the head of 1800 troops nearly all uniformed" had grandly marched out of the suburbs three months previous, wired Aguinaldo: [19]

"An American interpreter has come to tell me to withdraw our forces in Maytubig fifty paces. I shall not draw back a step and in place of withdrawing I shall advance a little further. I said (to the interpreter) that I did not want to have dealings with any American. War, War, is what we want. The Americans, after this speech went off pale."

Cailles' action was approved and applauded by the Insurgent President.

Subordinate Insurgent leaders were further coaxed and worked into a frenzy of hostility toward the Americans by promises of money, promotion, and the bestowal of titles of nobility such as the Marquis of Malate, Count of Manila, in the event the city was captured. [20] With an Insurgent Army of some 20,000 men surrounding the city, the Americans were finding themselves literally besieged and in a situation somewhat similar to that of the Spanish prior to August 13.

Realizing that something must be done if peace was to be maintained, Otis arranged on January 9 for the meeting of a joint Filipino-American commission for the purpose of "working out a plan for the adjustment of conflicting political interests of the parties concerned." Negotiating intermittently for over two weeks, the commission accomplished little, except to postpone the outbreak of hostilities. At the first session the Filipino representatives stated their basis for conciliation to be "absolute independence." They later deadlocked the conference by modifying their demands to an insistence upon a vague sort of American protectorate which would give them authority over the government without retaining the responsibility for defense against foreign aggression. Brigadier General R. P. Hughes, who was the Chairman of the American delegation, later said in testifying before a Senate committee: [21]

> "We met from time to time and spent hours trying to arrive at just what these men (the Filipino delegation) wanted. For instance, we asked them "What are we to understand by your demand for absolute independence? Do you mean that you wish the Americans to go out and take their transports and sail out of this harbor?" "Oh no; God's sake, no, no; we will make the laws and you will stay here and see that outsiders do not disturb us." And we never, from the day we began until the day we quit, could get the definition of what they really wanted. They did not know themselves."

Hughes also frankly admitted that he purposely dragged out the sessions pending the arrival of some expected American reinforcements. [22]

Impatient with the proceedings of the joint commission, the Malolos government anticipated its failure and on January 21 while the commission was still in session, promulgated the constitution for the Philippine Republic. The document was liberal and showed the handiwork of the brilliant Mabini and some of Aguinaldo's other well-educated advisors. Not dissimilar to the Constitution of the United States in many respects, it did, however, provide that a unicameral legislature should elect a president who was to serve a four year term and be eligible for reelection. [23] A week later, Aguinaldo, who had been elected President of the new republic, officially notified Otis of the new constitution and näively asked recognition of his government by the United States. Otis replied that he had cabled a copy of the constitution to Washington and made no other comment.

Necessary defensive measures on the part of the American troops, which were visible to the Insurgents, and growing excitement among the Filipinos, placed the time of actual outbreak of hostilities in the lap of fortune. An American sentry shot a Filipino captain who crossed his post wearing a pistol. The Provost Marshal seized Aguinaldo's telegraph office located in Manila and confiscated its files and equipment. Aguinaldo arrested an American engineer mapping party and imprisoned them at Malolos. Mistaking the feigned pacific demeanor which Otis enforced on his troops for cowardice, Filipino soldiers taunted American sentries, ignored challenges and crossed their posts at will.

On February 3, Otis wrote to Dewey: [24]

> "There has been a great deal of friction along the lines in

the past two days and we will be unable to tamely submit to the insulting conduct and threatening demonstrations of these Insurgents much longer. Insurgent leaders are constantly asking me to make concessions that they may be able to control their troops. The city is quiet, though there is a vast amount of underlying excitement. We are constantly losing our employees. Yesterday, seven of our men at the Malacanan quarters left us suddenly to join the Insurgents. They stole and took with them whatever they could find of value, one of them driving out of the lines Colonel Barry's carriage, which we consider lost property."

The following night the Insurrection broke.

NOTES ON CHAPTER V

1 cf H.D. No. 2 vol. 5, 56th 1st, p. 3.

2 cf Ibid, p. 6.

3 cf Compilation of Captured Philippine Insurgent Records p. 23. Hereinafter abbreviated P.I.R.

4 The proletarian members of the Katipunan. Those residing in Manila had been organized into a sort of secret Insurgent Militia.

5 cf P.I.R. p. 24.

6 cf Ibid. p. 25.

6a cf Hearings, Part I, p. 744.

7 cf H.D. No. 2, vol. 5, 56th 1st, p. 16.

8 cf Ibid. p. 22.

9 cf Ibid. p. 22.

10 cf P.I.R. p. 28.

11 cf H.D. No. 2 vol. 4, 56th 1st, p. 380.

12 cf H.D. No. 2 vol. 5, 56th 1st, p. 55.

13 cf Ibid. p. 55.

14 cf Ibid. p. 57.

15 cf Hearings, Part I, p. 781.

16 cf Ibid. p. 773.

17 cf H.D. No. 2 vol. 5, 56th 1st, p. 359 et seq.

18 cf H.D. No. 2 vol. 5, 56th 2nd, p. 200.

19 cf P.I.R. p. 39.

20 cf Ibid. p. 41.

21 cf Hearings, Part I, p. 618.

22 cf Ibid. p. 622.

23 For full text of this constitution see SD No. 208, 56th 1st, Part I. p. 107, et seq.

24 cf H.D. No. 2 vol. 5, 56th 1st, p. 90.

Chapter VI

THE MONTH of February, 1899 was to be highly eventful in respect to American-Filipino relations. The United States Senate was to ratify by a close vote the treaty with Spain, in which the Philippine Islands were ceded to the United States. A bloody battle was to take place at Manila in which the Insurgents were to be driven from their entrenchments and scattered into the surrounding territory. An Insurgent attempt to burn the city and massacre the foreign inhabitants was to fail. February was to mark the beginning of the three-year struggle in which the United States was forced to employ two-thirds of its armed forces to quell an insurrection and establish peaceful civil government in the Islands.

Before discussing the first, and what proved to be the most important battle of the insurrection in point of numbers engaged, it might be well to pause for a moment and cast a brief glance at the two armies who were confronting each other. How did they compare in the matter of discipline, training, equipment? Why was it that one army was to assert its superiority immediately and retain it throughout the balance of the Insurrection?

The American Army has never been noteworthy for strict discipline. The majority of the troops in the Philippines were state volunteers. Few had received prior military training and very little had been given them since they were mustered into the Federal Army. Many of the officers had been "elected" by their companies and most of them called their soldiers by their first names. Many of the soldiers had left home for the first time when they went to the Philippines.

The habit was prevalent among these civilian soldiers of writing exaggerated letters to friends in the United States. The accounts were usually highly colored for the purpose of impressing the people back home. Many were seized upon by newspapers anxious to exploit sensational news. More often the letters were compendiums of criticisms against the commanding officer of a dissatisfied soldier. In 1902 various allegations made by discharged soldiers were thoroughly aired in Congress and witnesses were called before a committee of the Senate.

As a rule these witnesses were unable or unwilling to produce facts when placed upon the stand. One ex-soldier who had made grave charges against General Funston concerning the "water cure" (which will be described later) answered a summons to appear before the Senate Committee with the following telegram "Will appear Friday but it will be of no use for I couldn't testify against anyone." Perhaps his answer was prompted by a statement which Funston had issued to the press shortly prior. The righteously indignant Funston announced that if this particular ex-soldier made under oath the same statement which he had given to the newspapers he would land in the penitentiary for perjury. Further evidence indicated that the man had never been a member of the organization to which he purported to have belonged.

Another newspaper article based on a letter written by a soldier in the 16th Infantry concerned the capture and execution of some 1000 Filipino prisoners in the province of Sorgoson. The matter was investigated to the point where it was determined that during the period mentioned the only operations in which that particular organization had been engaged had been confined to matters of the killing of two or three· (in a skirmish) and capturing a few others.

Another ex-soldier in a newspaper interview stated that his company commander had embezzled company ration funds and that the Ordnance Department had issued "dumdum" bullets to his organization. The company commander was able to exonerate himself by establishing the fact that during the period mentioned rations had been issued *in kind* and it would have been impossible for him to have access to ration funds. The same claimant called before the Senate Committee produced samples of the "dumdum" bullets which he had saved and brought back from the Philippines. It was necessary to call in the Army Chief of Ordnance to prove that the bullets were ordinary issue and in no wise of the "dumdum" type.

Shortly after the battle of Manila a private in the Kansas Volunteers stated in a letter home that he had seen four Filipino prisoners summarily shot on the orders of a company commander. The article was published in a newspaper at Minneapolis, Kansas, was reprinted in other papers and caused a furor throughout the United States. Four months later an investigation was ordered from Washington. Major John S. Mallory of the Inspector General's Department thoroughly investigated the matter and assembled the following evidence:

The soldier had not actually seen any Insurgent prisoners killed; the incident as mentioned in the letter was pure hearsay; that at least two prisoners who had been directed to accompany a guard to the rear had refused to move, and on the orders of an officer had been shot; that the evidence was conflicting and contradictory as to who had given the order.

Otis permitted the matter to be "whitewashed," principally because the officers involved had performed outstanding service since the incident had happened, and he felt that there was nothing to be gained by pressing charges. Soon the incident was expanded into a tale that Colonel Funston of the Kansas regiment had issued orders "that no prisoners would be taken." Three years later when Brigadier General Wilder S. Metcalf, who had been a major in the Kansas regiment at the time, was about to be appointed United States pension agent at Topeka, Kansas, political enemies revived the matter and charged that Metcalf had personally murdered the unfortunate Insurgents. A long Senate investigation took place, the report of which consumed over sixty pages in the Congressional Record. As a result of the thorough re-airing, Metcalf was completely exonerated, and given the appointment. The story then appears to have died a natural death.

The average soldier is apt, when he has money in his pocket, to imbibe freely of the "amber hued thirst quencher." No exception to the rule, drunken, undisciplined American soldiers finding themselves in a foreign land which they had conquered by the force of arms, often permitted unbridled instincts to overcome common sense. The result was the maltreatment on numerous occasion of the hapless Filipino natives. Stories of "atrocities" being committed by the Americans leaked back to the United States and caused numerous orders to be sent out from Washington. Investigations revealed that although the majority of reports of the alleged atrocities were exaggerations, many were matters of fact.

Mr. John Foreman, a scholarly writer of the day on the Philippine Islands, witnessed the occupation of Manila by the American troops. Later, called to testify on conditions there before the Peace Commission at Paris, he stated: [1]

> "Within a fortnight after the capitulation of Manila, the drinking saloons had increased fourfold. According to latest advices there are at least twenty to one existing in the time of the Spaniards. Drunkenness with its consequent evils is rife all over the city among the new white population. The orgies of the newcomers, the incessant street brawls, the insults offered with impunity to natives of both sexes, the entry with violence into private houses by the soldiery who maltreated the inmates and laid hands on what they chose were hardly calculated to arouse in the natives admiration for their new masters. Adventurers of all sorts and conditions have flocked to this

81

center of vice (Manila) where the sober native is not even spoken of as a man by many of the armed rank and file, but by way of contempt is called a Yu yu."

Aguinaldo complained of the American occupation of Manila as follows: [2]

"The searching of houses was carried on just as it was during the Spanish regime . . . It would make this book a large volume if I continued to state seriatim the abuses and atrocities committed by the American soldiery during those days of general anxiety."

Despite efforts of the military authorities to prevent "bulldozing" of the natives by soldiers, the practice continued in small measures. A year after the beginning of the Insurrection, an American interpreter serving in the captured town of Bangued wrote: [3]

"It was also my duty to regulate the price at which the market women sold their eggs and cigars to the soldiers and to present their complaints when the latter robbed or cheated them which was of no infrequent occurrence. Our soldiers are no better than those of other nations in this respect; a great many of them stole, cheated and even robbed whenever the opportunity presented itself. The officers were ever ready to listen to complaints but a few days in the guard house did not strike terror into the hearts of these bullies and when they came out they were ready to repeat their assaults on the helpless natives."

Strenuous corrective measures were applied by the military authorities. During the course of the Insurrection over 350 officers and soldiers were convicted by courts martial for offenses involving cruelties to natives. The list of offenses is a commentary on character and conduct of the American citizen soldier. A few typical convictions are interlarded here: [4]

"Assault and battery by wounding native woman on head with bayonet and creating disturbance in native shop by assaulting proprietor while drunk."
"Entering house and demanding money and striking native over eye."
"Entering house and assaulting native by pulling him out of bed and striking him with fist."
"Demanding a bribe of $12.50 from native woman."
"Wounding a native on head with heavy bottle without provocation."
"Intimidating and threatening to harm a native policeman."
"Striking native woman with revolver while drunk and attempting to rape her."

"Larceny of a barrel of beer, value $25.00."
"Obtaining money, merchandise and liquor under false pretenses from native by giving him a Confederate bill."

The punishments for these crimes varied from small fines for minor offenses to the sentence of death where murder or rape was proven.

It was true also that during the later stages of the Insurrection American officers and soldiers did inflict certain tortures on Filipinos for the purpose of making them divulge the hiding places of rifles. This will be discussed in a later chapter.

Perhaps the whole matter of the discipline of the American soldier can be summed up in the testimony of General MacArthur before the Senate committee: [5]

> "The standards of course are established by general orders and by advisory memoranda and by the reviews of courts martial. They are on a high ideal plane. There have been in the neighborhood I think of 125,000 men and soldiers in the islands. Some of these men have committed excesses under the provocation of hardship. That is not mentioned as an excuse but as a cause. Wherever any violation of the laws of war has been detected, the remedy has been instantly applied . . . but of course in conducting war all of the ferocity of humanity is brought to the surface and in individual instances, excesses have been committed.
>
> "But to say that the army committed excesses or that excesses were encouraged of course is to say that the character of Americans in the Philippines is immediately transformed by the question of latitude and longitude, which is not the fact. Individual men have committed individual outrages; but when we compare the conditions that exist in the Philippines today in that respect with what have existed in all modern wars between civilized states the comparison is absolutely in favor of self-restraint and high discipline of the American soldier."

And when it is considered that only 350 proven offenses against natives were committed by some 125,000 men, the actual percentage is low. It could be expected that if three hundred citizens of the United States were chosen at random the group would contain at least one malefactor.

In the matter of equipment, the American Army was in a more or less experimental stage. The United States had never before waged war in the tropics. Therefore a new type of clothing and field equipment was necessarily evolved. When they left the United States, the troops were issued cotton trousers, canvas leggings and blue woolen shirts. On the face of it, blue woolen shirts might seem impracticable for the tropics. In fact, they were very sensible because the wool absorbed perspiration and prevented chilling. A short time after the occupation of Manila, the so-called Hong Kong variety of cotton khaki was issued and proved very satisfactory for ordinary duties. The wearing of the cork helmet was authorized but not favored by the troops. It could be easily knocked from the head while moving through underbrush and its conspicuousness rendered the wearer an excellent target for the enemy. The felt campaign hat, hot as it was, could be used as a pillow at night and was found to be the most satisfactory headgear.

Prior to the declaration of the war the Army officially adopted the calibre .30 magazine type of rifle. The weapon not only used smokeless powder but was lighter and had a greater range than the older type calibre .45 Springfield of Civil War vintage. Sudden wartime expansion of the Army, however, revealed that the number of rifles of the new type available was strictly limited, limited in fact to regular army units. To their dissatisfaction, the volunteer units were issued the old calibre .45 rifles, modified model of 1869. This weapon was single shot, of short range, and gave a tremendous kick when fired. Possibly its greatest disadvantage was the fact that its cartridges were loaded with black powder. Everytime it was fired, it not only laid down a veritable smoke screen in front of the firer but definitely revealed his position to the enemy. Company commanders complained that among recruits its severe kick encouraged flinching with its attendant poor marksmanship. Complaints grew so numerous that production of the new type magazine rifle was rushed, and by October of 1899 all troops in the field were equipped with modern rifles.

The principal type of field artillery in use by the Americans was the 3.2 inch breech loading rifle, normally hauled by six horses. It was an efficient and handy weapon except when being pulled by hand over rice dikes. Officers who used it, complained that 60% of the issued shrapnel burst at the muzzle. Also used were a 3.00 inch and a 1.65 inch pack type of mountain gun. The hand operated Gatling and Hotchkiss machine guns were also issued and, when used, usually produced demoralization among the Insurgent troops.

One of the outstanding problems of the Army in the Philippines was the matter of supply. Between June 30, 1898, and June 26, 1899, twenty-nine regiments of Infantry, eight batteries of Field Artillery, more than one regiment of Cavalry, proportional parts of Engineers, Signal, Medical, Ordnance, and Quartermaster Corps personnel, were transported to the Philippines, making a total of 34,661 officers and men. By the following June the strength had risen to 63,426.

The principal article of food used by the natives in the Philippines was rice, a starchy cereal which would not sustain the average American soldier, even had he accepted it as the main article of diet. Fresh meat locally slaughtered was impracticable because of the humid tropical climate. It was found that to prevent deterioration, the meat had to be slaughtered at night and cooked the following morning. Hence most of the supplies had to come from outside the Philippines and receive a special treatment designed to make them suitable for tropical use. Early in the insurrection much of the non-tropical cured bacon imported from the United States spoiled shortly after arrival in the Philippines. Hard bread, one of the principal components of the ration, became a doughy mass after a few days campaigning during the rainy season. When fresh meat was not available, the canned variety was issued. Later frozen beef was shipped from the United States and Australia and distributed to the troops in the field by means of a special refrigerator car which the Quartermaster constructed. Fresh vegetables from the United States were distributed as quickly as possible, and, whenever feasible, were issued in lieu of the normally used dehydrated variety.

The principal mode of cargo transportation in the Philippines was a native cart pulled by the slow-moving water buffalo, or carabao. The carabao could be counted on to make about five miles a day under normal conditions. A serious obstacle to its military use was the fact that daily it must have access to water in which to wallow. This animal as a means of transportation was so unsatisfactory and slow that eventually American mules were shipped to the Islands and in a measure filled the gap in the supply system. The Medical Corps was assisted in the evacuation of wounded by the employment of Chinese coolie litter bearers.

2

Factual information concerning the Insurgent army is obscure, and can only be gained by a perusal of captured documents. As a rule no rosters, strength returns, or official reports of operations were kept. Apparently the army was organized on a territorial basis, the various units bearing such designations as "Cavite Battalion," or "Bulacan Battalion." On February 21, 1899, the Insurgent government at Malolos promulgated a decree establishing universal conscription of all men between the ages of eighteen and thirty-five,

The actual functioning of the system was placed in the hands of town mayors or "presidentes" who were permitted to grant exemption on the payment of money. The matter of subsisting the troops was made the responsibility of the barrios in which the troops were garrisoned at any particular time. Since the normal food of the Filipino consisted of rice, plus a little meat and fish perhaps, the food supply problem was not momentous.

In the matter of uniforms, the Insurgent army was nondescript. The normal one consisted of a thin blue and white cotton coat, trousers and a wide brimmed straw hat. The soldiers normally went barefoot. Later when Insurgent soldiers found it expedient to make quick changes from soldiers to "Amigos" the uniforms became nondescript.

In point of numbers, the Insurgent army was always strong. This very desirable feature was nullified, however, by the fact that there was never a sufficient number of rifles available for the existing personnel. The Insurgent army around Manila has been variously estimated as comprising from 20,000 to 40,000 troops. Of these possibly one-half were armed. The American Military Information staff estimated the total number of rifles in the hands of Insurgents throughout the Islands at 40,000.[6] However, around Manila there were so many more soldiers than rifles that an eye-witness[7] states that after an Insurgent soldier had done his tour of duty in the trenches he would turn his rifle and equipment over to the man who relieved him. In case a rifleman was wounded, there were alway many others nearby who would take his rifle and continue the fight. As General MacArthur testified before the Senate Committee:[8]

> "They have such an excess of men that their fighting line was accompanied by many men without arms. One of the great problems for solution in a modern war is to supply the firing line with ammunition, and the Insurgents did that admirably, because they had men bearing ammunition who had no guns and it was their duty to feed the firing lines with ammunition and to remove the wounded. The moment a man was wounded they would seize him and get him off the field and a man would seize his gun. We got very few wounded men around Manila. I could not account for it until I made some investigation and found out how they were organized to prevent exactly that thing. In front of my division were buried approximately 400 men and I looked around for the wounded and we found none."

It also appears that one unit at least of the Insurgent Army was composed of Negritos, the negroid, pygmy, Filipino aborigines, who were armed only with bows and arrows. In one battle, the Americans were opposed by a "battalion" of children, whose defense consisted of throwing stones at the advancing line. Of course all members of the army who did not carry a rifle were armed with bolos, weapons which at close quarters proved to be lethal and effective.

The matter of ammunition was also a paramount problem of the Insurgent Army. Several small arsenals were established throughout Luzon and empty cartridge cases carefully saved and refilled. However, the technical inefficiency of the reloading system rendered these arsenals virtually useless. On many occasions, bullets fired from reloaded cartridges carried only a few feet beyond the muzzle of the gun.

The Insurgent artillery was of a nondescript variety and consisted principally of muzzle loading cannon which had been captured from the Spanish. The few Hotchkiss and Gatling machine guns they possessed were considered so precious that, regardless of the tactical situation, they were often taken out of action at a critical time and withdrawn to the rear in order to avoid the possibility of capture.

The great weakness of the Insurgent army, however, was its lack of training, primarily in marksmanship. It appears that the majority of the Insurgents just simply could not shoot a rifle. Of course it is not easy for anyone to aim a rifle carefully at a moving target if that target is advancing and sending a shower of bullets at you. Shortage of ammunition made rifle marksmanship training entirely out of the question. Except for a few natives who had formerly been members of the Spanish Colonial army, the trigger squeeze was unknown. Insurgent ignorance of how a rifle should be shot is indicated by the fact that many of the soldiers removed the rear sights from their rifles.

The effect of the caliber .45 Springfield rifle bullets, which the volunteer regiments used in the battle of Manila, was particularly demoralizing to the Insurgents. This comparatively large slug carried a tremendous shock on impact and, in most cases when an Insurgent was hit, he was either disemboweled or the top of his head literally blown off. General Pantaleon Garcia, one of the Insurgent brigade commanders told the writer that, after the battle of Manila, it was very difficult to get the Insurgent troops to poke their heads above the parapet of a trench while being attacked by the American troops. They fired by sticking the rifle over the top and pulling the trigger, without taking any aim or even seeing at what they were shooting. General MacArthur later said "If the Insurgents had known how to shoot, the losses to the American Army would have terrified the nation." [8]

It is generally agreed that in no sense was the Filipino a coward. Poor shots that they were, it was often the case that they stood up against the advance of the American troops until there was no chance to escape and then essayed to fight it out with bolos. Many unnecessary casualties were occasioned among them simply because they would not retreat upon the orders of their leaders. Of course as the war progressed their morale reached a very low ebb and one hundred American troops could expect to rout five hundred or more Insurgents. As General Lawton said:

> "Taking into account the disadvantages they have to fight against in arms, equipment and military discipline, they are the bravest men I have ever seen."

3

Turning to a brief tactical discussion of the battle which took place at Manila on February 4th and 5th we find that Otis was confronted with three distinct problems in his defense of the city. (See map, page 89)

In the first place his lines were long and extended. The line of Insurgent trenches surrounding the city covered a distance of about sixteen miles. During the World War it was found that the normal front of an infantry division, containing some 28,000 troops, was from two to four miles. Taking out his provost guard of some 3000 and considering the 2400 troops at Iloilo and Cavite and the various members of the non-combatant branches, Otis had about 11,000 men with which to cover a front of some sixteen miles. The only feasible disposition was to hold out large reserves and rush them to danger points as the battle developed. In consequence of this principle, the Americans had no particular established line. Each regiment was assigned a sector. In the regimental sector an outpost was placed. Each regiment was then quartered within supporting distance of its respective outpost. A prearranged plan directed that, if and when hostilities broke out, each regimental commander would give his particular outpost the support it needed to repel any attack. Large brigade and division reserves were held out for emergencies. Telegraph lines were connected to all headquarters, so that calls for assistance could be answered promptly.

In the second place, unarmed Filipino soldiers had been permitted to enter Manila at will. This fact enabled Insurgent leaders to become fully acquainted with Otis' strength, the composition of his force and his dispositions.

In the third place, there was a probability that when the attack came from the outside, the Sandatahan within the city would arise and attack the American troops from the rear. It was also a possibility that this Insurgent proletarian militia would even attempt

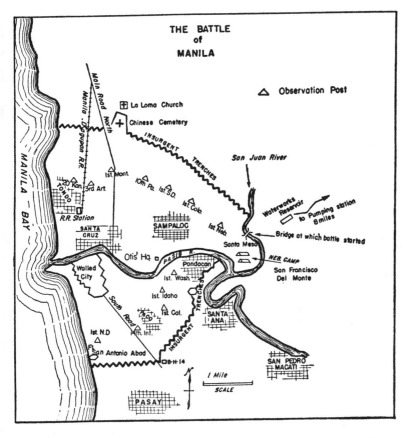

to burn the city. Hence it was necessary for Otis to weaken the force which he normally would have used for the defense of the city from attack without and maintain a strong provost guard in anticipation of an attack from within.

On the other hand, he had two distinct advantages. First, he knew the disposition of the Insurgent forces and could use that knowledge in planning his defense. Second, he was operating on interior lines. Because the Pasig River was unfordable, Insurgent troops moving from the south side of the city to the north, or vice versa, would have to use boats and march around the outer circumference of the circle of lines. Otis could use the three bridges over the Pasig in Manila and could quickly dispatch troops directly to threatened points.

General Anderson's division on the south side of the city consisted of the 14th Infantry, the 1st California, 1st Idaho, 1st Washington, 1st North Dakota Volunteer regiments, six troops of the 4th Cavalry, which were acting dismounted, one battalion of the 1st Wyoming Infantry and two batteries of the 6th Artillery. General MacArthur's second division, which protected the north side of the city, consisted of the 1st Nebraska, 1st Colorado, 1st South Dakota, 10th Pennsylvania, 1st Montana, and 20th Kansas Volunteer regiments, the 3d Regular Artillery, which was being used as Infantry, and two batteries of the Utah Light Artillery.

Otis had made arrangements with Admiral Dewey that in the event of hostilities, several gunboats would move in close to shore and enfilade the Insurgent lines. He had also further provided a rather unique weapon of defense in the "Laguna de Bay," a Pasig River steamboat which had been captured from the Spanish. This boat drew only four feet of water and was armor plated with sheet metal of sufficient thickness to resist rifle bullets. She was armed with two three-inch guns, two 1.65-inch Hotchkiss revolving cannon, four Gatling guns and carried a complement of about sixty armed infantrymen, who could fire from protected positions on her decks. The "Laguna de Bay" was placed under the command of Captain Grant of the Utah Artillery, an experienced steamboat captain. During the battle it cruised up and down the river causing much uneasiness to the Insurgents whenever it came in sight. It was handled fearlessly by Grant and was considered the equivalent of a regiment of infantry.

4

Because of the large amount of sickness in the regiment, the 1st Nebraska Volunteers had been moved in December from their quarters in the City of Manila to a camp site in the Santa Mesa district on the eastern edge of the city. The proximity of this camp to the Insurgent lines resulted in numerous verbal squabbles between the soldiers of the two armies. On February 2d a detachment of Insurgent troops deliberately entered the American lines and took possession of a small barrio in front of the Nebraska outpost. General MacArthur sent a note to the Insurgent local commander

SOLDIERS IN THE SUN

demanding their withdrawal and adding "From this date if the line is crossed by your men with arms in their hands they must be regarded as subject to such action as I may deem necessary." The Filipino troops were recalled and their action deprecated by Colonel San Miguel, their commanding officer.

On the night of February 4th, Private Willie Grayson of the Nebraska regiment was detailed on guard as part of an outpost patrol which was maintained in the village of Santol, a short distance in front of the Nebraska camp. The patrol was instructed to "allow no armed Insurgents to enter the town or vicinity. It was to halt all armed persons who attempted to advance from the direction of the Insurgent lines and order them back. If they refused to go to arrest them if possible or, if this was impossible, to fire upon them."[9]

Shortly before eight o'clock in the evening, Private Grayson and two other men of the patrol advanced a short distance ahead of the village to ascertain if any Insurgents were in the vicinity. Private Grayson suddenly saw four armed men appear in front of him. Perhaps it would be best to let Willie Grayson describe exactly what happened:[10]

"I yelled 'halt' . . . the man moved. I challenged with another 'halt.' Then he immediately shouted 'Halto' to me. Well I thought the best thing to do was to shoot him. He dropped. Then two Filipinos sprang out of the gateway about fifteen feet from us. I called 'Halt' and Miller fired and dropped one. I saw that another was left. Well I think I got my second Filipino that time. We retreated to where our six other fellows were and I said, 'Line up fellows; the niggers are in here all through these yards.' We then retreated to the pipe line and got behind the water work main and stayed there all night. It was some minutes after our second shots before Filipinos began firing."

It appears that Aguinaldo had not intended hostilities to commence when they did. On this particular night he and many of his higher ranking officers were absent from their headquarters, intending to be away for the week end. Impetuous or ignorant subordinates took advantage of the situation to precipitate the long suppressed outbreak of hostilities.

Since the Pasig River divides Manila into two distinct parts, the battle resolved itself into two virtually independent operations, starting in MacArthur's sector on the north side of the city on the night of February 4th and extending to the south side during the 5th. MacArthur's left flank rested on Manila Bay. His line then swung in a rough semicircular direction to the east, his right flank touching the San Juan River in the Santa Mesa district. The seven infantry regiments in the division were formed into two brigades and distributed along the sector in line. If General MacArthur had inspected the outposts of his division on the night of February 4th he would, moving from the bay in an easterly direction, have encountered successively the command posts of the 20th Kansas Volunteers, the 3d US Artillery (acting as infantry), the 1st Montana Volunteers, the 10th Pennsylvania Volunteers, the 1st South Dakota Volunteers, and 1st Colorado Volunteers and finally on his right (east) flank, the 1st Nebraska Volunteers. Behind each outpost were regimental reserves quartered in nipa buildings.

Shortly after Private Willie Grayson of the Nebraska Volunteers precipitated the battle by "getting his second Filipino," the Insurgents opened fire on the Nebraska camp. Rockets were then seen to go up from the Insurgent lines and the shooting soon spread along MacArthur's entire front on the north side of the city. On the American side the call to arms was sounded. Soldiers who had been attending the Manila theatres rushed to their barracks and supports moved out to the outposts.

The entire Nebraska regiment formed a line to protect their camp. In the Colorado regiment located next to the Nebraska camp, bullets poured into regimental headquarters. One officer was wounded while standing by his bed getting dressed. From a thick bamboo jungle in front of the 3d Artillery outpost, the men of this regiment suffered a severe sniping fire without being able to reply effectively in the darkness. Insurgents made two advances in considerable force in the sector of the 10th Pennsylvania Volunteers, but were checked without difficulty. Intermittent fire continued during the night. At 4:00 a. m. Colonel Stotsenburg of the Nebraska regiment reported that the Insurgents were closing in on him and requested reinforcements. By the time they arrived the attack had been beaten off. Despite several other piecemeal attacks made by the Insurgents during the night, the Americans were able by firing blindly into the darkness to hold their line of outposts.

As daylight of February 5th broke, MacArthur obtained permission from Otis to take the initiative. The terrain on the right of his sector was fairly open and sloped with a gradual rise to the hills northeast of Manila. The Insurgent troops there were limited to small groups occupying the old Spanish line of blockhouses. MacArthur ordered the 3.2 guns of the Utah Artillery brought up to the American outposts and trained on the blockhouses. The barrage which these guns laid on the Insurgent line was so effective that when the Nebraska, Colorado and South Dakota Volunteers swept forward at 8:00 a. m. the few Insurgents who remained scurried into the surrounding hills like rabbits. The Nebraska regiment crossed the stone bridge over the San Juan River, charged up San Juan Del Monte hill on the opposite bank and captured the Manila waterworks reservoir. With the assistance of a battalion of Wyoming Volunteers which had been thrown into the attack, the Nebraskans then turned south and moving along the east bank of the San Juan River captured the barrio of San Felipe Neri. Continuing past the junction of the San Juan and Pasig Rivers, they swept all Insurgents out of the area on the east bank of the Pasig to a point opposite the town of Santa Ana. The first scrimmage between Americans and Filipinos had been highly favorable to the Americans.

With success crowning the efforts of the right of his line, Mac-Arthur felt by noon that he could advance his center and left. The terrain in these parts of the line was much more difficult. Opposite the 10th Pennsylvania Volunteers and the 3d Artillery was the steep, broad La Loma Hill. On its south slope was a Chinese cemetery marked by a cluster of headstones. On its top was the stone La Loma Church, surrounded by a rock wall. On the sides of the hill the Insurgents had constructed elaborate entrenchments in which they had mounted several muzzle-loading cannon. Around the base of the hill was a dense bamboo thicket. Between the hill and Manila Bay, a mile and a half distant, was a swampy jungle.

To assist in the attack on La Loma Hill, the artillery was again brought into play. After a half hour bombardment the 10th Pennsylvania attacked the hill from the west. Better protected and better organized, the Insurgents on the hill remained to fight. Enfilading fire from the western slope of the hill caused men of the Pennsylvania regiment to fall like tenpins. The 3d Artillery and the 1st Montana moved to the attack from the east and after suffering numerous casualties, the three regiments finally carried the position.

Successful operations of the division for the day were capped by the 20th Kansas regiment which, assisted by artillery fire from the USS *Charleston,* advanced through the jungle on MacArthur's left flank for a distance of nearly two miles.

By late afternoon the Insurgents on MacArthur's front had been pushed beyond the line of Spanish blockhouses. The American troops were becoming disorganized and scattered. It was ascertained that a gap had been created in the American line. Also during the attack the 3d Artillery and Montana Volunteers had changed relative positions. A halt was called, a readjustment made and the gap closed before darkness set in, the new front resting approximately along the old line of Spanish blockhouses.

Except for a desultory fire throughout the night, Anderson's Division on the south of the city was not attacked on the night of the 4th.

As daylight broke on the 5th, large numbers of Insurgents could be seen in their trenches. The United States Navy Monitor *Monadnock* had moved in during the night until it was within 1000 yards of the shore. Anderson's troops having rested on their arms all night stood anxious to make an attack. At 8:00 a. m. Otis gave his authorization, cautioning Anderson however "not to advance too far and to look out for his flanks and the *Monadnock*."

On Anderson's left (east) flank, in the Pandacan District, a sharp bend in the Pasig River placed the troops of the Washington and Idaho Volunteers within a stone's throw of the Insurgent troops under the command of General Pio Del Pilar. Pilar was an erstwhile native bandit who had brought his gang into Aguinaldo's army. Poorly disciplined, Pilar's troops had particularly antagonized the American troops opposite. By unmistakable gestures and taunts, they had displayed their low regard for the potential fighting ability of these western volunteers.

An order to attack was what the troops opposite Pilar's brigade wanted most. On signal the Idaho and Washington Volunteers left their positions and, with shouts which resembled everything from a cowboy's "yippee" to an old Civil War rebel yell, and supported by Hawthorne's Mountain Battery, viciously charged Pilar's redoubts in Pandacan. In the face of muzzle blasts from Krupp Artillery pieces which the Insurgents had mounted in one particularly strong redoubt, the Idaho troops, at the cost of many casualties including a battalion commander, chased the Insurgents out of their trenches at the point of the bayonet and pushed them back to the bank of the Pasig.

Pilar's dispositions had not anticipated a retreat. When his troops reached the river bank, they realized that they were in a cul de sac, Americans to the front, the river on their rear. Many attempted to swim the river or cross in the few boats available; few elected to surrender. Consequently big game hunting, which the western volunteers had often found a practical necessity while at home, turned into pot shooting of Insurgents attempting to cross the river. The marksmanship of the western volunteers was so accurate that not a single one was seen to reach the opposite bank. It was estimated that some seven hundred Insurgents were killed, captured, wounded or drowned in this quick bloody attack.

While the Idahoans were chasing the Insurgents into the river, the California regiment on the right of the brigade charged and took the town of Santa Ana capturing in it an arsenal containing a large supply of rice, eight cannon, seventy-eight rifles and 34,000 rounds of ammunition. The optimism of the Insurgents before the battle started, is indicated by the fact that they had stored a large amount of war materials immediately in rear of their front lines.

The Californians then assisted by a battalion of the 1st Wyoming Volunteers and a company of Engineers, moved south and took the town of San Pedro Macati, about two miles distant. By noon the Insurgents on the left of Anderson's line had been entirely dispersed.

In General Samuel Ovenshine's brigade, on the right of Anderson's line, the attack did not go so smoothly. His troops occupied the front over which the Americans had advanced in their capture of Manila some seven months previous. It was swampy and so thickly vegetated with trees and bamboo thickets that deployed advance was most difficult. The Filipinos occupied the strong blockhouse No. 14 and poured a flanking fire on the 14th Infantry, whose line of advance was limited by the terrain. The 1st North Dakota Volunteers, who were on the beach at the extreme right of the line, were embarrassed by the fire of the *Monadnock,* the shots of which caused them to withdraw after making a slight advance. The advance being held up, the division reserve and a battalion of the Tennessee Volunteers borrowed from the provost guard in Manila, were rushed to the scene.

Lieutenant E. D. Scott, of the 6th Artillery, set up a three-inch gun on the front line and showered the Insurgent trenches with shrapnel at a range of 400 yards. After a desperate fight, in which serious losses were inflicted on the 14th Infantry, an attack led by Lieutenant Perry Miles carried blockhouse No. 14. The spirit of the attack was perhaps demonstrated by Lieutenant James Mitchell. As Mitchell fell, mortally wounded, he shouted "Forward men, advance; don't mind me." After the capture of blockhouse No. 14 and the trenches adjoining, the Insurgent resistance melted away. By evening the brigade had advanced to the town of Pasay, a mile beyond. At nightfall the division line was established through Pasay and San Pedro Macati, about three miles south of the walled city.

The operations of the 1st Division, particularly Ovenshine's brigade, had required all the resources of the American troops and had been replete with acts of individual bravery. One lieutenant colonel of infantry, recently arrived in the Philippines and temporarily without a command, was seen carrying a rifle and coolly and deliberately shooting at the Insurgents. A quartermaster sergeant left his duties of bringing up supplies and located and killed an Insurgent sniper who was harassing artillery gunners. Lieutenant Charles E. Kilbourne of the Signal Corps won the Congressional Medal of Honor because, (to quote his citation) "within range of 250 yards of the enemy and in the face of a rapid fire, he climbed a telegraph pole at the east end of Paco Bridge and in full view of the enemy coolly and carefully repaired a broken telegraph wire, thereby reestablishing telegraphic communication to the front."

During the afternoon of the 5th, American ammunition carts and ambulances, moving through the Paco district in the center of Anderson's sector, were subjected to a continuous sniping fire from within that barrio. The fire was so persistent that nearly all of the nipa houses in that district were necessarily burned before the snipers could be dislodged. Some fifty-three armed natives, dressed in civilian clothes were captured. Later General Anderson's command post received sharp musketry fire from the rear. It was determined to be coming from the Paco Church, well within the American lines. Artillery was turned on the church and shortly afterwards a battalion of California Volunteers sent to "clean it out." It took over three hours and the virtual destruction of the church to dislodge the one hundred odd Insurgents who had barricaded themselves therein.

The expected rising of the Sandatahan in Manila did not successfully interpose itself. Small groups of "bolomen" actually attempted to assemble during the night of the 4th. The three regiments of Infantry which General Hughes, the Provost Marshal, had judiciously placed at strategic points throughout the city easily broke up all gatherings. Some fifty recalcitrants were killed.

The battle over and the Insurgent Army dispersed for the time being at least, Otis took count of the toll on American troops. Considering the number of troops involved, it was surprisingly small. In the two divisions, the American casualties amounted to a total of fifty-nine killed and two hundred seventy-eight wounded. [11] Insurgent casualties were difficult to estimate because most of the wounded were carried from the field by their comrades. American troops buried six hundred and twelve Insurgent dead. General Otis estimated their total losses at 3000.

The battle of Manila proved two things. First it demonstrated that the comparatively untrained and undisciplined volunteers from the

Wreck of Bridge Over Paruao River, South of Bamban.

Fording Tarlac River, Nov. 17, 1899 (Troop E, 4th U. S. Cav.)

western United States were as a rule excellent marksmen and could be expected to advance fearlessly in the face of a hostile fire. Secondly, it proved that regardless of the protection of entrenchments or redoubts, the Insurgents either would not or could not stand up before the attacks of American troops, assisted as they were by light artillery and navy guns.

On the morning of February 6, Colonel John M. Stotsenburg, with a composite force consisting of the Nebraska, Tennessee and Colorado Volunteers, marched to the Mariquina River, seven miles east of Manila, and captured the waterworks pumping house. After it was found that the Insurgents had dismantled the machinery before retreating, a search revealed that the missing parts were hidden under a pile of coal, and in a short time the pumping station was again functioning. From then on the eight miles between Manila and the Mariquina River were guarded by strong patrols to prevent interference with the water system, which was operated henceforth without interruption.

Confusion existed on the south of the line. The California Volunteers, after capturing Santa Ana had, flushed with victory, pushed far beyond the objective selected by General Otis. Under the command of Lieutenant Colonel Duboce they had followed the highway contiguous to the Pasig River and, unopposed, had lost contact with the division. Fearing for their safety Otis sent hurried messages for them to return before they were cut off by the Insurgents who were reforming south of San Pedro Macati. They finally returned safely on the eighth.

Movements of the Insurgent army following this battle were ascertained by Otis to be as follows: [12]

"The demoralization of the Insurgents which the rough handling they had received from the American mode of conducting warfare hitherto unknown in these islands, and pronounced by them to be new and unsoldierly, continued for two or three days. The leaders confessing that their men were overmatched by our troops, contended that they could overcome by numbers what was lacking in individual characteristics. They commenced at once a reconstruction of their forces in all directions, hastening from the north by rail every available man whether armed with a rifle or bolo. There was no lack of subsistence or ammunition for the troops on the north, but those on the south had lost through capture all the rice and cartridges which they had stored near their original lines. The bolo men of the city who had remained quiet since the afternoon of the 5th began to show again a turbulent disposition and as early as February 8 became bold and defiant. It became necessary to make new combinations for the Insurgents still insisted in the intention to carry out their former preconceived plan of action which was to attack on our front, assisted by an overwhelming uprising of the city Insurgent militia."

Although, as far as Otis was concerned, the situation on the southern front was satisfactory, on the north side of the city the line was much longer and bent definitely to the rear as it reached the bay. The town of Caloocan, in front of the left of the line, contained an important maintenance plant for the railroad, the entire line of which was in possession of the Insurgents. Consequently on the 10th, MacArthur's division, after a half-hour's artillery bombardment in which the Navy guns participated, advanced its left flank, overcoming stubborn resistance from the Insurgents who were in strongly entrenched positions. This attack rectified MacArthur's line so that it now stretched in a general northwest direction and included the town of Caloocan. In Caloocan the Americans found five dismantled engines, fifty passenger coaches and over one hundred freight and flat cars. Possession of this rolling stock which was repaired by MacArthur's troops, enabled the division to make use of the railroad on its further advance to the north.

Meanwhile Otis had not forgotten the hapless expedition to the city of Iloilo on the Island of Panay. In accordance with the "peace at any price" policy enforced on him from Washington, Otis had, as will be recalled, directed General Marcus Miller, in command of the expedition, to stand by in the harbor until something happened. After the battle of Manila, Otis directed Miller to go ahead and take the city by force.

We now see a beautiful example of coordinated "uncooperation" between the Army and Navy. Standing with Miller in Iloilo Harbor were the cruiser *Baltimore* and the gunboat *Petrel*. As soon as Miller received instructions from Otis to attack the city he scoured the locality for water transportation with which to land his troops and the light battery he had brought along. Finally with difficulty he procured two barges and three steam launches.

On the morning of February 11, Miller held an officers' conference aboard the *Newport,* while the light battery was being loaded on the barges. Imagine his surprise upon hearing shots and seeing shells from the *Baltimore* and *Petrel* landing on the Insurgent fort outside the city while the conference was in session. Before he could do anything more, a few boatloads of blue jackets had been landed and the Insurgent fort taken. The middies hoisted the American flag and advanced on the town which was now in flames. Although Miller finally got some troops ashore in time to assist in the capture, the Navy had stolen the show.

As Miller later caustically remarked in his report of the incident: [13]

> "No arrangement or agreement with the senior officer of the Navy was made that he should open the attack without conferring with me . . ."

Distasteful as it was to Miller, the Navy's independent attack unquestionably prevented the complete destruction of the city. It appears that the Insurgents, anticipating their quick ejection as soon as force was employed, had planned to burn the city as they left. The sudden and unexpected attack of the sailors interrupted these preparations. The handful of sailors and Miller's men finally extinguished the fire and saved the majority of the permanent buildings.

In Manila, Otis anxious to restore normal conditions as soon as possible, authorized the opening of the Pasig River as far south as Laguna de Bay. It was hoped that such a move would permit the resumption of the trade in food products between Manila and the country to the south. However, as soon as traffic up the river was resumed, the Insurgent Army regathered itself and seized the towns of Pasig, Pateros, Taguig and Guadelupe. This advance brought them within rifle range of the American force at San Pedro Macati. These Insurgent forces, with the units which were being moved from northern Luzon, massed on MacArthur's front in the vicinity of the Manila-Dagupan railroad, and placed the Americans in a somewhat similar position to that which they had held before the battle of Manila. Cautious, Otis felt the necessity of awaiting reinforcements from the United States before he began further movement to the north or south. The Insurgents were thus given ample opportunity of reorganizing their army and entrenching themselves opposite the American lines.

The command of the Insurgent Army was now given to General Antonio Luna, a strong and striking character. An Illocano by birth, Luna had been fortunate enough to secure a European education. While finishing his studies on the continent, he had played with the study of military strategy. Upon his return to the Philippines in 1892, he set himself up as a pharmacist and, as a sideline, conducted a fencing school. In addition, he soon became prominent in the eyes of the Spanish by his anti-government and anti-Catholic sentiment. During the revolution of 1896 he had been tried and deported to

Spain. In prison there he publicly announced a retraction of all his former beliefs and was pardoned. Returning to the Philippines, he joined Aguinaldo's American sponsored Insurrection of 1898 and was soon made "Minister of War," with nominal authority as commander in chief of the Insurgent army. As Minister of War, he established his headquarters with the troops on the north side of Manila.

On February 9, the Provost Marshal of Manila came into possession of a rather nefarious document which was being circulated sub rosa among the members of the Manila Sandatahan. In part this document was as follows:[14]

> To the Field Officers of the Territorial Militia:
> By virtue of the barbarous attack made upon our army on the 4th day of February, without this being preceded by any strain of relations whatever between the two armies, it is necessary for the Filipinos to show that they know how to avenge themselves of the treachery and deceit of those who working upon our friendship, now seek to enslave us.
> In order to carry out the complete destruction of that accursed army of drunkards and thieves, it is indispensable that we all work in unison and that orders issued from this war office be faithfully carried out.
> Such measures will be taken that at 8:00 at night the members of the territorial militia under your orders will be ready to go into the street with their arms and ammunition to occupy San Pedro street and such cross streets as open into it.
> The defenders of the Philippines under your orders will attack the Zorilla barracks and the Bilibid guard and liberate all the prisoners, arming them in the most practical manner.
> 3. The servants of the houses occupied by the Americans and Spaniards shall burn the buildings in which their masters live in such a manner that the conflagration shall be simultaneous in all parts of the city.
> 4. The lives of the Filipinos will be respected and they shall not be molested with the exception of those who have been pointed out as traitors.
> All others of whatsoever race they may be shall be given no quarter and shall be exterminated, thus proving to foreign countries that America is not capable of maintaining order or defending any of the interests which she has undertaken to defend.
> 5. The sharpshooters of Tondo and Santa Ana shall be the first to open fire and those on the outside of the Manila lines shall second their attack and thus the American forces will find themselves between two fires . . .
> Brethren, the country is in danger and we must rise to save it. Europe sees that we are feeble, but we will demonstrate that

we know how to die as it should be done, shedding our blood for the salvation of our outraged country. Death to the tyrant. War without quarter to the false tyrants who wish to enslave us. Independence or death . . .

Malolos, February 7, 1899   A. Luna

At 8:00 p. m. on February 22 a fire started in the Santa Cruz district of Manila. Prepared for such an emergency, the fire department and the 13th Minnesota Volunteers repaired to the areas immediately, where they discovered that the flames were of incendiary origin. Due to the nipa construction of the houses, the fire, assisted by the wind, spread rapidly. It took the entire Manila Fire Department three hours to bring it under control. Firing stray shots from nearby buildings, the Sandatahan hampered the work of the firemen. However, the few who actually appeared with bolos and attempted to cut the fire hose were for the most part arrested or, in case resistance was offered, rewarded with a cracked skull from the butt of a rifle.

As the Santa Cruz fire was being brought under control, another fire broke out in the Tondo district, in the northwest part of the city. Hurrying to that area, the fire department, trying to enter the district, was halted by a fusillade of bullets. It was later ascertained that about 500 Insurgents under the command of Major Francisco Roman, one of Luna's aides, had managed to pass MacArthur's lines by going through the swamps which adjoined the bay on his left flank. These Insurgents had then infiltrated into Manila and barricaded themselves in Tondo. More provost guards were called, but the Insurgent force was so active that the Americans were forced to take up a defensive line and hope that they could confine the Insurgents to the Tondo district. The houses were necessarily permitted to burn to the ground.

At this time another fire started in the Binondo district, directly in rear of the force which was engaging the Insurgents in Tondo. The Binondo, one of the principal business districts of Manila, contained many permanent structures and large quantities of army supplies. Therefore, Santa Cruz was abandoned to the flames, and all efforts concentrated on the Binondo, the large market place of which faced destruction. By 2:30 a. m. the fire department was exhausted and discouraged and little headway was being made against the fire. As a last resort ten-inch powder cartridges were brought to the scene and exploded in buildings which were hopelessly on fire. When the walls of these buildings fell the flames were restricted and their progress arrested. By 7:00 a. m. it was evident that most of the Binondo had been saved.

The provost guard which had successfully resisted the efforts of Roman's force to advance from Tondo, was given a short rest and then six companies were sent to drive them out. During the night the Insurgents had securely barricaded themselves and it took an all day running fight to clear them out of the area. The majority were killed because they refused to surrender when cornered, and the few who did manage to escape, moved back through the swamps. Tondo was a mass of ruins.

NOTES ON CHAPTER VI

1 *cf* John Foreman in "The National Review," Sept. 1900 p. 56
2 *cf* Aguinaldo, Emilio, "The True Version of the Philippine Revolution," Tarlac, P. I. 1899, p. 46
3 *cf* Albert Sonnichsen "Ten Months a Captive among Filipinos" New York, 1901 p. 373 *et. seq.*
4 *cf* Hearings part III p. 2073 *et. seq.*
5 *cf* Hearings part II p. 870 *et. seq.*
6 *cf* SD 62 56th 1st p. 379
7 *cf* Millet *op. cit.* p. 63
8 *cf* Hearings part II p. 894 *et. seq.*
9 *cf* HD No. 2 Vol. 5 56th 1st p. 464
10 *cf* Statement of Private Grayson quoted by C. E. Russel in the "Outlook for the Philippines." p. 93.
11 *cf* Reports of Generals Anderson and MacArthur in HD No. 2 Vol. 5 56th 1st.
12 *cf* HD No. 2 Vol. 5 56th 1st p. 102
13 *cf* Ibid p. 106
14 *cf* Hearings part II p. 1912

Chapter VII

DURING THE LATTER part of February and the month of March, 1899, more American troops arrived in the Philippines so that American authority was gradually extended throughout the Archipelago. With the termination of the Spanish-American War, regular army units which had taken part in the expedition to Cuba became available for service in the Philippines and were dispatched there with the hope that the revolt would be quickly suppressed. Between February 23 and March 22, the 3rd, 4th, 17th, 20th and 22nd Infantry regiments arrived at Manila and were immediately put into active service. Between March 10 and 17 a provisional brigade, which was dubbed "Wheaton's Flying Column," moved southeast from Manila along the Pasig River and cleared Insurgents out of the area as far south as the Laguna de Bay, a large lake eighteen miles southeast of Manila. This movement opened the Pasig River to traffic from its source to Manila Bay. Between February 26 and March 3 the Islands of Cebu and Negros were occupied by American troops and American sovereignty partially established there. Between March 25 and 31 a reinforced division under the command of Major General Arthur MacArthur moved north from Manila and captured the Insurgent "Capitol" at Malolos, some twenty miles to the northwest. Since each of the movements gave some indication of the problems which would confront the army in fulfilling its mission of pacifying the Islands, It might be well to examine them in some detail.

Cebu is a small island some 357 miles south of Manila. As to size and the number of inhabitants, it closely resembles the state of Rhode Island, having an area of 1668 square miles and a population (at that time) of 518,000. The natives who lived there were Visayans, a Malay tribe who spoke a different dialect from the Tagalogs of central Luzon, and were isolated from contacts with the adherents of Aguinaldo to the extent that they were not necessarily sympathetic with the aims of the Insurrectos. Shortly after General Marcus Miller's troops had captured Iloilo on the Island of Panay, February 10, a ship of the United States Navy visited the city of Cebu on the Island of the same name, and its officers took quiet possession without difficulty. Arrangements were made with the business men of the city for the establishment of American sovereignty. Temporarily at least, the situation seemed to be well in hand and the battalion of the 23rd Infantry which was sent there to preserve order found little to do.

Within a short time, however, Tagalog agents representing the Malolos government arrived and stirred up dissension among the Visayan natives. Although the propertied classes were practically unanimous in their endorsement of the American rule, the urban and agrarian proletarians furnished fertile fields for the importunities of Aguinaldo's agents. Disaffected groups were given arms and encouraged to form bands whose basic purpose was to embarrass the Americans. The necessity of keeping all available troops on the Island of Luzon prevented Otis from dispatching a force to Cebu, which could have nipped the incipient rebellion in the bud. We will leave the situation with that status for the time being, with the Americans in control of the city of Cebu and being forced to watch the formation of an Insurgent army in the nearby mountains.

Negros was an island about the size of Massachusetts, but not as thickly populated. It contained 4839 square miles and about 372,000 inhabitants, also Visayan. It is located just west of Cebu and south of Panay. During February General Miller visited the island and held conferences with the leading citizens of Bacolod, the principal city. These citizens had accepted American sovereignty and emulating the action of the business men of Iloilo, had sent a committee to Manila to ask for assistance in maintaining law and order. Otis responded on March 2 by sending Colonel James F. Smith, a volunteer officer who was also an experienced lawyer, with a battalion of California volunteers to organize a government, with a measure of autonomy being given to the natives. Colonel Smith was also authorized to organize a native police force, which should eventually supplant the American troops. For the time being the natives on this force carried the status of quartermaster civilian employees and were furnished with arms and ammunition by the Ordnance Department. Colonel Smith was designated as Governor of the Island. Shortly thereafter the three islands of Panay, Negros and Cebu were organized into the "Visayan Military District" under the control of General Miller, who established his headquarters at Iloilo. In Negros, as in Cebu, events proceeded smoothly at first until Tagalog agents moved in and incited agitation among the lesser law-abiding elements. In a short time, as in Cebu, the principal city was under the control of the Americans and the majority of the surrounding country in the hands of dissident groups. With open rebellion rapidly developing, Otis was unable to send sufficient troops from Luzon to cope with the situation. How the Americans eventually pacified these southern islands will be discussed later.

Returning to the Island of Luzon, it may be recalled that at the conclusion of the fighting around Manila, on February 4 and 5, the American line on the south side of the city ran in a general northeast and southwest direction, from the hamlet of Pasay on the shore of Manila Bay to San Pedro Macati, a small town on the west bank of the Pasig River. Scattered to the south as a result of the battle on the 4th and 5th, the Insurgents had gradually reorganized themselves. Finding that temporarily at least the Americans showed no sign of aggressiveness, they had re-entrenched themselves opposite the American position and spasmodically maintained a harassing fire on the American trenches. While not causing casualities to any extent, this fire was annoying because it required that the troops in the line be constantly on the alert, with the attendant loss of sleep and sometimes wasteful expenditure of ammunition. Upon the arrival of the 20th and 22nd Infantry in the latter part of February and the early part of March, Otis felt strong enough to attack and clear the Insurgents out of this area.

For that purpose, he organized a provisional brigade consisting of the 20th and 22nd Infantry, two battalions of the Washington and seven companies of the Oregon Volunteers, three troops of the 4th Cavalry and light Battery "D" of the 6th Artillery. From 60% to 80% of the regular army troops were raw recruits.

In command was placed a recent arrival in the Philippines, Brigadier General Lloyd Wheaton, another product of the Civil War. In 1861 he had gone to the front as a first sergeant in the 8th Illinois Infantry. During the war he had been brevetted three times for "gallant and meritorious services" and had ended the war a brevet colonel. In 1865 he had been awarded the Congressional Medal of Honor for "Distinguished Gallantry in the assault on Fort Blakely, Alabama, springing through an embrasure against a strong fire of artillery and musketry, and first to enter the enemy's works." Following the war he had been commissioned as a captain in the regular army, a grade which he held for the next twenty-five years. After 1891, promotion being accelerated, he became a colonel and commanding officer of the 20th Infantry. With the expansion of the army because of the Spanish-American War, he had been promoted to the grade of brigadier general of volunteers. In appearance General Wheaton was heavily built and affected a full beard. Twenty-five years as a company commander had left him, mentally at least, a company officer. Regardless of the fact that he was a brigadier general, he spent most of his time on the front line.

Of the troops in the provisional brigade, the 20th and 22nd Infantry had taken active part in the campaign at Santiago de Cuba, both having seen service in the action at El Caney. Hence they had not only served their baptism of fire, but were conditioned for tropical field service. The other units in the brigade had taken part in the battle of Manila.

The Pasig River, which empties into the Bay at Manila, has its source in Laguna de Bay. The lake is thirty-two miles long in one direction and twenty-eight on the other. Its water is brackish and its shore dotted with villages, the inhabitants of which bring their agricultural products to Manila via the lake and Pasig River. On its eastern shores are the rugged Caraballos Mountains, virtually impassable to any kind of traffic.

Communication between the Insurgent forces on the north of Manila and those on the south was maintained along the Mariquina and Pasig Rivers, which skirted the western flank of the mountains. Control of these rivers, particularly the Pasig, would sever this communication and isolate the two groups of Insurgents. It was a similar situation to the position of the Hudson River in the Revolutionary War and Mississippi in the Civil War.

About eleven miles southeast of Manila the town of Pasig, with about 8000 inhabitants, is situated at the confluence of the Pasig and Mariquina Rivers, about three miles from the northern shore of Laguna de Bay. Also running into the confluence of the Mariquina and Pasig Rivers is the Taguig, which is about one mile southwest of and runs nearly parallel to the Pasig. Both rivers have their origin in the lake and meet at the town of Pasig to form the Pasig River, where their waters proceed northwest to Manila and empty into the sea. Along the Taguig River to the south are the towns of Pateros and Taguig. About three miles east of Pasig are the towns of Cainta and Taytay. These towns rest on the western slopes of the Caraballos Mountains.

Since the Insurgents had entrenched themselves facing the San Pedro Macati-Pasay line, opposition would be encountered as soon as the brigade left its entrenchments. A fairly large force was known to be entrenched in the town of Guadalupe on the Pasig, about three quarters of a mile east of San Pedro Macati. Hence the capture or destruction of this force was the first mission. Wheaton's plan contemplated placing his brigade in line, its right flank protected by the cavalry squadron, its left flank on the river, protected and assisted by the gunboat *Laguna de Bay* which was to move up the river with the column. In the early morning of March 13, the brigade moved forward. After advancing cross country about a mile, the 20th and 22nd Infantry on the right flank of the brigade were to execute a left wheel, entering Guadalupe from the south and preventing the escape of any Insurgents who remained there. An effective shelling of the Guadalupe Church by a platoon of the 6th Artillery before the attack was launched so discouraged the Insurgents that by the time the enveloping force entered the town, they had retreated along the river to the southwest. The brigade then formed on the road and proceeded towards Pasig, five miles distant. As the column approached the junction of the Mariquina and Pasig Rivers it came under two fires, one from Insurgent troops in Pasig and the other from the direction of Pateros, a mile to the south. Blocked by fire from two directions and by two unfordable rivers, the command was forced to bivouac for the night. As darkness fell the *Laguna de Bay*, which had been delayed by obstructions placed in the river by the natives, arrived and sent a few shots into Pasig.

On the following day Wheaton extended his lines to the south. Crossing the Taguig River in cascos the 1st Washington Volunteers, assisted by the cavalry, drove the enemy from Pateros. On the 15th, the 20th Infantry crossed the river and stormed the trenches in front of Pasig, driving the Insurgents to the northeast. One battalion of the same regiment, reconnoitering in that direction, encountered a large Insurgent force entrenched in front of the town of Cainta, two miles from Pasig. Although greatly outnumbered, the Americans charged this force and routed it to the extent that it was driven beyond the town of Taytay, one mile to the east. Other Insurgent forces on the same day in the vicinity to Taguig were routed by the Washington Infantry.

On March 18, a company of the Washington Volunteers, which had been assigned as a garrison at Taguig, was attacked by some 800 Insurgents. It took the battalion of the 22nd Infantry, which reinforced the Washingtonians, the entire day to disperse the enemy, during which the battalion commander, Captain Frank B. Jones, was killed. Exasperated, Wheaton the following day sent the 22nd Infantry, the Washingtonians and Oregonians to the south from Pateros and Taguig. This "Punitive Expedition" burned all Filipino villages and scattered all Insurgent troops encountered for a distance of fifteen miles around the west shore of the lake. On the 20th, the brigade returned to Manila, leaving the 1st Washington Volunteers to garrison Pasig, Pateros and Taguig.

In his brief and ungarnished style, General Wheaton summed up the accomplishments of the brigade as follows:[1]

> "This ended the operations of the provisional brigade. In one week, all his positions that (were) attacked (were) taken, and his troops killed, captured or dispersed; the towns from where he brought over troops or in which he resisted us (were) burned or destroyed. He burned them himself. His loss in killed, wounded or captured was not less than 2500 men."

The American casualties amounted to thirty-six killed and wounded.

2

While Wheaton was clearing the Insurgents from the Pasig River, MacArthur's division entrenched on the north side of Manila had also been subjected to periodic and annoying attacks. In order to protect the pumping station for the Manila water supply, the American line had been extended to the Mariquina River, seven miles northeast of the city. The isolated position of the right flank rendered it particularly vulnerable. On March 5th, 6th, and 7th detachments of the Nebraska, Oregon and Utah Volunteers, which garrisoned this portion of the line, were obliged to drive off Insurgent bodies attacking with the intent of capturing and destroying the pumping station.

The 3rd, 4th, and 17th, Infantry, having arrived in the Philippines, augmented the American strength by some 3600 men. It was reported that Malolos, the Insurgent capital, had become a war depot and contained a large quantity of rifles and ammunition; and that between Caloocan and Malolos the Insurgents had constructed a veritable "Hindenburg line" of entrenchments. Luna, the Insurgent Commander-in-Chief, boasted that he had 16,000 armed troops in his army. The American troops, impatient to be let loose, were in excellent health and spirits. Consequently Otis decided to move on to the Insurgent capital and if possible destroy Luna's army.

For the purpose of the movement, MacArthur's division which was designated to make the advance, was reinforced by the recently arrived regiments, a squadron of the 4th Cavalry and a battalion of the Utah Artillery. The composition of the division as augmented as follows:[2]

1st Brigade (Brigadier General H. G. Otis)
3rd U. S. Artillery (acting as Infantry)
20th Kansas Volunteers
1st Montana Volunteers
    2nd Brigade (Brigadier General Irving Hale)
1st Colorado Volunteers
1st Nebraska Volunteers
1st South Dakota Volunteers
10th Pennsylvania Volunteers
    3rd Brigade (Brigadier General R. H. Hall)
4th U. S. Infantry
17th Infantry (1 Battalion)
13th Minnesota Volunteers
1st Wyoming Volunteers

Brigadier General H. G. Otis, who commanded the 1st Brigade, should not be confused with Major General E. S. Otis, the Corps Commander. Harrison Gray Otis was a Los Angeles newspaper man of prominence who had served capably throughout the Civil War. In 1898 he had been commissioned from civil life as a brigadier general in the volunteers. Brigadier General Irving Hale, who commanded the 2nd Brigade, had graduated number one in the West Point class of 1884. Following graduation he had resigned from the army and at the outbreak of the Spanish-American war was a prominent electrical engineer in Denver, Colorado, and a brigadier general in the Colorado National Guard. Tendering his services to the government, he was sent to the Philippines as Colonel of the 1st Colorado Volunteers. After the capture of Manila he was promoted to brigadier general. Brigadier General R. H. Hall, who commanded the 3rd Brigade was a graduate of West Point of the class of 1860. In 1898 he was a colonel in command of the 4th Infantry and had been given temporary promotion to brigadier general of volunteers.

Consideration of the terrain to the north of Manila indicated that the easiest approach to Malolos would be, in a general way, along the Manila-Dagupan Railroad, which ran through the Insurgent capital. However, such intelligence service as the Americans had been able to organize, reported that the Insurgent line ran from the railroad possibly as far east as the Mariquina River. The right flank of any force advancing north on the railroad would therefore be vulnerable to Insurgent attacks from the east. In order to enable one brigade to remain near Manila and protect the right flank of the division, an additional brigade under the command of

General Wheaton was attached to MacArthur's division. This brigade consisted of one battalion of the 3rd Infantry, the 22nd Infantry and eleven companies of the 2nd Oregon Volunteers,

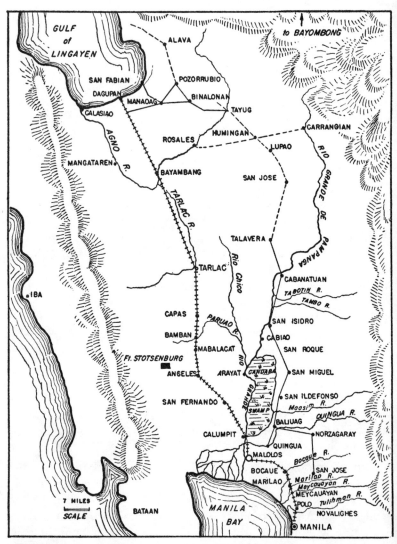

bringing the total strength of the division available for field operations to 11,780 officers and men.[2] The force was further augmented by a Colt 1-inch automatic gun taken from the USS *Helena* and manned by a Navy lieutenant and three Marines. Also accompanying the division was an "armored train," which consisted of three flat cars upon which were mounted a 6 pounder Navy Gun, 2 Gatling guns and a Hotchkiss revolving cannon.

The division field order for the movement prescribed that the advance would be by echelon from the right. Hall's Brigade on the extreme right was to demonstrate to the north, then stand fast and protect the water works line and the right flank of the division. Hale's Brigade on its left was to advance on the town of Novaliches, ten miles northeast of Manila and then swing to the west, cutting off Insurgent retreat to the north. It was to be assisted on its left by Otis' Brigade moving approximately in a northwest direction, just east of the railroad line. Wheaton's Brigade on the left of the Division was to advance slowly along the railroad, exerting only a mild pressure on the Insurgent lines until it was certain that Hale had swung to the left (west) and blocked the retreat of the Insurgents to the north. By this plan it was hoped that the Insurgent army would be not only defeated but captured.

At the outset the envelopment idea was a failure. It was premised on Hale's Brigade using a road which available maps indicated ran between Manila and Novaliches. When the brigade advanced on March 25th, it found that no such road existed and that its line of advance was through jungles, which precluded the movement of any wheeled transportation and over which even reconnaissance by mounted men was extremely difficult. As a result it was forced to swing to the left, some four miles south of Novaliches, which was too far south to block the Insurgents' withdrawal. The whole operation turned out to be a series of regimental combats, many of them bloody and devoid of either strategy or tactics.

Hale's brigade, which was to make the envelopment, moved forward from the trenches on the north side of the city at 5:30 a. m., March 25th. A picture of the brigade as it moved out may be formed from the following extract of the brigade order:[3]

> "Men will carry guns with straps and bayonets, belt, haversack, mess kit, canteen, filled with water or coffee. One days Field ration, 100 rounds of ammunition, poncho hung in belt. They will wear brown canvas uniform including blouse without blue shirt. Those not provided with blouses will wear blue shirts.
>
> "Two days additional field rations, 200 rounds additional ammunition, one blanket for each two men and necessary cooking utensils, tools, etc., will be transported in wagon and pack train.
>
> "Reveille will be at 3:00 a. m.; breakfast at 4:00 a. m.; and troops will be in assigned positions ready to start by 5:00 a. m. when each regimental commander will send a messenger to

brigade commander, to that effect. There will be no bugle calls, loud commands or shouting.

"Officers and non-commissioned officers will prevent men from throwing away accoutrements, rations, water and ammunition.

"Controlled volley firing by company, platoon or squad will be used except where enemy is scattered or retreating and individual firing when necessary will be closely regulated. Economize ammunition. Adjust sights to range. Aim low. Watch for dust and modify range accordingly. As a rule fire only at visible enemy or smoke.

"The advance will be pushed with energy and Insurgents driven from their positions without unnecessary hesitation. When under fire, advance by alternate rushes of companies or platoons, thus keeping the enemy down by a practically continuous fire, to proper distance and then charge. Impress upon the men that against the present enemy, the charge is the safest form of attack.

"Commanding officers will issue and enforce stringent orders against burning, looting and abuse of inhabitants or prisoners. Offenses of this nature will be severely punished."

This brigade in accordance with the above order left the line of American trenches one hour in advance of the other elements, moving in a general northeasterly direction on Novaliches. At the town of San Francisco del Monte, two miles to their front, they encountered spirited resistance from the Insurgents, who had entrenched themselves. In a hand-to-hand struggle for the possession of the town, one company commander, Captain Lee Forby, was killed and over fifty Insurgent dead or wounded left on the field. The Brigade then continued towards Novaliches. By ten o'clock in the morning the density of the jungle through which the advance was being made rendered the maintenance of contact between regiments impossible, and the brigade was unable to locate the road to Novaliches over which it had been intended to march supplies and ambulances. General Hale rode to division headquarters and explained the situation. At 12:15 p. m., upon MacArthur's instructions, he ordered the Brigade to swing to the left and move in a northwesterly direction. The change of direction soon brought it to the Tuliahan River which was crossed without opposition. The brigade then stopped and bivouacked during the night of March 25-26 on the north bank of the river.

Hall's Brigade, on the extreme right of the division, had made its demonstration to the north and halted about three miles north of the Manila-Mariquina road. It became evident that the Insurgents

Transporting Army Supplies in the Philippines by "carabao" (water-buffalo) Cart.

Macabebe Scouts.

were not extended in force as far east as Mariquina, so on the 26th this brigade was withdrawn and took no further active part in the movement.

Otis' Brigade, which was just to the west of Hale, had moved forward at 6:30 and encountered definite Insurgent resistance as soon as it left the American trenches. Advancing in the face of fire from the front and flank, it reached the Tuliahan River. There the fire from the Insurgents, who had entrenched themselves on the north bank, became so effective that the Americans were forced to stop and reconnoitre crossings. This river was about forty feet wide and five feet deep. With water up to their armpits and rifles held above heads, the 20th Kansans waded the river and chased the Insurgents out of the trenches. The 3rd Artillery, on the left of the Kansans, was forced to advance over open ground before reaching the river and in the first fifteen minutes of the advance experienced over thirty casualties. On reaching the river bank they were able to improvise a bridge by tying two nearby rafts end to end when they crossed without further difficulty. The brigade spent the night on the north bank of the river.

On the extreme left of the division, Wheaton's brigade had moved slowly because it was not desired to push the Insurgents back along the railroad until Hale's brigade had moved sufficiently far to the north to prevent their escape. Advancing from Caloocan along the railroad, Oregon Volunteers and the 22nd Infantry took line after line of Insurgent trenches. Bearing the brunt of the advance also was the 3rd Infantry which had arrived only three days previous from the United States and contained numerous recruits, many of whom had never before fired a rifle. However, by 11:30 a. m. the Insurgents had been pushed back to the north bank of the Tuliahan River. The Brigade did not attempt to cross the river on the 25th, but bivouacked in the vicinity of the railroad bridge. The division casualties for the day amounted to fifteen killed and ninety-one wounded.

The following day, March 26, saw the consummation of the modified flanking movement. As dawn broke, it was apparent to Wheaton, on the left flank, that the Insurgents were preparing to retreat. The town of Malabon to his left front was in flames. He immediately ordered the 22nd Infantry to cross the Tuliahan River and attack the Insurgents at Malinta, a mile and a half north of the railroad bridge. The Insurgents there had erected elaborate defenses, part of which consisted of a church surrounded by a two foot thick stone wall.

There also they had measured the ground from the railroad bridge to the church and at seventy-five yard intervals had erected large poles, bearing flags. By means of these markers they were able to determine the exact range to attacking troops. As the Americans passed the poles the Insurgents could adjust the sights on their rifles accurately. In some of the trenches rifles had been placed in fixed positions aimed at the height of a man's body. By this method it was not necessary for the defender to expose himself while firing and it was literally impossible for him to shoot over the head of advancing troops. The 22nd Infantry attacked this position in the face of a surprisingly effective fire. Within a few minutes after the attack began, the regimental commander, Colonel H. C. Egbert, and one first sergeant were killed and the first sergeants in two other companies had been wounded. However, the regiment charged, took the position and drove the Insurgents north along the railroad toward the town of Meycauyan.

At 8:40 a. m. of the same day, MacArthur sent the following telegram to Otis:[4]

> "I have just ascertained that by advancing to the Novaliches road, my artillery and wagons cannot follow me. Under these circumstances, propose to change front at once. This will threaten the Insurgent left, but somewhat farther south than intended. This movement which is the only feasible one in view of the character of the country, I propose to carry out at once. If you desire to make suggestions in the premises, please answer as quickly as possible."

At 9:25 a. m. Otis wired back "No suggestions."

The flanking movement now began from the bivouac occupied on the previous night. The 3rd Artillery on the left of Otis' Brigade entered Malinta just as the 22nd Infantry was clearing out the Insurgents. Hale's Brigade, which was to make the envelopment, swung to the left sharply and struck the railroad about two miles north of Malinta but not in time to prevent the withdrawal to the north of the retreating enemy. A defensive position at Polo was taken, and Hale pushed on towards Maycauyan three miles further north.

Maycauyan was situated on the Maycauyan River and was about eight miles north of Manila. There the Insurgents had again entrenched themselves on the north bank of the river, and it took a valiant charge, in which the Nebraska and South Dakota Volunteers were forced to wade the river and General Hale, the brigade commander, was wounded, before the Insurgents were dislodged. The advance element of the division bivouacked that night at Maycauyan. Casualties for the day amounted to two killed and twenty-nine wounded. On the walls of the railroad station in Maycauyan, the American troops found the following proclamation posted:[5]

> I, Antonio Luna, General in Chief of Operations, ordain and command from this date forward:
>
> First: The following will be executed by shooting without court martial:
>> a. Spies and those who give news of us to the enemy.
>> b. Those who commit robbery and those who violate women.
>
> Second: All towns which may be abandoned by our forces will be burned down. No one deplores war more than I do; I destest it, but we have an unalienable right to defend our soil from falling into the hands of the fresh rulers who desire to appropriate it, slaughtering our men, women and children.
>
> For this reason we are in duty bound as Filipinos to sacrifice everything for our independence, however great may be the sacrifices which the fatherland requires of us.   A. Luna.
> General Headquarters at Polo, February 15, 1899
> The General in Chief of Operations.

As a result of this order all Filipino barrios which were evacuated by the fleeing Insurgent troops were found to be in flames, an action which in no sense hindered the advance of the Americans and caused untold and unnecessary suffering and loss of property among the noncombatant natives.

On March 27, Wheaton's Brigade was detached and left behind to guard the railroad and line of communications, and Otis' and Hale's brigades continued to the north, one on each side of the railroad track. The Insurgents were retreating so rapidly that the advance became a pursuit.

The tactics of the pursuit may be summarized by the following extract from the 2nd Brigade Field order dated March 27:[6]

> "When advance party meets enemy in small force it will drive him out enveloping his flank. If in larger force, support and reserve (if necessary) of advance guard will turn flank. If in very strong force and position advance guard will hold front and main body will be used as may be most desirable. Firing pigs, chickens, etc., will be strictly prohibited at all times."

Contact with the Insurgents was reestablished at the town of Marilao, situated on a river by the same name, two miles to the north.

The South Dakota Volunteers, advance guard for Hale's Brigade on the east side of the railroad track, came under Insurgent fire and attacked immediately, losing three officers and four enlisted men killed and one officer and twenty-four enlisted men wounded. They forced the Insurgents across the Marilao railroad bridge and secured control of the bridge. Captain Clayton P. Van Houten of the South Dakota Volunteers became the subject of a special report by his regimental commander as follows:[7]

"Captain Van Houten, in command of Company D, which company was the first to cross the railroad bridge where he shot a Filipino Colonel with his revolver, went back to hurry forward the mountain gun which I had ordered up by my sergeant major. He found it across the bridge. He asked why it had not been taken over. The reply was that they couldn't do it. He told them to dismount it and take it over. They replied that two men could not carry the piece. Enraged at this answer, he had the piece dismounted, placed on his shoulders and carried it (weight about 250 pounds) over on his shoulders while four of his company carried over the carriage. Because of his energy the mountain gun was gotten over in time for a few parting shots at the retreating enemy although it was of no use in dislodging him. Captain Van Houten strained himself by his great effort of strength and has today been ordered to Manila by the surgeon."

Otis' Brigade on the west side of the railroad came under fire on their left flank from Insurgent trenches opposite where the river made a bend to the south. Colonel Fredrick Funston, of the 20th Kansas, finding the river unfordable at this point, called for volunteers to swim the river and bring back a raft which was moored on the opposite bank. One officer and four enlisted men volunteered, then disrobed and protected by a concentrated fire on the Insurgent trenches, swam the river and brought a raft back without a casualty. By the time that Colonel Funston and twenty-one men of the Kansas regiment had crossed on the raft, the Insurgents opposite had fled, leaving twenty-four dead and thirty-four prisoners, thirty-one Remington rifles and 4000 rounds of ammunition. Farther up the river a company of the 10th Pennsylvania Volunteers crossed in a similar manner and routed detachments of Insurgents.

At about 5:00 in the afternoon the Insurgents staged a counter attack. In full view of both brigades, a large body of Filipinos advanced within 2000 yards of the American lines and opened fire. Being beyond the range of the American Krag-Jorgeson and Springfield rifles and just within the maximum range of the Insurgent Mausers, shots that usually went over the heads of the Americans when they charged at close quarters were now landing in their ranks and causing casualties. The Insurgent left flank was charged by the 1st Nebraska and the entire line withdrew. The division casualties for the day were fifteen killed and seventy wounded.

The division was delayed at Marilao by the necessity of planking the railroad bridge for the passage of the supply trains and the construction of an entire new bridge over a small but deep stream which adjoined the river. The temporary bridge, which the division engineer detachment constructed from cascos, sank when the supply trains were about half over. MacArthur decided to get his supply system well in hand before continuing further and directed that the 28th be spent at Marilao.

On March 29 the division continued its movement along the railroad towards Malolos, eleven miles distant. The Insurgents had been pushed back so rapidly that they were demoralized and apparently had neither time nor inclination to damage effectively the railroad track or bridges as they retreated. By 10:30 a. m. on the 29th, Bocaue, three miles beyond Marilao, was taken with the railroad bridge intact. By noon the division had reached Bigaa, a mile and a half north, and after routing Insurgents entrenched on the north bank of the Bigaa River, moved to Guiguinto, two miles further on. There the command halted during the night of March 29-30.

The division was now less than five miles from Malolos, where it was anticipated that the Insurgents would offer a substantial resistance, principally because of the political effect that the capture of the capital would have on the Insurgent cause.

After spending most of the 30th distributing rations and ammunition, the division left Guiguinto and moved towards Malolos at 2:20 p. m. By 5:30 p. m., after overcoming what General MacArthur called "moderate" opposition from the Insurgents, they were within two miles of the Insurgent capital. There, in view of the formidable earthworks to his front, MacArthur halted and decided to attack the following morning.

For the attack on Malolos, MacArthur prescribed an artillery preparation of twenty-five minutes, to be followed by an envelopment of the Insurgent left flank.

At 7:00 on the morning of the 31st, following the artillery preparation, the 1st Nebraska, on the right of MacArthur's line, moved by the flank and pushed out weak Insurgent detachments. Apparently either the Artillery preparation had discouraged the Insurgents or it had been decided that the city would be evacuated without a struggle, for when the Kansas regiment advanced along the railroad it encountered no opposition.

Perhaps the capture of the city itself is best told by Colonel Funston, who was among the first to enter:[8]

> "When the advance was resumed on the morning of the 31st, the first trenches reached were found deserted, the occupants having fled during the shelling of their position by the field battery. An extensive trench near the railroad less than a quarter of a mile from the suburbs of Malolos was found deserted and here the regiment in common with the whole division halted. I received orders from the division commander to send a small reconnoitering party into the town and accordingly took second Lieutenant Colin H. Ball and two squads from Company E and taking charge of these in person advanced cautiously up one of the principal streets. We found the convent occupied by Aguinaldo as a residence in flames and were fired on by a dozen men behind a street barricade of stones. My detachment returned the fire with two volleys and charged, the enemy seeking safety in flight and we entered the plaza, being the first American troops in the enemy's capital. We were immediately followed by two guns under Major Young and shortly afterwards by several companies of the 1st Montana."

Aguinaldo's government and army had fled to the north the night before. General MacArthur wanted to follow up the Insurgent army at once and occupy the line of the large Rio Grande Pampanga, eight miles to the north. However, Otis sent out word from Manila for him to stop and refit. The total casualties to the division during the advance on Malolos amounted to 56 killed and 478 wounded. It is difficult to determine the Insurgent casualties, because as usual, the wounded were carried from the field. A conservative estimate places them at double those of the Americans.

Before we leave MacArthur and his division at Malolos let us make a brief glance at some of the problems which the Malolos campaign indicated the future might hold in store.

At the outset Insurgent military opposition may be eliminated as an obstacle of any importance. By the time they had been pushed back to Malolos, Insurgent morale was at such a low ebb that the signal for an American advance became automatically the signal for an Insurgent retreat. Casualties occurred to be sure, but they were more often than otherwise the result of chance.

Unquestionably the greatest problem in the Malolos campaign and what promised to be the greatest problem in the future was the matter of supply. A glance at the map will indicate that there were no less than six sizable rivers in the twenty miles between Manila and Malolos. Normally Filipino streams were not spanned by bridges suitable for heavy transportation. In this particular campaign, of course, the existence of the railroad solved the bridge problem. Partially dismantled bridges were planked and the supply trains crossed with little difficulty. Had the Insurgents been more adept at bridge destruction, however, the division would have been delayed until the few available engineer troops could have constructed bridges from local materials. During the dry season many of the shallow bridgeless streams could be forded without difficulty. What was to be done, however, when the streams became raging torrents during the rainy season? Native traffic normally subsided during that period, but military supplies must be moved regardless of season or weather.

What mode of transportation was to be used? The native carabao cart was capable of four or five miles a day, too slow for a fast moving infantry column. Either the column must slow down or transportation must speed up. It appeared that American-made wagons might shake to pieces moving over the rough, rocky tracks which the Filipinos called roads.

Troops deploying and moving cross country encountered special difficulties. The terrain did not consist of rolling corn or wheat fields. It was cut up into shallow rice paddies, each about a quarter of an acre in size. Each paddy was enclosed by an earthen dike at least a foot high. Crossing the dikes not only made the going hard for infantrymen but was tremendously exhausting to artillery horses or to the gunners when the guns were pulled by hand.

How were the wounded to be evacuated? Troops were sometimes deployed and men wounded in a bamboo thicket three miles from the nearest transportation. Who was to carry them over the dikes to the nearest ambulance? How was the health of the troops to be maintained? Potable water in the field was non-existent. Each soldier who drank from a native well or stream was inviting a first-class case of dysentery. Strange tropical germs, unfamiliar to American doctors, infected even the most minor cuts or abrasions, sometimes causing death within twenty-four hours.

The movement on Malolos was held during the dry season, with the troops moving along the only railroad line in the Islands. Campaigning away from the railroad during the rainy season would be an entirely different matter. If the Insurrection was to be broken, all territory in the hands of the Insurgents must be occupied without delay.

As these problems unfolded themselves, they caused General Otis to rub his chin in speculation. Their solution lay in the future, which held he knew not what.

Notes on Chapter VII

1 cf HD No. 2 Vol. 6 56th 1st p. 366
2 cf Ibid p. 377
3 cf Ibid p. 459 *et. seq.*
4 cf Ibid p. 382
5 cf Ibid p. 385
6 cf Ibid p. 461 *et. seq.*
7 cf Ibid p. 467
8 cf Ibid p. 393

Chapter VIII

THE QUESTION as to which army, Insurgent or American, was superior was settled by the battle of Manila, and confirmed by the easy capture of Malolos. American troops could, if supplied properly, advance in Insurgent territory at will. Occupation of the Archipelago should then be simply a matter of road marches to occupy key cities in Luzon, establish supply bases there and extend American authority into the surrounding territory from the bases.

Following the capture of Malolos, Otis had a golden opportunity to settle the Insurrection in short order. The rainy season generally commences in June, and he had two months within which he could have extended and consolidated American authority.

However, he failed to take advantage of his opportunity. Instead of sending small mobile columns in all directions to occupy Insurgent territory, he sent comparatively large forces on thrusts in two or three directions. The "thrust" idea would not have been so bad had the occupied territory been retained under American control. However, as soon as a key point was occupied, Otis required the expedition to return, bag and baggage, to Manila. Insurgent forces which had become scattered and disorganized were permitted to reorganize and reoccupy the territory without molestation. Then when their activities became embarrassing again, another expedition would be sent out to scatter them.

Probably the greatest fault of Otis' administration was his constant interference with his commanders in the field. Although a subordinate major general might be sent out on a campaign in command of 8 or 10,000 troops, he could not make a single move until he received authority from Otis in Manila. If a column moved too fast, Otis would make it retrace its steps and halt until he gave instructions to proceed. It took three years to do a job which most of Otis' subordinates thought could have been accomplished in two months. Had every officer in the American Army in the Philippines followed Otis' orders to the letter, the Islands might have never been pacified. Of course, Otis was the responsible commander and as such entitled to observe a certain amount of caution. However, a most tolerant estimation of his conduct of the military operations in the Philippines motivates this writer to say that Otis' policy was extremely over-cautious.

As far as the supply system was concerned, the two remaining months of the dry season were precious. Had the advance been pushed and bases established throughout the Island, the American troops would not have had to wallow their way through the mud of Luzon during the rainy season. But during April, MacArthur was forced to sit idly by at Malolos while the Insurgents destroyed railroad bridges to the north and harassed American outposts to distraction. The remainder of the American troops were utilized in abortive "sight seeing tours" in the vicinity of Manila. American authority in Luzon was not extended in any substantial manner whatsoever.

During May MacArthur was permitted to advance to San Fernando, Pampanga, a town about twenty miles north of Malolos. By that time his troops had been in the field so long that half the division went on sick report. More "thrusts" during the June rains emphasized the difficulties of operating during the wet season. As a result, the American Army was virtually immobile until November. Several of these abortive thrusts of Otis will be discussed, not because of their military importance on the Insurrection as a whole, but because they indicate some of the harrowing experiences which the American troops underwent while taking possession of the twenty millon dollar "gift" which Spain handed to the United States.

From the date of his arrival in the Philippines on March 10, 1899, to his death from an Insurgent bullet on December 18 of the same year, there was one man with whose name the Filipino Insurgents may have conjured apprehensively. He was Major General Henry W. Lawton, a soldier par excellence. At the age of eighteen he had enlisted for the Civil War as a sergeant in the 9th Indiana Infantry. During that war he took active part in no less than twenty-eight major engagements. He had been awarded the Congressional Medal of Honor for "Distinguished gallantry in leading a charge of skirmishers against the enemy's works, taking them with their occupants and stubbornly and successfully resisting two determined attacks of the enemy to retake the works, in front of Atlanta, Georgia, August 3, 1864." He ended the war as a brevet colonel of volunteers and was commissioned in 1866 as a second lieutenant of infantry in the Regular Army. In 1871 he transferred to the cavalry and between 1876 and 1883 was actively engaged in the campaigns against the Indians. During the Indian campaigns he was repeatedly mentioned in orders for "Vigilance and zeal," "rapidity and persistence of pursuit," and for "great skill, perseverance and gallantry." He was actively responsible for the capture of the Apache Chief Geronimo, in

1886. By the time the Spanish-American War occurred, he had reached the grade of colonel in the Inspector General's Department, and was immediately promoted to the grade of major general of volunteers and placed in command of a division in the campaign

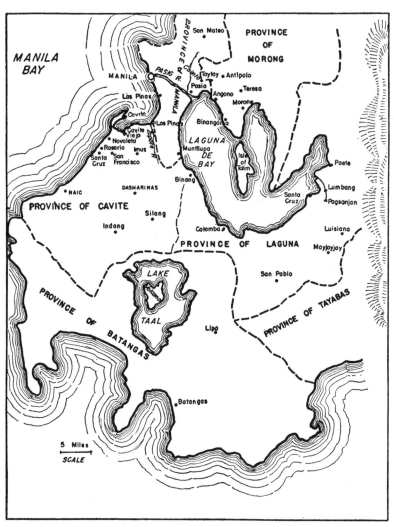

of Santiago de Cuba. In Cuba he took part in the battle at El Caney and was subsequently the Military Governor of Santiago. In January of 1899 he was sent to the Philippine Islands where he was placed in command of the 1st Division. A large man, well over six feet in height, he was entirely fearless. Noticeably conspicuous in the vicinity of the firing line in a white cork helmet, which he invariably wore, he was an excellent target for Insurgent bullets. Although of kindly disposition, he was frequently subject to violent fits of temper. On these occasions his staff found it expedient to disappear from his presence until the storm had passed. Had Otis permitted him to carry out the aggressive measures which he continually proposed, it is possible that the Philippine Islands might have been pacified at a much earlier date. A month after his arrival, Otis gave him command of an expedition into Laguna Province.

On the southeastern shore of Laguna de Bay is the city of Santa Cruz, one of the richest and most important in that part of Luzon. It was populated by 13,000 inhabitants and was the outlet for the produce of the fertile provinces to the south and southeast of Manila. It had been reported that the Insurgents were in force there. So in the early part of April, Otis decided to send Lawton with a provisional brigade to clear out the south shore of the lake. The expedition had for its immediate objects the following missions:[1] "To destroy or capture the enemy force at Santa Cruz; to distribute among the inhabitants of the country copies of proclamations setting forth the benevolent aims of the United States; to locate and capture several gunboats and launches which were rumored to be in the hands of Insurgents in that area; to reconnoiter the country to the east and north of Santa Cruz along the shore of Laguna de Bay; to make a landing on the west shore of the lake and capture the town of Calamba."

The expedition consisted of 1509 troops from the following units:[2]

One squadron of the 4th Cavalry (dismounted)
2 Battalions of the 14th Infantry
1 Battalion of the 1st Idaho Volunteers
1 Battalion of the 1st North Dakota Volunteers
2 mountain guns

They were organized into a provisional brigade which Lawton placed under the direct command of Brigadier General Charles King. Since by land the distance to Santa Cruz was sixty miles through Insurgent infested territory, and by water was some thirty-six miles, it was decided that the expedition would be transported to Santa Cruz by boats.

Seventeen cascos, two bancas, eight launches and the gunboats *Laguna de Bay, Ceste and Napidan* were assembled at San Pedro Macati on the afternoon of April 8, and the troops, carrying rations and ammunition in their packs, embarked. No tentage, animals or wheeled vehicles were taken. At 4:00 p. m., manned and piloted entirely by Army personnel, the flotilla cast off and started up the Pasig River. As a result of inexperienced pilots attempting to steer towed craft through the narrow winding channel, the boats frequently went aground and twelve hours were consumed reaching the Laguna de Bay, six miles distant. Starting across the Laguna at 4:00 a. m. on the 9th, sailing was easy and Santa Cruz was reached at 10:00 a. m.

The gunboats were distributed along the south shore of the lake and landing operations two miles west of Santa Cruz commenced during the afternoon of the 9th.

Because of the rough sea, many of the men were forced to wade ashore in water that sometimes reached their shoulders. The 55-year old brigade commander, Brigadier General Charles King, suffered a heart attack while the landing operations were in progress and his duties perforce were taken over by General Lawton. By five o'clock in the afternoon, however, the entire brigade was ashore and formed in line on the beach. A scattering fire from the nearby jungle was silenced by a few volleys and a brigade wheel to the left facing Santa Cruz was effected. Then, darkness coming on, a halt was made and the brigade bivouacked for the night about two miles from the town.

During the evening Captain C. C. Walcott, a quartermaster officer on Lawton's staff, started out with an orderly to locate the front line. The two walked blindly through a gap between the 14th Infantry and the Idaho Volunteers, and guided by a wily Filipino whom they met, were led right into the town of Santa Cruz. An Insurgent patrol armed with bolos was encountered and after a short but decisive fight, the Insurgents were disarmed and made prisoners. An hour of hide and seek with other Insurgent patrols in the city followed before Walcott, his orderly and the Insurgent prisoners were able to regain the American lines, only slightly the worse for wear.

On the morning of the 10th the brigade stormed a barricade across the bridge leading into the town, and swept the Insurgents through the town into the open where they came under an effective fire from the *Napidan*. Ninety-three Insurgent dead were picked up on the streets and seventy-one captured. Some forty-two wounded Insurgents, who had been carried away by their comrades, were subsequently found dead in nearby thickets. American casualties were six wounded.

Except for a few Chinese shopkeepers, Santa Cruz was found denuded of inhabitants, and Lawton immediately took steps to protect the captured city from burning of buildings and looting. Proclamations were freely distributed in the houses of the city to be found by the inhabitants when they returned.

The following morning the brigade proceeded at 6:00 a. m. to the town of Pagsanjan and after a short fight entered the town about 8:00 a. m. Six steam launches and two cascos were captured. Meanwhile the gunboats which had been sent to enter the Pagsanjan River had been blocked by a sand bar. Upon Lawton's request to Otis, a dredge was sent out and the bar removed.

Moving via Lubang the brigade, on April 12, followed the shore of the lake northeast, occupying Longos without difficulty. Early that afternoon a battalion of North Dakota Volunteers was sent further along the shore to reconnoiter the town of Paete as a possible embarking place for the command upon its contemplated movement to Calamba, across the lake.

During this movement, while marching through the jungle which adjoined the road, a flank guard of the North Dakotas was ambushed. Of the five men in the group three were killed outright and one seriously wounded. The sole uninjured member of the patrol, Private Thomas Sletteland, won the Congressional Medal of Honor by remaining with his comrade and "By his cool and unerring aim successfully holding the enemy back until reinforcements came."

Despite the thick underbrush, the flanking parties were sent up a 45 to 70 degree hill which adjoined the road and forced the Insurgents back through Paete.

Short as had been the campaign, Lawton's command was tired. Since no wheeled transportation had been taken along, every requisite to military operations—rations, blankets, shelter tents, ammunition, medical supplies and water—were of necessity carried on the individual. The extra weight made it particularly difficult for the officers, whose duties required them to change position rapidly up and down a skirmish line during any action.

The gunboats had proved to be a valuable asset. Standing off shore a short distance, they were able to throw retreating Insurgent bodies into a panic by dropping shells in their midst.

Lawton's instructions had contemplated that he next cross the lake to the town of Calamba on the south western shore. However, while his troops were in bivouac at Paete for a couple of days' rest, he received word from Otis to return to Manila immediately. Five Americans had been killed and 135 Insurgents buried by Lawton's troops during the "sight-seeing tour" of the lake. As soon as the expedition returned to Manila on April 17, Santa Cruz, Pagsanjan,

Longos and Paete were reoccupied by the Insurgents. If viewed merely as a reconnaissance, the expedition was worth while; otherwise the sole fruits were the capture of a few Insurgent water craft.

2

The next episode of the war was an exchange of proclamations rather than bullets. There had arrived in Manila on March 4 two civilian members of the First Philippine Commission. This body had been appointed by President McKinley during January of 1899 for the purpose of "ascertaining without interfering with the military authorities what amelioration of the condition of the inhabitants of the Philippines could be accomplished and what improvements in public order were practicable."[3] It was to study attentively the existing social and political conditions in the Islands, particularly the forms of local government, administration of justice, collection of customs, taxes, means of communication, and need of public improvements. It was to report the results of its observations with such recommendations as it cared to make to the President through the Department of State.

The Commission consisted of Jacob Gould Schurman, the President of Cornell University as Chairman, Charles Denby, who had served as the United States Minister to China for fourteen years, Dean C. Worcester, Professor of Zoology at the University of Michigan who, in 1890 had headed a Zoological expedition to the Philippines, General Otis, and Admiral Dewey. Hostilities had broken out before the Commission assembled at Manila so that at the outset its field of activities was limited. However, it did, as the occasion presented itself, interview Filipinos from all elements of the native population and discussed subjects which ranged from racial problems to church property.[4]

On April 4, in view of the fact that "It became convinced that the Tagalog rebellion was due to the ambitions of a few and the misunderstanding of the many," the Commission issued a proclamation[5] which enunciated the beneficial aims of the United States towards the Filipino and set forth several principles by which the United States would be guided in dealing with them. It commenced with the statement: "The supremacy of the United States must and will be enforced throughout every part of the Archipelago and those who resist it can accomplish no end other than their own ruin." It promised "most ample liberty of self government"; religious freedom; prevention of exploitation; an honest civil service; a sound, economical tax system; a pure, speedy, and effective administration of justice; the promotion of an advantageous public works program; the fostering of domestic and foreign trade; the establishment of a modern educational system; and reform in all branches of the government.

As was customary, the proclamation was printed in English, Spanish and Tagalog and copies were posted in prominent places throughout Manila. Within twenty-four hours the majority were so torn or mutilated as to be unrecognizable. It was even reported that Insurgent leaders had forbidden Filipinos to read the document upon penalty of death. However, judging from the response that the proclamation received from some of the more educated and conservative Filipinos, as a whole it was beneficial, though apparently it made little impression on the Insurgents themselves. On April 15 Mabini, "In behalf of the Philippine Government," issued a manifesto which indicated no intent to give credence to the beneficent aims of the Americans. In referring to the Proclamation, Mabini said:[*]

> "The American Commissioners who to inspire greater confidence have not hesitated to have recourse to falsehood, shamelessly asserting that my government by not having understood the good will and fraternal sentiments of their ambitious president, has provoked war when everybody is aware that President McKinley had to decree war in order to force the American Senators of the opposition to ratify the cession of the Philippines stipulated in the treaty of Paris.
>
> "If the North American people is great and powerful, far greater and more powerful is Providence which watches over the unfortunate and chastises and humbles the proud. Thus if we should lay down our arms, we should leave our sons without liberty and without the means of retrieving our fortune and moreover we should bequeath to them all the penalties and sufferings of a conflict which of necessity they would have to face today if we do not release them from this task.
>
> "Open your eyes, my dear countrymen, while there is yet time. Fight without truce or respite, without faltering or desponding, without measuring the duration of the conflict, the forces of the enemy or the greatness of the sacrifices.
>
> "Annexation in whatever form it may be adopted will unite us forever with a nation whose manners and customs are different from our own, a nation which hates the colored race with a moral hatred, and from which we could never separate ourselves except by war.
>
> "It matters not whether we die in the midst or at the end of our most painful day's work; the generations to come, praying

over our tombs will shed for us tears of love and gratitude and not of bitter reproach."

Otis decided that the most effective proclamation was the bark of a Krag-Jorgenson rifle.

3

To the north of Manila, the Insurgents were becoming bold again. On the night of April 11 a determined attack under the personal command of Aguinaldo was made on the railroad line between Bocaue and Marilao. Upon the small detachment guarding the line calling for help, Wheaton with the armored train loaded with troops moved along the railroad line and drove the Insurgents off. The principal damage had been the destruction of four miles of telegraph line. The following morning a "punitive expedition" was sent to Santa Maria, three miles east of Bocaue, and although they did not realize it, the Americans nearly captured the Insurgent President.[7]

On April 13 the Insurgents attacked an outpost occupied by the 3rd Artillery at Paomban, a barrio east of Malolos. Two Americans were killed, five wounded and one captured before the marauders were driven off. It became evident that if the Americans did not take the offensive, their losses on small outpost attacks would reach disconcertingly substantial figures.

The total strength of the American forces in the Philippines at this time was 26,003 officers and men. Of this number 5000 were at Cavite or in the Visayan Islands; 836 were members of noncombatant branches; 2739 were sick or in confinement; some 1500 were on special duty or performing civil functions. The available fighting force then numbered about 16,500. Volunteer organizations which had enlisted for the duration of the war with Spain were beginning to clamor for discharge and return to the United States. If Otis was to use these volunteer troops, he would have to do it quickly; so an advance was decided upon before the rainy season set it.

About thirty miles northeast of Manila lies the southern tip of the large Candaba swamp, which is inpassable during the rainy season. It is roughly triangular in shape and extends north about twenty miles to the boundary between Pampanga and Neuva Ecija. In its widest place it traverses about ten miles, its eastern borders roughly following the boundary between Pampanga and Bulucan. The important strategic town of Calumpit is on its southern tip. At Calumpit the large Rio Grande of Pampanga, which follows the western edge of the swamp in an almost north and south direction, turns southwest and empties into Manila Bay about thirteen miles distant. Any force advancing along the Manila-Dagupan Railway had to cross the Rio Grande de Pampanga. The railroad itself ran through Calumpit.

It was not known exactly whether the Insurgent army under Luna had retreated along the railroad due east of Malolos, or whether it had cut back to the northeast. The fact that the majority of the natives spoke no English and were either sympathetic with the Insurgent cause or feared to divulge information, made it particularly difficult to trace his movements. In order to contact Luna's army whichever route it had taken, Otis decided to send two expeditions to the north. One under Lawton was to move through the Tagalog provinces of Neuva Ecija and Bulacan, while the other under MacArthur was to move north along the railroad into the province of Pampanga. As a matter of fact, Luna's army had actually retired north along the railroad line, while the Insurgent government had moved to the northeast and set up a new capital at San Isidro in the province of Nueva Ecija. Otis planned to have the two divisions effect a junction at or near the town of San Miguel de Mayumo. The plans did not materialize, as will be seen later, because MacArthur was unable to advance as rapidly as had been anticipated.

The movement of Lawton's division north was a perfect example of another wasteful "sight-seeing expedition" hampered by fussy interference from Otis at his desk in Manila.

Lawton assembled his force at La Loma Church on the outskirts of Manila. His immediate purpose was to be almost due east of Malolos by April 24, which date MacArthur's column was to move on Calumpit.

Lawton's column, which was designated as the 1st Division of the 8th Army Corps, was composed of the following troops:

22nd Infantry
1st North Dakota Volunteers
1 Squadron of the 4th Cavalry (dismounted)
2 Battalions of the 3rd Infantry
6 Mountain and 2 field guns from Battery D of the 6th Artillery

Two battalions of the 2nd Oregon Volunteers and two battalions of the 13th Minnesota Volunteers and a troop of the 4th Cavalry in bivouac near Bocaue, were detached from the 2nd Division with instructions to march from Bocaue on the 23rd and effect a junction with Lawton's column at Norzagaray on the 25th.

Lawton's division left La Loma church on the 22nd, marching on Novaliches about ten miles to the northeast. Minor Insurgent opposition was brushed aside, and the troops marched into Novaliches about 10:00 a. m. the same morning. The greatest problem of the march had been the difficulty in getting the trains over the Tuliahan River, which was not bridged and had steep approaches to its rocky banks. Novaliches was found abandoned by its inhabitants, who had taken with them all property of value. That night the American troops slept in deserted nipa huts.

Leaving Novaliches the following day, the command moved on San Jose about six miles north. The road now became a mere footpath and great trouble was encountered moving the wagon train over a succession of hills and deep valleys. No enemy was met, but the difficulties of the road, combined with the intense heat, slowed progress to such an extent that it took the column from five o'clock in the morning until 3:30 in the afternoon to reach the Sapangalat River, about four and a half miles north of Novaliches. It is thus apparent that the rate march of the column, with no delays caused by the enemy, was less than one half mile per hour. Utterly exhausted, the division camped for the night at the Sapangalat River.

The whole next day was spent getting the column into San Jose. The animals of the wagon trains were subjected to such heavy draft that many died in the traces, and the soldiers were forced to take their places, pulling the wagons and carts in some places and literally carrying them along the road in others. The mounted troops of cavalry accompanying the detachment from Bocaue had arrived in Norzagaray the same day and then moved south to San Jose, where they established contact with the main body. The wagon train did not reach San Jose until late that night. It had consumed two full days in covering a distance of six miles.

The following day the advance guard of the main column reached Norzagaray, eight and a half miles to the north, and joined there the Oregon and Minnesota Volunteers who had marched from Bocaue. Colonel Owen Summers, in command of that column, reported that he had been forced to drive the Insurgents out of Norzagaray before his column was able to enter.

The united division now had a strength of 116 officers and 4473 men. The troops of the Bocaue column were formed into a "provisional brigade" and placed under the command of Colonel Summers.

Norzagaray is situated on the Quingua River which winds to the east at this point. On the 25th a reconnoitering force occupied the town of Angat, two miles east. On the 27th the remainder of the division moved into Angat, its advance elements continuing along the river as far as Marunco in an effort to locate a road to the north. No road worthy of the name could be found; so on the 29th the march was continued along the Quingua River towards San Rafael. There a force of 300 entrenched Insurgents were brushed aside and the town occupied.

Meanwhile the Signal Corps had established telegraphic communication between Angat and Manila. From his desk in Manila Otis thought that Lawton was moving too fast for his supplies; on the 29th he directed him to return to Angat until more supplies could be moved to that place. Lawton was forced to withdraw his troops at San Rafael and retire to Angat where the division remained for three days. Then on May 1, having been authorized by Otis to move out with Baliuag as an objective, the division retraced its steps down the Quingua River.

While at Angat waiting for "permission" to advance, Lawton had organized a company of scouts, recruited from picked riflemen of all organizations. They were placed under the command of W. H. Young, an American ex-frontiersman and prospector, who had found his way to the Philippines. Despite the fact that he was a civilian, Young proved his capabilities and justified the confidence which Lawton had reposed in him. Always in front of the main column, the scouts bore the brunt of the advance, reconnoitering and maintaining contact with the enemy. Their work was so fearless and effective that a large number of them reaped their reward in the form of a Congressional Medal of Honor.

As the division, moving along the river, approached San Rafael on May 1, opposition was offered by some 1000 Insurgents who had occupied the town after Lawton's withdrawal. A flanking movement by the provisional brigade forced them back through, and to the west of, the town. The division bivouacked for the night at San Rafael, having lost one killed and four wounded in the recapture of the place.

On May 2, the division continued the march towards Baliuag, four miles distant. After a short fight at Bustos, Baliuag was entered at noon, the irrepressible Americans announcing their arrival by ringing the Cathedral bells. Though large numbers of Insurgents followed by native civilians had been seen fleeing in wild confusion to the north, any pursuit was precluded by the extreme heat which had caused more casualties than Insurgent bullets.

Located near the southern tip of Candaba Swamp, Baliuag was at the junction of seven roads, converging from various directions. Being about seven miles from Quingua, which had been taken by MacArthur, the division could now establish communication with, and be supplied from, Malolos through Quingua instead of the roundabout route through Bocaue and Norzagaray.

In Baliuag, Lawton seized some 150,000 bushels of rice and 265 tons of sugar which the Insurgents had confiscated from the natives and assembled there. These supplies were issued to the native civilians of Baliuag, who were now returning to the town in large numbers. Lawton also authorized the installation of the first native government in the Philippines under the jurisdiction of the United States. The plan is best explained by quoting the following Division Order:[8]

> General Field Orders   Hdqrs. First Division 8th Army Corps
> No. 8   In the Field, Baliuag, May 7, 1899
> For the purpose of official and just representation of the inhabitants of this town with the Military authorities, as well as for temporary convenience in restoring and maintaining order among the former, the citizens were authorized to meet and elect a mayor, (Captain Municipal). The result of such meeting has been the election of Senor Francisco Guerrero, who is therefore announced as Mayor and authorized to select a council and such other assistants or officers as may be necessary to properly administer municipal affairs. He will be accordingly respected and obeyed.
> The United States will in no way be held accountable or responsible for any salaries or compensation.
> By Command of Major General Lawton.
> Clarence R. Edwards
> Assistant Adjutant General

As long as the Insurgent Army was retreating and unable to influence the natives living in the various Filipino barrios, the American-sponsored, native-ruled municipal regime worked well. However, as will be seen, after the Insurgent army was broken up and the erstwhile Insurgent soldiers returned to their homes they were able to stir up discontent and trouble among more peaceably inclined elements. At any rate, having established a local government in a fairly prominent Filipino town, Lawton was able to lay plans for further advance to the north.

A fairly good dry-weather road ran north from Baliuag to San Miguel, fourteen miles distant. Since the swamp prevented any movement of troops to the northwest, it was apparent that the remnants of the Insurgent division which had opposed Lawton's advance had escaped to the northeast.

SOLDIERS IN THE SUN

On May 2nd Otis wired Lawton as follows:

"Remain at Baliuag watching San Miguel road until you receive rations via Malolos. Enemy now concentrating supplies in large storehouses some five miles east of Maasin on Maasin River, northeast of you. Look in that direction; main force there."

To which Lawton replied on May 3:[9]

"I will send men to look up enemy constructing storehouses as indicated in yours of last evening. I find enemy's strength always exaggerated. They have offered no determined or effective resistance. Are greatly demoralized and are breaking into small parties and disintegrating. With a squadron of mounted men I could have destroyed the whole outfit from here yesterday, but our men on foot cannot stand the extra exertion in this awful heat. Those who suffered sunstroke yesterday fell as though shot. The mounted troop did excellent work but could make but slow progress because very small detachments of enemy's rear guard could stop them. It has rained nearly every day and the country off the roads is impracticable for vehicles."

In accordance with Otis' telegram the provisional brigade moved north on May 3 towards the town of Maasin. A force of about four hundred Insurgents entrenched on the north side of the Maasin River was driven out and Maasin occupied. The scouts were then sent to the north and northeast to locate any Insurgent supplies and, if possible, the "storehouses" which Otis had mentioned in his telegram. Otis' information was correct and in the vicinity of Maasin the scouts ferreted out and destroyed over 100,000 bushels of rice, 40,000 bushels of corn, two hundred eighty-three Insurgent uniforms, a large quantity of uniform material and several sets of rifle cartridge reloading tools.

On May 6 the advance was again delayed from Manila. Otis wired Lawton that 5000 Insurgents under Generals Pio Del Pilar and Geronimo were reported proceeding from the towns of San Mateo and Antipolo with the intent of attacking him in flank and rear. Further movement to the north was to be halted until the truth or falsity of this rumor was verified. Annoyed, Lawton sent reconnoitering parties back as far as San Jose, but was unable to find enemy troops or even locate a road by which they could march except that over which his division had just passed.

The search for the phantom army of Pilar continued until the 12th, and then convinced that the rumor was false Otis authorized reconnaissance towards San Miguel, seven miles north. The reconnaissance party, consisting of a mapping detail and a few scouts, protected by two companies of the Oregon Volunteers, gained contact with the enemy at San Ildefonso. A sharp fight ensued and the Insurgents were driven out of town towards San Miguel.

The following day, led by the scouts, the reconnaissance party pressed its advantage. About one mile south of San Miguel it was met by volleys from an Insurgent band numbering about three hundred. Led by Captain William E. Birkimer and W. H. Young, the civilian chief, the group of eleven scouts charged the Insurgents without hesitation and drove the whole three hundred into San Miguel. In this charge, Mr. W. H. Young was mortally wounded. Captain Birkimer and the eleven scouts received the Congressional Medal of Honor. The small band then entered San Miguel and drove the few Insurgents who remained northeast towards San Isidro and east towards Biac-Na-Bato. The entire reconnaissance force was posted at San Miguel to hold it until the remainder of the division could be brought up.

It appeared that the Insurgent morale was rapidly degenerating and that the Insurgent troops under General Gregorio Del Pilar, who had been opposing Lawton's advance, were becoming demoralized. From San Miguel, Captain John Case, of the Oregon Volunteers, who had entered San Miguel with the scouts, wired Lawton, who was still at Baliuag:[10]

> "From residents here I learn that there were 900 Insurgents at Baliuag but only 600 arrived here, the balance having deserted. He (Pilar) has desertions daily, soldiers have received no pay and are discouraged. Insurgent troops have gone to San Isidro, which town is reported fairly well entrenched. Aquinaldo passed through here April 19th."

Meanwhile the strategic town of Calumpit, having been taken by MacArthur's division, Otis dispatched the 17th Infantry and one battalion of the 9th up the Rio Grande with instructions to unite with Lawton at San Miguel or San Isidro. This expedition was accompanied by two gunboats, which pulled cascos loaded with rations. Shallow water and obstructions placed in the river prevented the steady movement of the column so that it did not reach either of its objectives.

Despite the fact that detachments held San Miguel, fourteen miles to the north, the slow cautious advance ordered by Otis kept Lawton's headquarters at Baliuag. The delay become so onerous to Lawton, however, that on May 13 he sent the following wire to Otis:[11]

"The delays in my movements disturb me very much. The rice fields are now in places covered with water and twenty-four hours rain will render travel with transportation impossible. The weather is now favorable and every day lost may cost us dearly. I am possibly mistaken, but the enemy has not impressed me as being in very great force or as showing much pertinacity."

On May 15, having received permission to move, Lawton left one battalion to garrison Baliuag and the entire division moved forward and occupied San Miguel.

Otis then named San Isidro, about twenty miles north of San Miguel and on the Rio Grande, as the next objective of the expedition. San Isidro, a town of about 9,000 inhabitants, was the capital of Nueva Ecija Province. Upon the evacuation of Malolos, Aquinaldo had designated it as the Insurgent "National Capital." Also, information had been received that an ammunition factory was located there.

The provisional brigade under Colonel Summers moved north on the 16th and occupied San Roque without incident. A group of scouts reconnoitering for water discovered a small wooden bridge in flames over an unfordable river just south of San Isidro. The scouts realizing the importance of saving it despite an enfilading fire from six hundred entrenched Insurgents on the north bank, rushed it, extinguished the flames, and drove the Insurgents out. For this gallant charge, twenty-two Congressional Medals of Honor were awarded, of which eleven went to members of the 1st North Dakota Volunteers. Following their advantage, the scouts pushed the Insurgents back into the outskirts of San Isidro.

On the following morning the Americans entered San Isidro without opposition, and a second Insurgent "Capital" had been captured. Although the delay caused by the Insurgents was negligible, the average rate of advance had been little more than two miles a day and the division had consumed twenty-seven days to advance some fifty-eight miles.

At San Isidro the Americans were to get their first definite information as to how their comrades who had been captured by the Insurgents were being treated. An aged Spaniard brought the following letter to Lawton's Headquarters:[12]

San Isidro, May, 1899
Commander of the United States Army:
    Sir: Through the kindness of the bearer, Senor Ramon Rey, we, fourteen prisoners held by the Philippine Government are enabled to send word through the lines and notify you of our presence here. The following is a list of our names: Lieutenant

J. C. Gillmore, USN, W. Walton, Chief Q.M., P. Vandvit, J. Ellsworth, L. Edwards, S. Brisolose, A. Peterson, F. Anderson, USS Yorktown captured at Baler, Apr. 12, 1899. W. Bruce, E. Honeymen, Nevada Cavalry captured January 30, 1899. H. Huber, Hospital Corps, J. O'Brien civilian. A. Sonnichsen, civilian captured January 27, 1899.

We are about to march northward. Where, we do not know. Up to Lieutenant Gillmore's arrival we have been treated in a most barbaric manner, starved, beaten, bound, but since the advance of the American troops, our treatment has been a trifle better. We have been living on five cents a day and most of us nearly naked. The Spaniards have been treated even worse than we, being tortured in the stocks and starved. Some hundreds are dying of dysentery and various other diseases, but whether incapable or not caring the government does nothing for them. The bearer, Senor Ramon Rey, has been a true friend to us; in fact, had it not been for him and his countrymen we probably should have been starved to death on the retreat from Malolos. He is therefore entitled to the best consideration of every American.

Very respectfully,
Albert Sonnichen
Formerly Quartermaster, SS Zealandia.

The writer of the above letter had been captured by the Insurgents while visiting within their lines around Manila. He was held a captive by the Filipinos for some ten months, before the advance of the American troops in northern Luzon enabled him to escape. He later wrote a most interesting book regarding his experiences.[13]

The capture of the naval officer, Lieutenant J. C. Gillmore, and seven sailors merits more than a passing glance.

On the northeastern coast of Luzon practically inaccessible from Manila by land stood the town of Baler. The lofty Sierra Madre Mountains to its immediate west, made steamer travel the only feasible means of communication between Baler and the outer world.

During the Spanish regime the garrison at the place was normally a handful of soldiers. With Aguinaldo's insurrection arising in 1898, the native populace of the town attacked the garrison and forced it to take refuge in the small, but substantially built, town church. There, largely through the perseverance of its commander, a young Spanish second lieutenant named Don Saturnio Martin Cerezo, this handful of Spaniards withstood determined attacks from the Insurgents for three hundred thirty-seven days. Sustaining themselves with water from a well dug in the church yard and eating sparingly of their meager rations, the beleaguered garrison steadfastly refused to surrender.

On one occasion they repelled an Insurgent assault by pouring boiling water on the attackers. When their Spanish flag on the cupola of the Church was shot to shreds a new one was fashioned from a monk's cassock, coverings for the church relics, and a yellow mosquito bar. After the Spanish-American War had ended the Insurgents attempted to obtain the surrender by telling Cerezo that Spain had ceded the Philippine Islands to the United States. He refused to believe them and henceforth refused to parley. Occasionally his men were able, under the cover of darkness to make a quick foray into the surrounding jungle and obtain a few green leaves which they used for food. In an attempt to overcome the numerous cases of beriberi which appeared among the soldiers, a few green vegetables were grown in the churchyard, behind the shelter of a wall. Two soldiers who attempted to desert were tried by Cerezo and shot within the Church walls. As the Spanish troops were evacuating the Islands, a lieutenant colonel in the army was sent to Baler in an effort to convince Cerezo that as far as Spain was concerned, the war was over and to direct him to surrender and return to Spain with his comrades. Cerezo believed the officer to be an imposter or traitor and refused to discuss the matter with him. He was convinced that Manila newspapers, which were thrown into the church and which explained the true state of affairs in the Islands were spurious imitations which the Insurgents had specially printed to deceive him.

Towards the end of the siege the conditions under which the group was living is perhaps best described by quoting Cerezo himself:[14]

> "On the 24th, the beans and coffee gave out. I mean the last remains of them. There was now nothing left to eat but a few handfulls of rice flour, the dust of the Palay we had hulled and a few dozen tins of sardines, problematically edible. Our food was now reduced to a kind of poultice made of pumpkin leaves mixed with sardines and a little rice. But we had to reduce even these articles. Those same men who at first would not eat the leaves, because as they said, they lay like a lump in the stomach, soon had to be restrained from devouring those leaves, raw, sprouts and all.

> "For the mornings, we had in place of coffee, a decortication of orange leaves which we gathered from the trees that were in front of the church. So great was our hunger in fact that if a dog came within our reach, a dog was eaten. If a cat, a cat; if reptiles, reptiles; if crows, crows. A certain kind of snail was abundant. The natives loathed them, but it was soon apparent that they were disappearing. All around the church there was an abundance of leafy shrubbery and it was all stripped, the

men not being deterred by the risk, not improbable of eating some poisonous plant."

The story of this amazing defense of a lost cause had permeated throughout the Islands and had become legendary even while the garrison was still holding out. Aguinaldo sent one of his most capable officers, General Manual Tinio with a modern field gun to take the church. The Spaniards poured such a devastating fire on the Insurgents manning the gun that they could not aim and Tinio advised Aguinaldo that the church could not be taken by assault with the artillery then in the hands of the Insurgents.

In April of 1899 the Americans decided to attempt the relief of this brave garrison. The USS *Yorktown* was sent to Baler and anchored off the coast. Lieutenant J. C. Gillmore and seventeen blue-jackets were sent in a small boat up the river on which the town was situated to communicate with Cerezo. There they were ambushed by the Insurgents and suffered nine casualties. The oars of the boat were shattered, and it drifted ashore where the survivors were captured and taken to San Isidro.

Cerezo continued to hold the church, the wooden roof of which was riddled by bullets. Finally on June 6, his supplies utterly exhausted, he and thirty-three survivors surrendered only after the Insurgents had promised to give them their liberty. After an overland journey full of vicissitudes the valiant band reached Manila. Upon its return to Spain the survivors were showered with honors by the Spanish government.

Returning to Lawton and the American forces at San Isidro, indications appeared that now the Insurgent government as well as the rank and file were becoming discouraged. Two residents of San Isidro, who had been members of the Philippine Insurgent Congress, reported that the Insurgent President had left San Isidro on the 15th and had moved to Cabanatuan, fifteen miles to the north. It also appeared that the Philippine Congress had met and voted for peace with the Americans under the provisions of the plan outlined by the proclamation of the Schurman commission. Lawton's advance on San Isidro had caused the rather precipitate adjournment of the Congress, but these particular members felt that at any time the Insurgent Government would make representations to the Americans looking towards peace and the establishment of American sovereignty. A few days prior to this Otis had attempted to ease the road to peace by authorizing the payment of $30.00 for every Insurgent rifle turned in to the American troops. However, the response was not particularly encouraging.

By this time, MacArthur had pushed Luna's Army back along the railway to San Fernando. From San Isidro, Lawton could have effectively struck this army in flank. However as Otis reported:[15] "The rainy season had now come and the volunteer organizations must be hastened homeward. Occupation of Tarlac by Lawton would be seriously complicated by the difficulties of supply. We must keep what we had gained and could do that by establishing a line from San Fernando on the left and Baliuag on the right, from which it would be easy to resume operations. Lawton was recalled and a sufficient force placed at Calumpit and Baliuag to hold the country in rear." The story goes that Lawton vigorously opposed the withdrawal from territory that had been captured, but was preemptorily ordered to do so by Otis.[16] A few months later Lawton was forced to fight his way back to San Isidro at the cost of American and Insurgent lives.

At San Isidro the division was now about fourteen miles north of the northern tip of the Candaba Swamp and on the Rio Grande de Pampanga. On the afternoon of May 18th the return journey began. Cabiao was entered on the 19th and Arayat on the 20th. At Arayat a junction was effected with Kobbe's "Gunboat expedition". On the 21st the march was continued to Candaba where the division was disbanded. Lawton's division had marched some eighty miles and made a complete circuit of the Candaba Swamp.

In this campaign the Americans received a forceful intimation of the devastating effects of a tropical climate on the health of troops operating in the field. There were in Lawton's division during the circuit of the Candaba Swamp a total of 515 casualties. Of those only nine were killed and thirty-five wounded by Insurgent bullets. Nearly 40% or 187 of the casualties were caused by dysentery or diarrhoea; over 20%, or 108 were caused by malaria. Mosquito bars had not become an article of issue, and a soldier sleeping in the open had absolutely no protection against the bite of the anopheles mosquito. There were thirty-seven cases of heat exhaustion, the sun proving to be as dangerous an enemy as the Insurgents' bullets. Twenty-six cases of "sore feet" also went to make up the list of casualties.

Among the regiments the lowest percentage of casualties was in the 1st North Dakota Volunteers. Despite the fact that they were actively engaged throughout the campaign and the scouts were largely drawn from their ranks, only fifty-one casualties occurred in this regiment. One medical officer attributed the low sickness rate to the fact that the regiment never missed a meal and never had one served more than an hour late. Every company carried coffee boilers and other cooking utensils and two days rations on small pony carts which were kept closed up with their column, no matter what the state of the roads or what opposition was encountered by the enemy or other commanding officers. These carts were not issued by the Quartermaster Corps, but had been procured through the initiative of the regimental officers.

Upon his return to Manila, Lawton called upon Otis and told him in the presence of a witness that if the latter would furnish him with two regiments, would allow him to arm, equip, and provision them to suit himself and would turn him loose, he would stake his reputation as a soldier and his position in the United States Army on the claim that within sixty days he would end the insurrection and would deliver to General Otis, one Emilio Aguinaldo, dead or alive. Otis laughed at him.[17] Very possibly Lawton was optimistic in the matter, but as later events proved, it was unnecessary and an overcautious move to withdraw garrisons from San Isidro and the towns between there and Baliuag. With Lawton's expedition disbanded, we can now turn to General MacArthur's second division and follow it through its movement north from Malolos.

4

About five miles north of Malolos the Bagbag, Quingua and Calumpit Rivers merge. Two miles north of this confluence flows the large Rio Grande De Pampanga. To the east of the area was the impassable Candaba Swamp. To the west was a maze of small rivers, estuaries, and arroyos running into Manila Bay, which made operations in that quarter highly unfeasible. Reference to the map will indicate that MacArthur's division advancing against the main Insurgent army under Luna would be forced to cross at least two of these four rivers. Thus Luna occupied an almost ideal defensive position: a double line of rivers and both flanks protected. The nature of the terrain also made it impracticable for the American troops to leave the railroad or main roads for any distance to attempt flanking movements. The division was faced with the difficult task of making a frontal attack on Luna's army if it was to advance to the north.

Planning the attack to the north in conjunction with Lawton's advance fifteen miles east, it was believed that first resistance would be encountered along the north bank of the Bagbag and Quingua Rivers. A second line was believed to be along the north bank of the Rio Grande.

For the movement, MacArthur's division was divided into two brigades as follows:[18]

1st Brigade (General Wheaton)
20th Kansas Volunteers
1st Montana Volunteers
1 battalion 51st Iowa Volunteers
1 squadron 4th Cavalry
3 guns Utah Artillery
The "armored" train

2nd Brigade (General Hale)
1st Nebraska Volunteers
1st South Dakota Volunteers
2 battalions of the 51st Iowa Volunteers
2 field guns, 6th Artillery

The 3rd Artillery was directed to remain at Malolos and guard the line of supplies.

The First Brigade was assigned the mission of advancing up the railroad and forcing the Bagbag, at the point where the railroad crossed. The Second Brigade was to cross the Quingua River near Pulilan, then swing to the left and enter Calumpit from the east.

It was originally planned for the movement to start on April 24. However, early on the morning of April 23, a troop of the 4th Cavalry reconnoitering towards Quingua became involved with the Insurgents to such an extent that successive reinforcements built up a firing line of considerable proportions, involving both the Nebraska and Iowa regiments. In a charge which captured the town, Colonel Stotsenburg of the Nebraska Volunteers was killed. He had brought the Nebraska regiment to the Philippines and was popular with his men. One member described him as the type who, when an attack was being launched, shouted, "Come on boys, I'm going," instead of "Go on boys, I'm coming." A monument was erected on the spot where he fell, and Fort Stotsenburg, one of the larger army posts in the Philippines, was named in his honor.

The following morning the brigade forded the Quingua River under fire and swinging to the left swept through Pulilan and moved along the wagon road towards Calumpit. Insurgent barricades along the road slowed the advance, and the brigade was forced to bivouac for the night about two miles west of Pulilan.

The 1st Brigade remained in the vicinity of Malolos until the

SOLDIERS IN THE SUN

25th. It then advanced along the railroad, encountering no opposition until the Bagbag River was reached. It reached the junction of the three rivers about the same time that the 2nd Brigade advancing from Pulilan came under fire from the Insurgent trenches on the west bank of the Calumpit River. Both brigades were deployed at right angles to each other, and each found itself opposed by fire from the Insurgents entrenched on the opposite bank of the two rivers.

At this point the rivers merge at nearly right angles. The Insurgents entrenched on the inside of the angle found themselves enfiladed from two directions. The 20th Kansas Volunteers led by their regimental commander, Colonel Frederick Funston, were able by wading and swimming to cross the Bagbag. A company of Nebraskans swinging well out into the Quingua River, forded it and advanced to Calumpit, a town of 16,000 inhabitants located on the south bank of the Rio Grande River.

Reconnaissance of the town of Calumpit led to the belief that it was untenable unless the Insurgent forces entrenched on the north bank were defeated.

The Rio Grande de Pampanga at this point was a deep stream, some eighty yards wide and with a five mile current. Luna's troops had carefully removed all boats; with the absence of a pontoon train the only apparent means of crossing was by the partially dismantled railroad bridge. On the north bank of the river on both sides of the bridge were some 6000 Insurgents securely protected in thickly embrasured entrenchments. The situation presented by far the most difficult obstacle yet encountered by the American troops.

The manner in which the crossing was forced was in General MacArthur's words "a remarkable military achievement well calculated to fix the attention of the most careless observer and to stimulate the fancy of the most indifferent." Indeed the crossing was probably unique in the annals of military operations in all time.

Credit for the feat must be given to Colonel Funston, who conceived the plan and carried through its execution. Let Colonel Funston describes the operation as embodied in his official report:[19]

"When darkness came (on the 26th), I asked Corporal A. M. Ferguson of Company F, who has on numerous occasions shown himself to be a fearless and reliable man, if he would be willing to attempt a reconnaissance of the railroad bridge, telling him that the work was so hazardous that I would not order him to undertake it. He consented to go at once. Under the cover of darkness, Captain Flanders of Company I and myself accompanied him to the end of the bridge. Ferguson took off his shoes and armed only with a revolver crawled along through the network of iron braces underneath where the floor had been and then inch by inch worked his way, hand over hand until he was underneath the Insurgent outposts stationed on the other end of the bridge and returned with a complete description of the bridge which was afterwards verified in every particular. He was gone two hours. A single misstep would have meant a fall of forty feet into the river, while the chances were greatly in favor of discovery by the enemy which would have meant certain death or capture. He reported that all of the ties, rail and planks were gone from the bridge and at its further end all but one of its steel girders. This utterly precluded a plan that I had for carrying the bridge by assault.

"During the night I took a force of 120 men, a mile down the river with the intention of attempting a crossing by means of rafts, but we were discovered and fired upon and so returned to camp at one o'clock in the morning. The next day, the 27th at noon, I determined to make an attempt to force a passage about 600 yards below the railroad bridge.

"A hundred picked riflemen were posted with instructions to cover the enemy's trenches on the opposite bank so that they would not be able to interfere with our operations. A raft which the enemy had unsuccessfully attempted to burn was moored on our side of the river. A rope 300 feet long had been obtained and it was necessary to get this fastened on the opposite bank before operations could proceed further. A dozen men volunteered to swim the river although they would be under fire. From these men I selected Privates Edward White and W. B. Trembly of Company B. These men, naked and unarmed, swam the river with the end of the rope, although fired upon repeatedly and landed within twenty feet of a small work containing several of the enemy who did not run out until the men actually crawled up on all fours and tied the rope to one of the uprights on the trench, whereupon three armed Filipinos ran out. I got on the raft with eight men and we hauled ourselves over by hand. The raft was at once returned and made several trips. As soon as I had three officers and forty-one enlisted men, I attacked the enemy's strong entrenchments at the end of the bridge in flank. After a sharp fight in which the enemy turned a Maxim gun on us, they fled in disorder, abandoning the most elaborate fortifications I have seen in this war, with a rifled bronze howitzer, numerous Mauser and Remington rifles and thousands of rounds of ammunition which were found scattered everywhere."

Shortly thereafter the remainder of the division scrambled across the bridge or crossed in improvised rafts. That most difficult of military operations, the crossing of an unfordable stream in the face of a hostile force, had been accomplished without a casualty. In his memoirs, written thirteen years later, Colonel Funston states that when White and Trembly reached the opposite bank of the river, they threw mud balls into the Insurgent trench with the result that the few who remained fled. White and Trembly, whose names belied their courage, were awarded the Congressional Medal of Honor for the exploit. Colonel Funston was not only awarded the Congressional Medal but was promoted to the grade of Brigadier General of Volunteers.

General Funston was, from a regular army officer's standpoint, the perfect paradox of the war. As an adventurous youth of twenty-six he had accompained a botanical expedition into California's Death Valley. Two years later he went to Alaska and floated down the Yukon River in a canoe, alone. In 1896 he accompanied a filibustering expedition to Cuba and fought against Spain. Wounded and a victim of malaria he returned to the United States in 1898. When the 20th Kansas Volunteers was organized in that year, the Governor of Kansas appointed this comparatively young man of thirty-three, who had experienced a total of eighteen months' pseudo-military service, colonel of the regiment. Of diminutive height, he was absolutely fearless in regard to his personal safety. His height and youth often made it difficult to convince strangers that he was a colonel in the American Army. A most capable, practical soldier in every sense of the word, his ability and exploits soon made him sought by division commanders, among whom Lawton was numbered. More was heard of him as the Insurrection progressed.

Few words of praise can be spoken for the Insurgents in their defense of a virtually impregnable position. Had one Insurgent soldier in the vicinity of the point at which White and Trembly crossed had the courage to put his head above the trench and shoot the two Americans, the whole plan would have been a failure. Even a well aimed stone could have incapacitated the naked, unarmed, and well-nigh exhausted swimmers as they stood alone on the river bank within pistol shot of the Insurgent trenches. As a nation the Filipinos should not be proud of their defense of the Rio Grande de Pampanga.

On April 29, two days after the capture of Calumpit, the Insurgent Government at San Isidro sued for an armistice for fifteen days in order[20] "To justify itself before the people as having employed all the means in its power to avoid the ruin of the country" and to "offer the Schurman Commission a means of putting an end to the war in the manner most honorable to the American Army." Otis agreed to permit an Insurgent delegation to go to Manila and appear before the Philippine Commission, but refused an armistice.

In this refusal he was justified, because as later events proved, the Insurgent "diehards" desired the armistice merely for the purpose of gaining time for their arsenals to produce sufficient cartridges to continue the war. An Insurgent representative, Colonel Aguelles, actually did go to Manila to confer with the commission. While there he was permitted to visit the wounded Insurgent prisoners hospitalized by the Americans, and returned to the Insurgent lines definitely "pro-American." Owing to his importunities, at the next meeting of the Insurgent Congress at San Isidro, the anti-American group led by Mabini fell from power and the congress definitely resolved to change the policy of the war with the United States to one of peace.

A new commission was organized to go to Manila and treat further with the Americans. Enroute on May 18, it was intercepted by the definitely anti-American Luna, who by force arrested the pro-American members and substituted three others of his own choice.

This "packed" commission passed through Lawton's lines enroute to Manila. Through his efficiently functioning spies, Lawton had full knowledge of the situation and on May 18 wired Otis:[21]

> "I find that the former commission named by General Aguinaldo to treat for peace has been dissolved by General Luna. The latter arrested Buencamino and Arguelles in Cabanatuan and has this afternoon sent them to Talavera. Luna evidently desires to be dictator and has the greater part of the Army (5000 or 6000 men) under his influence. Aguinaldo fears Luna and is only nominally in power. The present commission bears no more power than a request for a suspension of hostilities for a short time to call an assembly of the congress for further action and this proposition is from General Luna."

Luna's delegation was received by Otis, who informed it that the cessation of hostilities depended entirely upon the surrender of arms and the disbandment of their military organizations. It then appeared before the Schurman Commission and after discussing American and Filipino aspirations left Manila, promising to return within three weeks. It never returned. Luna's attempt to gain control of the Insurgent government was to result some three weeks later in his assassination.

The second division stayed in the vicinity of Calumpit a week for the purpose of allowing the men to rest and to permit the supply trains to catch up. Then on May 4 the advance to the north was continued. The First Brigade, moving along the railroad, was blocked at

the Taong River near the town of Santo Tomas. The ground adjoining the tracks was swampy, the large three-span railroad bridge
over the river was partially destroyed, and the opposite bank held
by entrenched Insurgents. The river was deep and unfordable and
presented another serious obstacle, if held in a determined manner.

In the meantime, the Second Brigade had anvanced north along
a wagon road. A short distance from Apalit they dispersed an Insurgent working party preparing "traps," which consisted of a series
of conical pits containing sharpened bamboo stakes hidden by light
earth-covered bamboo mats. Destroying the traps and continuing
on, the Brigade reached the Santa Monica River, where Insurgent
opposition forced the Nebraska Volunteers to deploy in a swamp.
Fording the river under fire, the line pushed on, following the general direction of the road which converged on the railroad at the
Taong River. Being forced to remain in extended order, the brigade
advanced through the swampy ground in water to their waist, the
Nebraskans fording as many as eleven streams. However, their direction of advance brought them upon the left flank of the Insurgents
who were holding up the advance of the 1st Brigade on the railroad.
At this threat the entire Insurgent line withdrew, permitting the
First Brigade to cross the Taong River and continue the advance.

At the Santo Tomas railroad station, near the barrio of San
Matias, more Insurgents were found, strongly entrenched. A brilliant
charge of the Kansans, led by General Wheaton in person, dislodged
them, however; and with Luna wounded, they withdrew towards
San Fernando.

Despite their wet, dirty condition, the morale of the Americans
was high as is indicated by the following remark of Captain William
Albright of the 20th Kansas Volunteers. May 4 happened to be
this officer's birthday. As he was receiving some instructions from
Colonel Funston for the deployment of his company, an Insurgent
bullet struck Albright in the leg. As he went down, the unfortunate
officer remarked to Funston, "Isn't this a hell of a birthday present?"

The division bivouacked for the night near the Santo Tomas
railroad station. The work for the day had been extremely arduous.
The difficulties of the terrain can only be apparent to one who has
examined it and seen the large number of streams and the swampy
ground over which many of the units were forced to advance. A
prisoner stated that Luna had expressed the opinion that the
Americans would not be able to advance through the swamp.

The following day, scouts reported that the important town
of San Fernando, two miles distant, was held by a small force only.

Consequently two battalions of Iowa Volunteers were dispatched to occupy it. They entered San Fernando without difficulty, driving what few Insurgents they encountered towards Bacalor. The remainder of the division then moved up and occupied the town, which enjoyed the reputation of being a "resort," and which contained many permanent buildings.

MacArthur's division had now been intermittently on the go since February 4. Between the battle of Manila and the advance on Malolos, the combat units had been in trenches a short distance from the Insurgent lines and forced to "sleep on their arms," so to speak. Following the five days of forced marching and fighting to Malolos, they had been harassed constantly by small Insurgent bands, who attacked the line of supply. Outposts were harried to the extent that the troops were continually answering calls for support. During the advance from Malolos to San Fernando, the movement over difficult terrain in the heat of the day further debilitated the already worn-out troops. At San Fernando the division began to go to pieces. A condition which Civil War veterans called "irritable heart" developed in a large number of the personnel. Hearts became weak, pulses quickened. Medical officers noticed that the condition resembled typhoid fever convalescence. Stomachs refused to digest food; men were nervous and jumpy; some could not sleep at night. Perhaps it was a forerunner of what was known during the World War as "shell shock." At any rate, so many men went on sick report that the division had to pause and take stock of itself.

The "bullet" casualties in the division for April and May had amounted to thirty-two killed and two hundred nineteen wounded. These figures become inconsiderable when compared to the casualties from "sickness." On May 12, a week after San Fernando had been captured, of the 4800 combatant troops in the division, 2160, or 45%, were on sick report. In one regiment 70% were in hospitals at Manila or San Fernando. Of the remaining 30% in this regiment there were not eight men in each company able to endure one day's march. [22] The condition in other regiments was little better.

Otis minimized the condition to newspaper correspondents and attributed it to "The great strain attendant upon constant fighting with lack of needed rest, the indiscriminate consumption of the abundant native fruit, the drinking of unpotable water and general neglect of person." MacArthur laid the blame on "The sun, field rations, physical exertion, and abnormal excitement arising from almost constant exposure to fire action" and proposed that:[23]

"For prolonged field operations in this climate, a sufficient force must be maintained to afford frequent relief for the troops at the front. Otherwise the complete collapse of entire regiments may be expected to follow exposure and exertions such as have attended the movable column of this division since February 4th."

With half their number on sick report, the volunteer regiments who had enlisted only for the duration of the war with Spain, reiterated their clamors for discharge and return to the United States. Otis had received instructions from Washington to return them as soon as possible. Consequently he decided that until more regular army regiments arrived from the United States he would have to suspend operations against the main Insurgent Army. In the meantime he could give some attention to the bands who were harassing him on the south side of the city.

5

About seven miles east of Manila flows the Mariquina River, which follows a general north and south course. It empties into the Pasig River at the town of Pasig. Farther east of the Mariquina River, rises a series of rugged hills which form the Mariquina Watershed. Eight miles further east rise the Caraballos Mountains, a range so wild, rugged, full of tangled undergrowth, and devoid of roads that military operations therein are virtually impossible.

Twelve miles southeast of Manila in the Mariquina valley are situated the towns of Cainta and Taytay. These two towns had been captured by General Wheaton's expedition to Pasig in March. Upon the withdrawal of Wheaton's outposts to Pasig, however, both had been reoccupied by the Insurgents. Sixteen miles east of Manila was the town of Antipolo, a hotbed of Insurgent activity. Nearest American force to Antipolo was the waterworks guard on the Mariquina River. Southeast of Antipolo and Taytay, the Morong peninsula, eight miles in length, jutted into Laguna de Bay. On the northeastern shore of this peninsula lay the town of Morong.

During the latter part of May it was reported that the native inhabitants of the Mariquina Valley were suffering heavily on account of the various crimes committed by the Insurgents in that area under the nominal command of General Pio Del Pilar, whom we have noticed before and who prior to the insurrection enjoyed the reputation of being the bandit chief in that section of the country. Either through fear or because he was one of the few Insurgent leaders capable of keeping his troops together, Pilar stood high in Aguinaldo's favor and the many depredations which the troops committed on the native citizenry were accomplished in the name of the Insurgent government. After Wheaton had driven the bandit away from Manila and Pasig in March, Pilar had simply transferred his activities further east.

Consequently on June 3, an expedition was organized to drive the Insurgents out of the Mariquina Valley as far east as Antipolo and into the Morong Peninsula where, surrounded on three sides, capture would be inevitable.

This expedition was placed under the command of General Lawton and consisted of two brigades totaling 2500 men. One brigade was to move east from the Mariquina pumping station and occupy Antipolo. The other was to move east from Pasig and reoccupy Cainta and Taytay. After the capture of Antipolo, the north group was to swing south and march on Morong, establishing an east and west line which it was hoped would prevent the Insurgents from escaping to the north.

The northern column, which was placed under the command of Brigadier General Robert Hall, consisted of the 2nd Oregon Volunteers, six companies of the 1st Colorado Volunteers, one battalion each of the 9th (regular) Infantry and 1st Wyoming Volunteers, a dismounted squadron of the 4th Cavalry, two battalions of the 4th Infantry and a provisional battery of artillery. The Pasig brigade was composed of two battalions of the 1st Washington Volunteers, the 1st North Dakota Volunteers, one battalion of the 9th Infantry, and one platoon of light artillery. It was placed under the command of Colonel James Wholly of the 1st Washington Volunteers.

On the morning of June 3, Hall's Brigade left the pumping station at 5:00 a. m., hoping to reach Antipolo, twelve miles distant by 1:00 p. m. The route followed by the main column, under the guidance of Filipinos, was due east over the hills and then by a trail to Antipolo. Soon after leaving the pumping station, however, the road was found to be so poor that in places it was impracticable even for foot troops. The onslaught of the rainy season had caused ravines which were normally dry to become raging streams. Instead of a march, the movement became a series of halts for the construction of small bridges which would permit the passage of wheeled transportation.

The farther the expedition progressed, the worse the road became. Finally one escort wagon which was carrying ammunition was perforce abandoned. Shortly thereafter it became evident that the ambulances were in danger of being shaken to pieces. Hall directed them to return to the pumping station and join the column via Pasig. By 4:00 in the afternoon, after struggling in humid air and in the hot sun for eleven hours, the column had advanced only eight miles. Then as it debouched from a sunken road it was attacked by some three hundred Insurgents who were so placed in the hills as to concentrate their fire from three directions. Exhausted though they were, the Oregon Volunteers, the 4th Infantry, and the 4th Cavalry squadron attacked and in an engagement, which lasted an hour and a half, drove the Insurgents towards Antipolo. The American casualties amounted to three killed and ten wounded. The brigade bivouacked for the night on the battlefield.

Meanwhile Colonel Wholly's southern column had moved from Pasig at 1:00 p. m. the same day, advancing on Cainta. Opposition encountered outside the town was overcome with the assistance of the fire from gunboats which had been strung along the Pasig River, The brigade entered Cainta the same day.

On June 4, the following day, virtually devoid of wheeled transportation and carrying their wounded and dead in litters, Hall's Brigade completed the remaining four miles to Antipolo. No Insurgents appeared to dispute its entry. Some 3500 rifle cartridges and a small number of 80 mm shells which were found in the village church were disposed of by throwing them down a well. The brigade then marched towards Taytay, six miles to the southwest, hoping to meet its trains which were moving by that route. Two miles from Antipolo the brigade met not only its trains but General Lawton, who directed that it retrace its steps to Antipolo and march on Morong by way of Teresa. Teresa was six miles southeast of Antipolo and the weary brigade reached it at 8:30 that night. Insurgent opposition appeared to have melted away.

Early that same morning the Washington Volunteer regiment had been withdrawn from Wholly's column at Taytay and sent by cascos up the river into Laguna de Bay. Following the shore of the lake, the regiment reached the Morong peninsula opposite the town of Morong on the morning of the 4th. Protected by gunboats, which had accompanied the casco fleet, the regiment waded ashore and despite a sharp fire from Insurgents in Morong, captured the town without a single casualty. Spending the night there, the Washingtonians were joined the following morning by Hall's Brigade, which had marched from Teresa. Leaving a squadron of the 4th Cavalry as a garrison in Morong, Hall's Brigade then commenced a circuit of the peninsula. At Cardona, five miles south, it met the North

Dakota Volunteers who, in opposite direction, had marched around the peninsula from Taytay. The North Dakotas continued their march to Morong for the purpose of strengthening the garrison there, while Hall's command continued on. Following the only existing road, it reached Binangonan on the western shore during the afternoon. There it met the remainder of Wholly's column and the whole group then marched back to the pumping station on the Mariquina River, where the units resumed their normal duties "on the line."

Unsubstantiated information indicated that Pilar and the remnants of his force had scattered and escaped to the north through the Carrabalos Mountains and its adjoining hills. Considering its purpose to be that of cooping Pilar's force up in the Morong Peninsula, the expedition had been a failure. However, it did advance the outpost of American sovereignty in the area southeast of Manila by nearly twenty miles. In Hall's Brigade, although only three men were killed and ten wounded, eighty-four men became casualties principally from heat exhaustion. In Lawton's next campaign the heat was to be a paramount factor.

6

In the province of Cavite directly south of Manila, the convergence of Manila Bay and Laguna de Bay have combined to form a virtual isthmus. Five miles wide as its narrowest point, it is in effect a "bottleneck." The narrow stretch extends about seven miles south of the city after which the bay and lake recede from each other. Otis had long hesitated to attack the Insurgents in this area. It was here that the staunchest resistance to the American attack had been effected during the battle of Manila in February. East of the main road which ran south from the city, the terrain was a maze of bamboo thickets and swamps, and in other places was overgrown with thick, waist-high, rank weeds called cogon grass. The whole area was wild and inhospitable and known to the natives as "El Desierto."

In the battle of Manila the previous February, the Insurgents had been pushed back along the road to a line running east through the barrio of Pasay, but had thereafter been left unmolested. Farther around the bay, isolated by land from Manila, two regiments still garrisoned Cavite. Following the return of Lawton's expedition from Morong, frequent Insurgent "attacks" from Pasay caused Otis to feel the necessity of making the force of American arms felt in this portion of the line. Also the area had been the center of Insurgent activities during the rebellion against the Spaniards in 1896, and contained Aguinaldo's home.

Two days after his return from Morong, Lawton's division was reorganized and assembled in preparation for a movement to the south. Consisting of some 4000 men, it was divided into two brigades as follows:

1st Brigade (General Wheaton)
8 companies of the 9th U. S. Infantry
8 companies of the 21st U. S. Infantry
6 companies of the 1st Colorado Volunteers
1 troop of the Nevada Volunteer Cavalry
1 battery (composite) of Light and Mountain Artillery
2nd Brigade (General Samuel Ovenshine)
2 companies of the 12th U. S. Infantry
9 companies of the 14th U. S. Infantry
13th U. S. Infantry
Battery of Field Artillery (composite)

The plan was for the division to advance with its brigades in column, south from the center of the San Pedro Macati-Pasay line. After the first line of Insurgents had been dispersed, Wheaton's Brigade was to swing to the left (east) and continue down the shore of Laguna de Bay on the town of Muntilupa, some thirteen miles distant. Ovenshine's Brigade was to swing to the right when opposite the town of Las Pinas and there form a barrier which should prevent the escape of Insurgents along the main highway running south of Manila.

As planned, the division left the line at 4:30 a. m. June 10, Wheaton's Brigade in the lead. Besides his rifle and bayonet each man carried his mess kit, canteen and a roll over his shoulder consisting of a blanket, a poncho and fifty rounds of ammunition. In addition he had 200 rounds of ammunition in his belt and two days rations in his haversack. Except for the artillery, no wheeled transportation accompanied the troops. Kitchen and cooking utensils were carried by Chinese coolies.

Brushing aside Insurgent opposition on a ridge running through Guadelupe, the division continued south through the cogon grass and rough terrain. As the day wore on, the motionless heat of "El Desierto" rose to 110 degrees. By 7:30 a. m. the panting soldiers had drained their canteens—in a country destitute of wells and springs. By 8:30 they were parched. Gasping and staggering under their smothering loads of equipment, they repeatedly deployed to return

Insurgent fire. Then men began to throw away their rations, their clothes and even their rifles. They plodded on to topple over from heat exhaustion, and weaved off the trail to search hopelessly for water and rest. Unique in the history of American armies, an entire division disintegrated.

At 10:30 a. m. Wheaton's Brigade came under a sharp fire from its right and was forced to swing in that direction to meet it. General Lawton sent a hurried message to Ovenshine to close his brigade in on Wheaton's right. When Ovenshine was finally located at about 11:00, he pointed to where about 150 men had been and said, "That is all that is left." At noon, a fresh water well having been located, the entire division was halted at a point just east of the town of Paranaque. A check revealed that Wheaton's Brigade had 526 men missing and Ovenshine's 372. Nearly 50% of the command had fallen behind. One company of the 12th Infantry, to its credit, did not have one straggler.

After resting for two and a half hours, during which many stragglers rejoined, the division continued the march towards Las Pinas, Wheaton's march on Muntilupa having been abandoned. Insurgent opposition was soon encountered, and after a fight, which consumed the remainder of the afternoon, the Insurgents were forced back towards Las Pinas. The division, exhausted, bivouacked for the night one mile southeast of the town. Battle casualties for the day amounted to one killed and twenty-three wounded. Ninety-six Insurgent dead were found. The division surgeon, bringing up the rear of the column, picked up one hundred fifty stragglers from the 13th Infantry. A check made that night, after many stragglers had rejoined their organizations, revealed that the 14th Infantry still had 182 men missing, the 13th, 167 out of a nominal strength of 900.

That evening within rifle range of the American camp, the Insurgent army marched through Las Pinas towards the south. Lieutenant Scott, of the 6th Artillery, wandering away from camp on an unofficial reconnaissance, saw the Insurgent army moving towards Las Pinas and hurried back to camp for the purpose of appraising General Lawton of the situation. There he found Lawton still in a rage over the day's happenings with none of his staff officers daring to approach him. So fearsome was Lawton while in these moods that not even the irrepressible Scott dared to enter the Commanding General's tent. The Insurgent army was thus allowed to escape unmolested. Later, as if in answer to a soldier's prayer, a heavy rainfall cooled the air and permitted canteens to be filled from pools on the ground. In the middle of the night the sleep of the exhausted

Americans was interrupted by a stampede of the Chinese coolies who accompanied the division. They ran over the sleeping troops shouting "Insurgents"—"Bolos." An imminent panic of Ovenshine's brigade was fortunately checked by officers. The day and night of June 10, 1899 was long remembered by the members of that expedition.

During the following forenoon, which was somewhat cooler, the division marched unopposed into Las Pinas, seven miles south of Manila. Lawton halted his command and returned to Manila for a conference with Otis. Upon his return in the afternoon, the 13th Infantry was relieved and returned to the city. The regiment had arrived in the Philippines only twelve days previous and apparently was in no condition for tropical field service. Two days later a quartermaster detachment searching the area over which the division had advanced picked up two wagon loads of clothing and miscellaneous equipment. Other organizations were directed to send back searching parties to recover whatever equipment they could find.

After resting one day, Lawton felt that his command had recuperated sufficiently to permit further movement against the Insurgents. So aboard the U. S. gunboat *Helena,* he reconnoitered the shore of the bay where south of Las Pinas the shore line takes a bend to the west. Near the point where the Zapote River emptied into the bay it was discovered that the Insurgents had taken up a position on the west side of that stream. That day Lawton sent the following telegram to Otis:[24]

> "Condition of command satisfactory. Men fast recuperating and ready to proceed. The enemy are apparently in force on the Zapote River. Men of the 13th Infantry sent to the city yesterday should be sent over their trail to recover property abandoned by them. Evidence accumulates that punishment on enemy much more severe than first thought. Twenty-six additional dead bodies found this morning. Inhabitants of Pananaque and Las Pinas remain, welcoming command with enthusiasm. Food supply in this section extremely short, the Insurgents having stripped the country. I am informed by the local priest that upward of $75,000 in cash was taken by Insurgents from this district alone."

Early the following morning, Lawton with a battalion of the 21st Infantry advanced along the road towards the Zapote River, to make another personal reconnaissance. He ascertained that the Insurgents had a strongly fortified position across the river, about one half mile inland from where the river emptied into the bay. With the assistance of a Filipino guide, he was able, by crossing the salt marshes and swamps, to move completely in rear of the Insurgent position. Seeing this force behind them, some 1000 Insurgents attacked, attempting to isolate the lone battalion. Lawton hurried back to Las Pinas and ordered a frontal attack on the main Insurgent position on the west bank of the Zapote River. Occupying it were some 4000 Insurgents in trenches that Lawton described as being "five feet thick." In its rear were some six inch smooth bore cannon. In 1896 the Insurgents had repulsed a Spanish attack at this point and, as was later determined, a great many of them had made religious vows, assumed under superstitious rites, to overthrow the Americans there or die in the attempt. The intense fire which covered the partially dismantled bridge over the river made American advance difficult. In the face of this fire, a 3.2-inch gun finally advanced to the bank of the river and poured shells on the Insurgent trenches at a range of 30 yards. In this heroic use of artillery, two of the gunners were killed and seven wounded. At 3:20 p. m. Lawton wired to Otis:

"We are having a beautiful battle, hurry up ammunition, we will need it."

Meanwhile, the 21st Infantry on the Insurgent left flank had run short of ammunition and had signalled the *Helena* for assistance. Two officers and thirty-eight men with a Colt gun came ashore and were followed an hour later by forty-two men from the *Monadnock*.

By 4:00 p. m. the Americans had control of the bridge and Lawton gave the order to rush the Insurgent position. From two directions, several units fording the river, the American line, assisted by the sailors, went forward. The pressure was too great, and the Insurgents fled, having lost 150 killed and an estimated 375 wounded. Insurgent opposition here, so different from that at the Rio Grande de Pampanga, resulted in American casualties of fourteen killed and sixty-one wounded. That night Lawton sent outposts along the road towards Bacoor and Imus.

The following day the town Presidente of Imus came to Lawton's headquarters at Las Pinas and stated that the inhabitants of that town, population 15,000 and headquarters of Aguinaldo during the Rebellion of 1896, desired the Americans to enter their city. He also stated that the Insurgents were demoralized and had fled south and west in the direction of Dasmarinas and San Francisco de Malabon respectively. The two battalions of the 14th Infantry which Lawton sent forward occupied Imus without difficulty. Meanwhile a reconnaissance of the 10th Pennsylvania Volunteers from Cavite on the

15th had indicated that Insurgents were in force at San Francisco de Malabon. Lawton made two attempts to reach this town via Imus but both were frustrated because of the marshes and deep streams in this area. From Manila, Otis ordered that operations in that direction be suspended.

On June 19th one battalion of the 4th Infantry with a strength of 288 men reconnoitering from Imus towards Dasmarinas, was attacked and nearly cut off by some 2500 Insurgents. Like Sheridan at Winchester, Wheaton at Imus heard the shooting and hurried to the assistance of the harried battalion, arriving at a critical time. The report of this engagement is given by the battalion commander Major John W. Bubb as follows:[25]

"I proceeded leisurely towards Dasmarinas for about six miles. There were dwelling houses pretty much all along the road on both sides and the inhabitants appeared very friendly freely supplying our men with water. During the last mile or two of the march I noticed the absence of nearly all the male inhabitants and suddenly I discovered all fleeing before me. My flankers discovered what appeared to be Insurgents on my flanks, particularly on my right. Halting my command I made a careful investigation by reports and personal examination and discovered a line of skirmishers being conducted by a mounted officer about 300 or 400 yards on my right flank, marching parallel with my own line of march. As soon as I could make a hurried disposition of my command, I opened fire. Immediately there was a heavy return fire, which soon developed across my front and it was apparent that the enemy was there in force at least equal to my own and having been instructed not to bring on an engagement, I after a hurried consultation with a number of my officers, decided to withdraw. After making a proper disposition of my command, I began the movement. It was not long before I was completely surrounded, so much so that I didn't deem it prudent to send a message back to the brigade commander without detaching more of a detail for the purpose that I could spare, particularly as the enemy's fire seemed to be increasing. Keeping my command well in hand, I succeeded in getting back about three miles, when I received word that a battalion of my regiment was coming to my assistance and I immediately held my ground although I was nearly out of ammunition. Captain Robinson with his battalion of 4th Infantry arrived about 4:00 o'clock deploying on the right and left of the road advancing in the face of a heavy fire, relieving the situation at once. During the engagement which lasted without any cessation from 11:30 a.m. until 4:30 p.m. I lost four enlisted men killed and twenty wounded."

Following the charge by the relieving troops, fifty-five dead Insurgents were found on the battlefield. The following day Wheaton in person led the 4th Infantry and a battalion of the 9th Infantry into Dasmarinas, dispersing weak Insurgent opposition there. After reconnoitering the surrounding countryside for two days, he returned on the 21st to Imus.

Although for the time being it appeared that the Insurgent forces in the area had been dispersed and that the natives were satisfied with municipal governments which Otis permitted to be established under American supervision, peaceful conditions in the south were short lived.

7

During August and September the Insurgents under General Manuel Trias reassembled. Not only Imus and Bacoor, but Calamba, an important town of 7000 inhabitants on the south shore of Laguna de Bay, were attacked. Calamba had been occupied in June by a boat expedition from Manila. Otis was anxious to turn his attention against the main Insurgent army under Luna and Aguinaldo in the north, but did not feel it advisable to concentrate his troops in that area while the Insurgents still appeared to be in force to the south and were constantly harassing the American garrisons.

A determined attack on Imus early in October motivated Otis to give the matter serious attention. General Lawton visited Imus and ascertained that the erstwhile Insurgent army in that area had been resurrected and now was able to muster a strength of some 1700 men. Consequently on October 6 a temporary brigade for an expedition further into the province was organized and placed under the command of Brigadier General Theodore Schwann. Its assigned mission was to "punish and if possible destroy and break up Insurgent forces in the province of Cavite."

General Schwann was a native of Germany. An immigrant to the United States, he had in 1857 enlisted in the American Army. The Civil War came, and by 1863 he had been commissioned as an officer in the 10th Infantry. He was twice brevetted for bravery, and in 1864 awarded the Congressional Medal of Honor for "most distinguished gallantry at Peebles Farm, Virginia, while in command of his regiment which was on the picket line, and falling back before a superior force of the enemy, at the imminent risk of his own life, in dragging a wounded and helpless officer of his regiment to the rear, thus saving him from death or capture." Following the war Schwann had retained his commission and remained in the regular army. By 1898 he had reached the grade of colonel. The Spanish-American War brought his promotion to the grade of brigadier general of volunteers and command of a brigade in the Cuban campaign. A favorite of Otis, he had been made Corps Chief of Staff upon his arrival in the Philippines. He was given command of the expedition into Cavite as a "diversion" from his office duties at Manila.

Schwann's provisional brigade consisted of the 13th Infantry, 3 companies of the 14th Infantry, 2 troops of cavalry, Reilly's Battery of the 5th Artillery and a company of "Scouts." Its total strength was about 1800 men. Assembled at Bacoor on October 7, its first objective was designated as the town of Cavite Viejo, three miles to the west.

Leaving Bacoor on October 8, Cavite Viejo was entered by the brigade without difficulty. However, on continuing one mile west, some 300 entrenched Insurgents were encountered and managed to kill two officers and wound thirteen soldiers before they were dislodged.

Next town along the shore of the bay was Novaleta, two miles distant. Novaleta was at the base of the narrow Cavite Peninsula and was supposed to contain a large number of Insurgents. Since Cavite was garrisoned by United States Marines, it was arranged that while Schwann's brigade attacked the town from the east, the Marines would move in from the north. The advance guard of Schwann's column reached the outskirts of Novaleta at 3:30 p. m. November 8. After weathering a few scattered shots from houses, the Americans found the town deserted. A quantity of Insurgent uniform cloth, clothing, flags and insignia was located and destroyed. During the morning the battalion of Marines had dispersed a band of Insurgents on the north outskirts of the town and then waited the arrival of Schwann's column.

Such information of the Insurgents as Schwann had been able to obtain, indicated that they had retreated south to the town of San Francisco de Malabon. Although the indicated move was to follow the Insurgents, Schwann was so apprehensive of the ability of his trains to follow along the flooded roads that he changed his plans and marched west to the town of Rosario where his troops could be supplied by boat from Manila.

Between Novaleta and Rosario there was almost constant opposition from small Insurgent bodies. It was not organized, however, and as the Americans advanced, unmistakable signs indicated that the Insurgent troops were hiding their uniforms and rifles, shortly thereafter appearing in ordinary native clothing and professing to be "amigos." Fighting its way into Rosario at 8:00 p. m. the brigade arrested some 200 suspicious civilians who gave indications of being erstwhile Insurgents. In line with the American policy of "attraction," these prisoners were later released with the hope that they would return to their normal civil pursuits.

After receiving supplies by boat, the column moved on the 9th towards San Francisco de Malabon. This city, which had been reported as an Insurgent stronghold, was entered with little difficulty and on the 10th Schwann wired Otis as follows:[26]

> "Enemy, with an estimated strength of 1500, abandoned this town last night and early this morning, leaving behind detaining forces concealed in thicket. He is retreating southward. I am sending out strong reconnoitering party to watch his movements. He seems disinclined to fight and can easily evade fighting. The roads for wheeled vehicles are most difficult, making the problem of supply a hard one. We find maps of the country south of Rosario very inaccurate. Conditions of the roads to this place so bad that wagon belonging to signal corps, though carrying a light load, had to be abandoned. Question of garrisoning this place as well as Imus and thus establishing a southern line, perhaps worth considering at this time."

Natives told Schwann that the Insurgents had been so discouraged by the steady advance of the Americans, that Trias had disbanded the mass of his soldiers and preserved the organization of only six or seven companies for harassing purposes.

Otis however refused to entertain the idea of establishing a garrison in San Francisco de Malabon and directed Schwann to return his wagon trains to Bacoor, via the Rosario-Novaleta road and to move cross country to Dasmarinas, about eight miles south. (It may be recalled that in June attempts to cross this area had been abandoned because of the swampy nature of the ground.)

Complying with Otis' instructions in regard to the return of the wheeled transportation via Rosario and Novaleta, Schwann assembled his tired troops at San Francisco de Malabon and made preparations for what promised to be a most difficult cross country march.

Anticipating the debilitating effects of heavy packs, each soldier's personal equipment was limited to three days rations, a small supply of ammunition and a blanket. No wheeled transportation whatsoever was to accompany the mobile column. The start was made at daybreak on October 12.

At this season of the year rice was growing, and by means of irrigation ditches the natives kept the rice fields, which comprised a large part of the area, flooded to a depth of about three inches. The brigade marched in several columns of files along the dikes, which enclosed each field, but as described by General Schwann, the march for the infantry was most difficult. The rice dikes being narrow and the footing most insecure, falls and slides into the mud on either side were very frequent. Large irrigation ditches with soft bottoms and located at frequent intervals, also added to the difficulties of marching. By afternoon, despite the difficulties, the main road running from Imus to Dasmarinas was reached, and the command marched into Dasmarinas that night after dispersing a weak Insurgent resistance. The following day, upon Otis' orders, the expedition returned to Bacoor, where the units were sent to their normal stations.

In regard to the accomplishments of the expedition, General Schwann is quoted as follows:[27]

> "Notwithstanding the difficulties of locomotion, the expedition accomplished the objects for which it was set on foot with thoroughness and dispatch. The enemy though assembled in large bodies and occupying positions whose natural strength had been still further increased by artificial means was easily defeated in a province in which he had scored some of his greatest successes in the rebellion against Spain, and where since February 5, he has held almost undisputed sway. It is impossible for a column, absorbed in keeping its opponent on the run to estimate the number of casualties. But is appeared that the loss of the Insurgents amounted to not less than 100 killed and 400 wounded. The effect of the punishment is evidenced by the quiet that has since its administration, prevailed on the south line, where as reported not a shot had been fired for fifteen days. It is further reported that many Insurgents have returned to Rosario and Novaleta, laying aside their arms. It is undoubtedly a fact that those of the inhabitants of these towns who did not quit their homes, had occular demonstration of the fact that American troops respect the rights of noncombatants."

The situation in the south quiet, apparently, Otis could now turn his attention to political developments and to what he considered the main seat of Insurgent activity, the Army in the north.

8

By this time the Congress of the United States realized that the 5000 troops which Dewey had stated would be sufficient to take and hold Manila were is no sense sufficient to suppress the rebellion which the assumption of American sovereignty over the Islands had kindled. Arrangements were in progress for the return of the state volunteers to the United States. Of the 34,661 troops in the Philippines in June, 1899, over 50% were volunteer troops, and their departure would leave the American forces at a dangerously low level. A steady stream of regular regiments was arriving in the Philippines, but the small regular army had reached the limit of its capacity to furnish troops.

Considering the Insurrection in the Philippines a temporary emergency and imbued with the idea of keeping the regular army small, Congress authorized in July of 1899 the organization of twenty-five new volunteer regiments. The infantry of these new troops were to carry numerical designations from 26 to 49, inclusive, and were to be enlisted for the specific purpose of service in the Philippines. The 36th and 37th Infantry and 11th Cavalry were authorized to be recruited in the Philippine Islands from discharged state volunteers. The 48th and 49th regiments of Infantry were to be composed of colored troops. The officers for these new volunteer regiments were to be secured largely from the regular army.

Between June 14 and October 8, the state volunteer regiments were returned to the United States and their points of origin, Oregon, Nebraska, Utah, Pennsylvania, Colorado, California, Wyoming, North and South Dakota, Idaho, Minnesota, Montana, Kansas, Washington, Iowa, Nevada, and Tennessee. These volunteers had done their work nobly and had borne the brunt of the heaviest fighting during the Insurrection. Because of ignorance of the Philippines, they had been in effect War Department "Guinea Pigs" in regard to clothing, equipment and weapons. Undisciplined perhaps, when judged according to regular army standards, they showed throughout their campaigns the initiative so necessary to the successful winning of battles. As a final testimony to their efforts, two quotations are here cited:

Major J. S. Mallory, Inspector General of MacArthur's division reported:[28]

"Nearly every volunteer organization I inspected at San Francisco I have inspected in the Philippine Islands under actual service conditions and have had the good fortune to witness the conduct of many of these regiments in battle. . . . . I wish to add my testimony that these volunteers although not thoroughly trained and disciplined soldiers, have in the present war proved themselves to be magnificent fighting men."

A British Army Officer, acting as observer with the American troops, paid the following tribute to the volunteers in referring to their capture of Manila in August of 1898:[29]

"The advance took place between 11 and 12 mid-day and by 5 p. m. every road, bridge and gateway of the town was carefully picketed and held by American troops, who the whole of that night, Sunday and Sunday night uncomplainingly remained in the streets under heavy tropical rains, good-temperedly carrying out the difficult and troublesome duty of preventing armed Insurgents from entering the town and carefully abstaining from coming into unnecessary conflict with the large mass of Spanish officers and soldiery who were rather aggressively parading the streets. The most careful inquiries failed to elicit any report of a complaint being made of any act of pillage or assault committed by an American soldier."

On their return to the United States, these volunteer regiments took with them some twenty-five Congressional Medals of Honor and a fund of stories (many exaggerated) concerning "service in the Philippines."

While the volunteers were being sent home, a unit rare to American arms was organized, namely a battalion of "Macabebe Scouts." The Macabebes were a native tribe living in an area about 10 miles square to the east of Calumpit. It appears that in the distant past their ancestors had been imported by the Spanish from Mexico, so that in addition to a Malay strain gained by intermarriage, they were also part American Indian. Contrary to the majority of Filipino tribes, they had remained loyal to the Spanish, a large number of the men enlisting in the Spanish army and some rising to high positions in the church. The Tagalogs were their pet aversion and when the Spanish left the Islands, the Macabebes transferred their loyalty to the Americans and offered their services. Otis refused until the frequent forays on MacArthur's lines from the Tagalogs, who lived in the maze of swamps and estuaries bordering the north shore of Manila Bay, made him realize the feasibility of organizing the Macabebes into an American military unit for the purpose of punishing these forays by the use of natives familiar with the terrain. A company was organized under the command of Lieutenant Mathew Batson, and was so effective that it was expanded to a battalion and used for scouting purposes throughout the island. The antipathy of the Macabebes towards other Filipinos in general was so great that it was necessary to exercise a strong restraining hand to prevent the robbery, rape and torture of native inhabitants. However, the Macabebe Scouts were a valuable adjunct to the American army and were loyal to the core. It was largely through their efforts that the capture of Aguinaldo was finally accomplished. The native scout idea was so successful that later other native troops, even including Tagalogs were organized into "scout units." Today the Philippine Islands are garrisoned by some 5000 Philippine Scouts.

Between June and October the 6th, 16th, 19th, 24th, and 25th U. S. Infantry regiments arrived in the islands. Despite the return of the state volunteer regiments, the strength of the American troops still amounted to 35,683.[30] In October, the newly constituted volunteer regiments recruited in the United States commenced to filter over, continuously augmenting the American forces to such an extent that by March of 1900 they numbered nearly 56,000.

In his cabled reports to the War Department, Otis had invariably assumed an optimistic view. He had deprecated the necessity of the War Department sending him the large number of troops which were arriving in a steady stream from the United States. His dispatches minimized the stability of the Insurgent government and by a strict censorship of the press, he had systematically prevented information regarding the large amount of sickness among American troops from reaching the United States. The newspaper correspondents in Manila, disgusted with what they considered an unnecessary curtailment of their activities, created no little excitement in the United States at this time by publishing a "round robin" dispatch which had of necessity been taken by boat to Hong Kong and cabled from there. The text of this unusual message was as follows:[31]

> The Undersigned, being all staff correspondents of American newspapers, stationed in Manila unite in the following statement:
>
> We believe that owing to official dispatches from Manila, made public in Washington the people of the United States have not received a correct impression of the situation in the Philippines, but that these dispatches have presented an ultra optimistic view that is not shared by the General Officers in the field.
>
> We believe that the dispatches incorrectly represent the existing conditions among the Filipinos in respect to internal dissention and demoralization resulting from the American campaign and to the brigand character of their army.
>
> We believe that the dispatches err in the declaration that the "situation is well in hand" and in the assumption that the Insurrection can be speedily ended without a greatly increased force.
>
> We think that the tenacity of the Filipino purpose had been

underestimated and that the statements are unfounded that the Volunteers are unwilling to engage in further service.

The censorship has compelled us to participate in this misrepresentation by excising or altering uncontroverted statements of fact on the plea, as General Otis stated, that "They would alarm the people at home" or "have the people of the United States by the ears."

Specifications: Prohibition of hospital reports; suppression of full reports of field operations in the event of failure; numbers of heat prostrations in the field; systematic minimization of Naval operations; and suppression of complete reports of the situation.

The dispatch was signed by John T. McCutcheon and Harry Armstrong of the Chicago *Record,* Oscar K. Davis and P. G. McDonnell of the New York *Sun,* Robert M. Collins, John P. Dunning and L. J. Jones of the Associated Press, John F. Bass and William Dinwiddie of the New York *Herald,* E. D. Skene of the Scripps McRae Association, and Richard Little, of the Chicago *Tribune.*

Otis was furious with the press representatives. He called them to his office, accused them of conspiracy, and threatened to have them tried by a court martial. In the United States the dispatch caused much comment, particularly in Congress and among the anti-imperialist groups. In September the Adjutant General of the Army in Washington announced that censorship of news from the Philippines had been abolished. However, three months later newspaper men complained that it was still being exercised.

Both Otis and the representatives of the press had legitimate reasons for their viewpoints. From Otis' standpoint, he knew that many of the cases of heat exhaustion in the field were pure straggling and that many of the soldiers in the hospital were shirkers. The Navy had antagonized him by attacking and capturing Iloilo in February, in advance of the prearranged plan. Further, the retention of the Philippines was a major issue in the ensuing presidential election, and a minimization of the disorders was a matter of loyalty to the administration. On their part, the newspaper men wanted to get accurate information to their papers, and they were not being permitted to do so, or were required to color their reports to such an extent that they felt they were not doing their duty to their employers. Eventually, after Aguinaldo's Army was dispersed, the matter was finally ironed out and correspondents were permitted to telegraph facts, being required, however, to carefully differentiate between facts and opinions particularly in regard to the political situation in the Islands.

9

In San Fernando, Pampanga, forty-three miles north of Manila, MacArthur's division was perforce granting the Filipinos, actually if not officially, the armistice which they had requested in May. It will be recalled that the physical condition of the troops in the second division was so bad that nearly 50% of the command was on sick report, and operations were suspended.

Aguinaldo took advantage of the temporary breathing spell to rectify the dissension within the Insurgent ranks. When the commanding general of the Insurgent forces, Antonia Luna had dissolved the pro-American Peace Commission while enroute to Manila and substituted a delegation of his own choice, it had constituted a definite challenge to Aguinaldo's authority as head of the Insurgent government. Understood as it was that Aguinaldo was a cat's-paw to the importunities of the rabid anti-American paralytic, Appolinario Mabini, the Insurgent Congress and Cabinet had met in May, ousted Mabini as President of the cabinet and adopted a program designed to establish peace. Aguinaldo appears to have concurred with the majority, but was apprehensive as to the attitude which might be assumed by Luna and the Insurgent Army. Shortly thereafter he received definite information that Luna was laying plans for the overthrow of the "Peace Cabinet" by means of a military *coup d' etat* and intended to assume the dictatorship of the Filipino government himself. After the capture of San Fernando by the Americans, Luna had withdrawn his military headquarters to Bayambang, a town on the railroad in the province of Pangasinan, and some eighty miles north of the scene of military activities. From his capital at Cabanatuan Aguinaldo decided to strike first.

It appears that in order to allay suspicion, he had intimated to Luna that the latter would be made head of a new Filipino cabinet soon to be formed. On June 5, Luna was requested to proceed to a conference at Cabanatuan. Arriving there with a small bodyguard, he proceeded to Aguinaldo's headquarters where he had been advised that he would find the Insurgent President. As he and his aide, Colonel Francisco Roman entered the house they were met with a hail of bullets which proved fatal to both. Aguinaldo was not in the town at the time, and had that day gone to Tarlac, where following Luna's death he assumed command of the Insurgent Army. It was a well planned and executed assassination. But doubt remains as to Aguinaldo's responsibility therefor. Illocano troops in the Insurgent Army, who he thought might dispute his assumption of

command, were disarmed by Tagalogs and held under guard until
it became evident that they had no intention of causing trouble.
Before the Filipino people, Aguinaldo gave justification for the
crime as a "state necessity." Although universally indignant, Luna's
Illocano tribesmen permitted their feelings of patriotism to overcome their anger and as a whole remained loyal to Aguinaldo.

Discords among the Filipinos were not entirely to cease, however,
as is indicated from a letter written in July by a well-to-do citizen of
Tarlac, the then Insurgent capital, to a friend in Manila:[32]

> "For some days, I have been trying to get into your city and
> leave this band of thieves, but with my numerous family it is
> impossible to travel off the road and they watch us here so
> closely that it is impossible to get away, which I very much
> regret. However, I believe that this will all end up some way
> or other and a great many of the people here long for the
> American troops to advance, for everyone is desperate with so
> much savagery committed by our army. Quiet citizens are never
> left in peace, nor anyone in fact who has as much as a grain of
> rice put aside. . . . I will not go into details as to occurrences
> here as this letter will be too long. I do not sign this letter or
> put down the address, as to do so might bring disagreeable
> consequences."

In a measure, this letter expressed the opinion of the majority of
the Filipinos of means, many of whom had been forced to contribute
to an Insurgent bond issue amounting to $500,000. However, to
quote Otis:[33]

> "It did not voice the sentiments of Army officers who were
> enjoying a license of action never anticipated before its realiza-
> tion and of the ignorant masses who composed the enlisted
> strength of the army and preferred to gain subsistence through
> exaction rather than the severe manual labors of former days.
> The army offered an excellent field of operations for the La-
> drones. They had been gathered from all portions of Luzon and
> were of great service in recruiting diminished Insurgent ranks
> by drafts on the people."

From the mountains south of Manila, the bandit chieftain Pio
Del Pilar wrote to a friend in Manila stating that for $1,000,000 he
would hand over to the American authorities Aguinaldo and his
entire government.

Even though the rabid anti-Americans, Mabini and Luna had
been removed from the picture, the idea of peace with the Americans
faded. Taking command of the army and government, Aguinaldo

appeared to have become imbued with the idea of continuing the struggle to the bitter end.

The effect of this change in Insurgent authorities was manifested on June 16, a few days after Luna's death. While MacArthur's troops were still recuperating, Aguinaldo personally directed an attack of some 7000 Insurgents on San Fernando.

No military man, Aguinaldo spread his entire force in a seven-mile arc which practically surrounded the city. During the attack telegraph communications with Manila were interrupted and fifty feet of the railroad track between San Fernando and Calumpit were removed. The attack of the thin over-extended Insurgent line, however, was easily repulsed by the Americans. In the sectors occupied by the Kansas and Iowa Volunteers, several Filipino units were scattered by vigorous counter attacks. Henceforth, Insurgent tactics were to follow a Fabian policy—a series of defensive positions, which were quickly abandoned when attacked. They contented themselves with occupying trenches opposite the American lines and harassing the American outposts with occasional unorganized attacks.

Between Aguinaldo's attack on San Fernando on June 16 and August 9, the situation on MacArthur's front was, to quote the division commander himself, "an exceedingly languid period." However, the contiguity of the opposing armies was such that the outposts frequently descended to useless wrangles, the total sum of American casualties for June and July amounting to two killed and twenty-four wounded.

Early in August Otis, realizing that the backbone of the Insurrection lay in the Insurgent army on the railroad, conceived the plan of having MacArthur contain that force until another column could move around in its rear and cut off retreat. In order to hold the forces on the railroad while the details of the plan were maturing, MacArthur was directed to push his advance on August 9 to the town of Angeles, ten miles north of San Fernando. For the movement the 2nd division was reconstituted as follows:

1st Brigade (General Hale)
3 Battalions, 9th Infantry
12th Infantry
1 Battery, 3rd Artillery
2nd Brigade (General Wheaton)
17th Infantry
51st Iowa Infantry
22nd Infantry (1 battalion)
1 battery of 1st and one battery of 3rd Artillery

The division was to straddle the railroad, with one brigade on each side of the track. The 36th Infantry, one of the new volunteer regiments which had been organized in the Philippines and placed under the command of Colonel J. Franklin Bell, was to protect the left flank of the division and to demonstrate towards the town of Bacalor.

Moving with difficulty on account of rain followed by steamy sunshine, and the poor condition of roads, the division left San Fernando at 5:00 a. m. on August 9. At Calulut, a small town about seven miles north of San Fernando and three south of Angeles, it surprised and dispersed some 3000 Insurgents who occupied the town. At noon that day MacArthur telegraphed Otis:[34]

> "Movement commenced at 5:00 this morning. Command now occupies a line extending right and left from railroad at Calulut. The movement has been entirely successful up to this time. We have contact at almost every point on line but opposition has not been desperate. Weather conditions have been favorable except as regards heat. Command is now halted to rectify alignments which have been badly broken by usual jungles and ditches. Casualties number possibly thirty. Losses inflicted have been considerable, probably fifty or sixty killed and proportionate wounded. So far as can be determined, enemy have retired in direction of Porac and not directly up railroad. Everybody nearly exhausted but we are getting rest while lines are being rectified."

Porac was a town seven miles to the east of Calulut and at the base of the Zambales Mountains.

Anticipating further American advance along the railroad, the Insurgents had taken advantage of the breathing spell granted them between May and August to make the railroad as useless as possible. Between San Fernando and Calulut they had removed some five miles of track. They had destroyed all bridges and culverts and had plowed grades in places, with the view of making a water course which would wash them out. At the end of the day MacArthur felt that even if he did take Angeles, it would be impossible to supply his troops there until the railroad was repaired. The wagon road along his route of advance had been so boggy that all but two artillery pieces had been returned to San Fernando.

Two companies of the Iowa Volunteers, who had been left to protect his right flank on the Mexico road northeast of San Fernando, had been attacked by some 500 Insurgents and had driven them off with difficulty. Perceiving the necessity of dispersing the Insurgents from his flanks, if he was to advance unmolested, MacArthur proposed to Otis that his division halt for the time being at Calulut. Then while the railroad line was being repaired, he could use this time to clear out the Insurgents on his flank. Otis approved, and on August 11 reconnoitering detachments sent out on his left flank reached Guagua, a town about twelve miles southwest of San Fernando and situated on the Guagua River, a navigable stream which emptied into the bay.

On August 10, Colonel J. Franklin Bell, with a detachment of the 36th Infantry, reconnoitered the road between Angeles and Bacalor. Encountering no opposition, he soon found himself on the outskirts of Angeles itself, some three miles in advance of the American front lines. Determined to carry the reconnaissance as far as possible, he and a small group of mounted men galloped on, yelling and firing their pistols like a band of cowboys. In the heart of the town they were stopped by a scattering fire. They returned to Calulut to report that Angeles was lightly held. The following day an exploring party of fifty men from the Iowa regiment entered the city and found it deserted. Another reconnaissance on the 13th indicated that the town was now held by some 500 Insurgents. It appeared that they were debating in their councils as to whether or not they should oppose American advance into the town. At any rate MacArthur decided on the 16th that the town should be occupied by at least a regiment to prevent opposition when the railroad had been repaired and the division advanced. He made the decision about five days too late. When the 12th Infantry advanced on the 16th they were opposed by some 2500 Insurgents, and it necessitated a charge by ten companies of the 12th Infantry before they were dislodged from their entrenched positions and the town taken. Indecision as to the occupation had caused the deaths of five Americans and the wounding of thirteen. In Angeles the 12th Infantry captured three railroad locomotives, twenty-five cars and a large quantity of rice. The town normally contained some 12,000 inhabitants, most of whom had departed upon the advance of the Americans. Reconnaissance groups were sent to the west of the town, reaching the site of the present location of Fort Stotsenburg. The following morning at 5:00 a. m. Angeles was attacked from two directions by about 800 Insurgents, but the 12th Infantry was able to drive them off without casualties.

Although the division then held the railroad line between San Fernando and Angeles, it by no means controlled the surrounding country. To the west were the Zambales Mountains which furnished ample refuge for small bands of marauders. During the next three weeks repair on the railroad was interrupted and the American troops were constantly harassed by Insurgent attacks. On September 9 outposts at Santa Rita and at Guagua were attacked.

On September 19 the railroad line between San Fernando and Angeles was finally repaired, and steps were taken to make Angeles the base for the division. On the 22nd, the Insurgents slipped through the American lines and placed a mine under the railroad track a mile and a half south of Angeles. As the next train passed over it, the mine exploded, derailing five cars, killing two and injuring five Americans.

Since the town of Porac, six miles southeast of Angeles seemed to be the center of Insurgent activity, MacArthur sent, on the 28th, two columns, one from Angeles and one from Bacalor, to attack Porac from two directions. The coordinated movement was a success, and in a charge the Americans entered the city at the cost of one killed and four wounded. Ten of the 600 Insurgents who defended the town were killed before they scattered into the mountains or to the north.

On October 9 a detachment of the 36th Infantry under Colonel J. Franklin Bell, moving out from Guagua entered Florida Blanca, a town fifteen miles west of San Fernando. After capturing six Insurgents it returned to Guagua by way of Lubao, scattering several small Insurgent bands encountered along the route of march.

At 2:00 a. m. October 16 some 3500 Insurgents made a night attack on Angeles. Supported by artillery fire, detached bands attempted to enter the town from all sides. Although the attack was repulsed, artillery shells were responsible for the death of one and the wounding of eight Americans.

During the balance of October repeated attacks on the Insurgents at Porac, Guagua and vicinity had completely disorganized and demoralized the Insurgent brigade under General Tomas Mascardo which had been operating from the Zambales Mountains. Mascardo himself was temporarily forced into hiding. Reconnaissance to the north indicated that the main Insurgent force opposing MacArthur's division numbered some 6000 men and was extended from Magalang, about eight miles northeast of Angeles, through a line north of Angeles to entrenched positions north of Porac. With the Insurgents on his flanks dispersed, the stage was now set for further advance to the north.

Notes on Chapter VIII

1 *cf* HD No. 2 Vol. 6 56th 1st p. 31
2 *cf* Ibid p. 32
3 *cf* Worcester, "The Philippines, Past and Present" p. 301
4 For complete minutes of the meetings of the first Philippine Commission see SD No. 138 Vol. 44 56th 1st
5 For full text see Ibid p. 3 ff
6 *cf* Facts about the Filipinos Vol. 1 No. 6 p. 50
7 In an interview in 1932 Aguinaldo told the writer that in this instance he was forced to hide in a bamboo thicket with a handfull of followers. An American patrol passed within 150 yards of his hiding place but did not observe him.
8 *cf* HD No. 2 Vol. 6 56th 1st p. 88
9 *cf* Ibid p. 164
10 *cf* Ibid p. 219
11 *cf* Ibid p. 209
12 *cf* Ibid p. 243
13 *cf* Sonnichsen, *op. cit.*
14 *cf* Cerezo, "Under the Red and Gold"
15 *cf* HD No. 2 Vol. 5 56th 1st p. 120 *et. seq.*
16 *cf* Worcester, "The Philippines Past and Present" p. 322
17 *cf* Ibid p. 323
18 *cf* HD No. 2 Vol. 6 56th 1st p. 400
19 *cf* Ibid p. 424
20 *cf* SD 208 Vol. 12 56th 1st p. 69
21 *cf* Ibid p. 72
22 *cf* HD No. 2 Vol. 5 56th 1st p. 121
23 *cf* HD No. 2 Vol. 6 56th 1st p. 410
24 *cf* HD No. 2 Vol. 6 56th 2nd p. 298
25 *cf* Ibid p. 354
26 *cf* HD No. 2 Vol. 7 56th 2nd p. 488
27 *cf* Ibid p. 477
28 *cf* HD No. 2 Vol. 4 56th 1st p. 443
29 *cf* Ibid
30 *cf* HD No. 2 Vol. 5 56th 2nd p. 210
31 *cf* Robinson "The Philippines, The War and the People" p. 81
32 *cf* HD No. 2 Vol. 5 56th 2nd p. 206
33 *cf* Ibid
34 *cf* HD No. 2 Vol. 9 56th 2nd p. 21

Chapter IX

NOVEMBER AND DECEMBER, 1899, were to be Armageddon as far as the American and Insurgent armies were concerned. These two months were to witness the denouement of the drama being played 7000 miles from the shores of the United States; the government of the "Philippine Republic" was to be broken up, its members either captured or chased into hiding; Emilio Aguinaldo, the President, was to become a breathless fugitive in the Benguet Mountains; northern Luzon was to be overrun with a tattered, unkempt, shoeless, but determined force of American soldiers. Whereas between February and October, a period of eight months, no American soldier had ventured more than sixty miles from Manila, these last two months of November and December were to see venturesome expeditions reaching Aparri, on the northern tip of the Islands, 354 miles distant. Subordinate commanders out of touch with the restraining hand of Otis ventured into areas which even the Spanish in their three hundred years of possession of the Islands had avoided. The whole affair was a brilliant testimony to the initiative, courage and endurance of the American soldier.

It may be recalled that the American lines north of Manila ran through the towns of Angeles and Baliuag. They were not straight lines by any means, because the Candaba Swamp was between the two towns, which were garrisoned by American troops and may be considered to be the limit of American advance into Insurgent territory. It may also be recalled that during the previous April Lawton's division had advanced as far north as San Isidro, Nueva Ecija, a town thirty miles north of Baliuag. Lawton had wanted to garrison the town and establish a base for future operations to the north. However, the cautious Otis had required him to withdraw to Baliuag. As might be expected, the Insurgents immediately reoccupied the intervening territory as soon as Lawton withdrew.

During October, the new volunteer regiments began trickling into the Philippine Islands and Otis decided that he was sufficiently strong to deliver one sweeping *coup de grace* to the will o' the wisp Insurgent army. The Fabian policy which the Insurgents had adopted after the first few fights with the Americans, made the capture extremely difficult. It is axiomatic that an enemy which will not stand up and fight cannot be decisively beaten. And the farther the Americans advanced into Insurgent territory, the greater became the supply problem and the number of troops required to protect the lines of communications. Eventually the Insurgents might be driven into the mountains of northern Luzon, but what then? The mountains were completely impracticable for military operations of a large scale. Native forces scattered through them could have prolonged the rebellion indefinitely.

Consequently, with his map spread in front of him at his Manila desk, Otis conceived a plan for capturing the Insurgent Army, which was little less than brilliant in its conception. It was known that the main Insurgent force was in front of MacArthur's division at Angeles. The logical line of its withdrawal was along the railroad line which had its terminus at the town of Dagupan, on Lingayen Gulf, 150 miles north of Manila. If MacArthur's division could pin Aguinaldo until an encircling force could get around his rear, access to the mountains in the north would be denied. The Insurgent Army, including its leader Aguinaldo, would be caught in a virtual *cul de sac*.

The geography of central Luzon was especially suited to such a plan. The broad, flat Pampanga plain extended from the mountains in the north to Manila. While the main Insurgent Army was pinned by MacArthur at Angeles, one mobile force, predominant in cavalry, could sweep around the Insurgent left (east) flank, and block all passes to the east and northeast. Another expedition moving by boat into Lingayen Gulf in the vicinity of Dagupan could block all escape to the north. Then when the stage was set, MacArthur would push the Insurgents back into the waiting arms of the blocking forces and the Insurgent army as such would either be captured or destroyed. The plan appeared more practicable when it is noticed that the large Rio Grande de Pampanga cuts diagonally across the Pampanga Plain. This river, normally navigable, could be used as an artery for supplying one encircling force.

Specifically the plan was as follows: General Lawton's division, operating from a base at San Isidro, was to move north through the providence of Nueva Ecija, closing as he went all passes into the Caraballos and Sierra Madre Mountains.

Another force under General Wheaton was to move by boat from Manila, land near the town of San Fabian, extend its lines to the east and close all movement north along the coastal cities on the west shore of Luzon and block all passes into the Benguet Mountains. When the two encircling forces were in position, MacArthur was to start advancing along the railroad and push Aguinaldo and his army into the waiting hands of Lawton or Wheaton.

An inexplicable weakness of the plan was that Otis does not appear to have specified where the two encircling forces would join hands. Since the success of the whole movement depended on the passes to the mountains to the north being blocked, it is hard to understand how a man as meticulous of details as Otis, would have permitted such a detail to be overlooked. A glance at the map would indicate the town of Tayug as a logical point. If the forces met at Tayug, it would have meant that Lawton's force, which contained cavalry, would have made a march of about sixty miles, while Wheaton's infantry column would have had to move only twenty miles from its base. Possibly Otis intended for once to leave the matter of uniting up to the commanders in the field, trusting to their initiative and aggressiveness. If he did, Wheaton was the wrong man to send.

Having outlined the general plan, let us see how it worked. Since each of the three forces was operating virtually independently, a separate discussion of the operations of each would be in the interests of clarity.

Lawton's mission was by far the most difficult. His base was to be thirty miles from the railroad. He was advancing into a strange country, where the amount of opposition to be encountered was problematical. He was operating in a portion of the Islands where the roads were known to be notoriously bad. He was supposed to cover much more ground than either of the other forces. He had not only the usual supply problem of furnishing rations for the troops, but also of hauling or finding forage for his animals. To make matters more difficult, the rainy season was a long and heavy one.

Insurgent opposition to Lawton's advance can be dismissed as inconsequential. His battle casualties were too small to be worthy of mention. His big problem was that of supply. From the time his division left San Fernando early in October, until it became scattered all over Luzon late in December, Lawton considered the problem of sufficient importance to "act as his own chief quartermaster." The longer the campaign continued, the more difficult the supply system became and, as we shall see, finally broke down completely.

The Manila-Dagupan Railroad crosses the Rio Grande at Calumpit. If Lawton established a base at San Isidro, thirty miles up the river, supplies could be hauled by rail from Manila to Calumpit, then placed on boats and hauled to San Isidro. As far as his advance to the north followed the river, the water supply system should still be efficacious. A glance at the map indicated that his advance would follow the river at least as far north as the town of Cabanatuan, a distance of twelve miles. From then on the column would have to be supplied by mule-drawn escort wagons or carabao carts. On paper the plan for supply seemed feasible. It was excellent in every respect except one, and that was that it didn't work.

Lawton's force assembled at Calumpit and San Fernando during the early part of October, consisting of eight troops of the 3rd Cavalry, nine troops of the 4th, the 24th Infantry (colored) and two battalions of the 22nd Infantry. All of these were regular army units, and with the exception of the 4th Cavalry all had seen service in Cuba. The 4th Cavalry had been in the Philippines since the beginning of the war. The artillery for the division consisted, strange to say, of two companies, G and H, of the 37th Infantry. One of these was armed with 12 pounder Hotchkiss guns, while the other, armed with rifles, habitually accompanied the "Battery" as protection. A rather peculiar arrangement for the "divisional artillery," it was the crystallization of experience as to the most effective employment of artillery during the type of warfare being waged. This artillery was placed under the command of Captain Ernest D. Scott of the 37th Infantry. An artilleryman who had graduated from West Point in 1898, the strapping Scott had, despite his youth, proven himself to be the artilleryman ne plus ultra of the Insurrection. He had participated in virtually every campaign since the beginning. His fearless handling of the guns, in some cases within a stone's throw of the Insurgent lines, had attracted the favorable attention of many high officers, particularly Lawton who cited him repeatedly for bravery and efficiency. When the volunteer regiments were organized, Scott was commissioned as a captain in the volunteer infantry and at Lawton's request assigned to his division. Also assigned to the division was the 16th Infantry, garrisoning Baliuag, and the 34th Infantry which was marching to join it at the earliest possible moment. The division was further augmented by a battalion of Macabebe scouts, under the command of Lieutenant Matthew Batson, and two companies of "Tagalog" scouts under the command of Lieutenant Joseph C. Castner. The majority of both the Macabebes and Tagalog scouts had been members of the Spanish army, and as such had received what might be called "western military training"—had been taught to shoot. Both units were worth their weight in gold.

The cavalry was formed into a brigade and placed under the command of Brigadier General Samuel B. M. Young. Six feet four, weighing 250 pounds, General Young had enlisted as a private in the 12th Pennsylvania Infantry in 1861. By 1865 he had been brevetted four times for gallantry and promoted to the grade of brevet briga-

dier general of volunteers. In 1866 he entered the regular army as
a second lieutenant of Infantry and had reached the grade of colonel
of the 3rd Cavalry by 1897. With the declaration of war against
Spain, he was commissioned as major general of volunteers and
commanded the 3rd Army Corps in the expedition to Cuba. The war
over, he was reduced to the grade of brigadier general of volunteers
and ordered to the Philippines. Prior to his departure from the
United States, he had addressed a communication to the War Department, stating his views as to how the pacification of the Islands
should be accomplished, and criticizing in a measure Otis' administration and methods. The War Department forwarded the communication to Otis. The story goes that when Young arrived in the
Philippines Otis immediately called him to headquarters and gave
him a thorough "dressing down" for interference and criticism of
military superiors. Later Young told at least one officer[1] that Otis
was attempting to ruin him professionally.

Moving from San Fernando on October 12, the 24th Infantry
drove entrenched Insurgents from Arayat, with but one casualty. The
engineers constructed a cable ferry over the Rio Grande de Pampanga at Arayat and, after crossing the river, the division proceeded
on the 18th towards San Isidro. At Cabiao the 22nd Infantry captured an Insurgent blockhouse and seventy prisoners and on the 19th
marched into San Isidro, after routing some 900 Insurgents under
the command of General Pio Del Pilar. The first step had been accomplished with little difficulty.

Established at San Isidro, and having ordered the movement of
supplies from Calumpit via boat to begin, Lawton immediately
found himself faced with an unexpected and exasperating struggle
with the fickle Rio Grande River. By October the steady rains of
June, July and August had changed to intermittent cloudbursts. On
the days that it rained, the river overflowed its banks with a current
so strong that the overworked launches, which Otis had furnished,
were unable to tow the laden cascos upstream. On alternate days,
the river dropped so quickly that the launches and cascos frequently
went aground on the numerous sand bars which formed in the river.
Since most of these rains occurred in the nearby mountains, the
condition of the river was unpredictable. The first convoy of boats
illustrated the difficulty of shallow-water transportation. Abandoning the towing launch, a detachment of troops undertook to pull
the cascos to San Isidro by means of shore lines. Although a detail
of men was sent ahead to cut a path through the jungles for the pul-
lers, they strained at the tow ropes for an hour and a half to gain

only 300 yards. The bank on the opposite side of the river looked better, so the casco was poled across the river, but in the crossing, the casco drifted some 400 yards downstream. After two hours of work the casco was actually behind the point from which it had started. It then being nearly dark, the detail quit in disgust. Starting at daybreak the following morning, a back breaking, heartbreaking day ensued. The bank was in some cases a vertical bluff twenty feet high, making the towing extremely difficult. At other points trees extended out so far into the water that a man would have to take the tow rope, jump into the river, swim around the tree and clamber up the bank again. At one point the casco went aground and the whole party had to take to the water in order to effect its release. After two days of this toil during which a detail from the 22nd Infantry was of necessity sent to assist, the bedraggled party finally waded through the waist-deep mud flats at San Isidro and brought the boat to its destination. If all the supplies for San Isidro had to be hauled by this method, the command would starve.

The work of pulling up the river was also embarrassed by the intermittent fire received from Insurgents hiding along the river bank. One man lying in the bamboo thickets which lined the bank could fire to his heart's content at a slow moving barge. If the barge became stuck on a bar, as was a frequent occurrence, this sniping made the task of removing it extremely onerous for the men working in the water. By the time a detail could reach the bank, the malefactor would have disappeared.

With the river at a low ebb, Lawton realized the crying need for shallow-bottomed launches which could go over the sand bars. He sent his quartermaster, Colonel Guy Howard, to Manila with instructions to "beg, borrow or steal every shallow-bottomed launch he could put his hands on." Enroute to Manila via boat, Colonel Howard was killed by a fusillade of bullets from the shore.

On the 24th of October a heavy rain caused the river to rise ten feet. Taking advantage of the situation, the entire division worked day and night for three days assembling 10,000 rations at San Isidro. Although he regarded the supply as entirely insufficient, Lawton felt that the movement towards the north must start. So, as a feeler, he issued orders for detachments to push out towards Cabanatuan, twelve miles to the north. Although he invariably marched with the leading elements of his division, he realized that the critical feature of this campaign would be supplies and remained with the rear units for the purpose of personally pushing them through.

When two cavalry squadrons, a battalion of the 22nd Infantry, Scott's mounted Infantry-Artillery, and a company of Tagalog scouts, all under the command of General Young, moved out of San Isidro on October 27, the supply problem entered upon a new phase. Heretofore the river had furnished the principal obstacle. Henceforth the problem would be to push wheeled vehicles over poor roads.

At San Isidro Lawton had assembled a supply train which consisted principally of twenty-two four-mule-team escort wagons and 110 bull carts drawn by carabaos. This train was to follow Young's column. The bridge over the Tambo River about eight miles north of San Isidro being out, the men of the 22nd Infantry stripped and working in water from five to eight feet deep, constructed a floating bamboo bridge in order that the trains could pass. At the Tabotin River a few miles further on, the advance was held up for some time by 400 Insurgents entrenched on the north bank. In the ensuing fight, Scott's artillery was brought up to the river bank and fired at point-blank range. The 22nd Infantry waded and swam the river under fire. The Tagalog scouts crossed the river on the flank of the Insurgent position and advancing through the water-soaked rice fields forced the Insurgents to retire. American casualties amounted to two killed and one wounded. The gunboat *Laguna de Bay* which had steamed up the Rio Grande and the Tabotin River to assist in the attack went aground on a sand bar and lay there helpless until rains nearly a week later enabled it to disengage itself.

Late that afternoon, the column marched into Santa Rosa without opposition. A number of the infantrymen had been prostrated by heat exhaustion. Many of the cavalry horses had become mired in the rice fields and extricated with difficulty. The clothing of every member of the command was not only soaking wet but covered with mud.

The signal corps had followed despite the difficulties of marching and established telegraphic communication between Santa Rosa and San Isidro.

Young stopped at Santa Rosa for two days awaiting the supply train which had been held up at the makeshift bridge over the Tabotin. Then on the 29th, Ballance's battalion of the 22nd Infantry moved forward and brushing weak Insurgent resistance aside entered Cabanatuan. Captured in the wake of the fleeing Insurgents was a large amount of rice and a small "arsenal."

Back at San Isidro, Lawton was having his hands full keeping the supply system from bogging down. The river was falling rapidly. Although he had expressly asked Otis for shallow-draft launches, those which were sent continually went aground. It appeared impossible to accumulate a surplus of supplies. Tired, worried, Lawton became so irritated that he sent the following message to Otis:[2]

"All boats sent to me draw too much water. The question of supplies is the only serious one confronting me and this should have been solved long since. I have been able so far only to maintain supplies for current use and have no supplies of consequence. Supplies should have been placed here during the rainy season when for more than three months there was from ten to twenty feet of water in the river. The supply question has to this time occupied my whole personal attention . . . ."

Then as if to lend emphasis to his point he placed the entire division on half rations of bread and meat.

At Cabanatuan the advance stopped. Rain washed out the makeshift bridges over the Tambo and Tabotin Rivers, and the heavy wheeled supply wagons simply could not reach Cabanatuan until these bridges were repaired. Young's column was supplied via the river; but, since the contemplated advance was to leave the stream at Cabanatuan this procedure was only a temporary stopgap. In addition the Engineers had arrived on the scene. Although they were repairing the bridge with all possible dispatch, frequent rains, during which the rivers reached flood stage, slowed the work down to such an extent that it was finally decided to construct new bridges, which it was hoped would be floodproof. Young bided his time by sending out detachments on each flank and clearing the Insurgents out of the towns of Bongabong and Aliaga.

On November 4 another heavy rain fell, and the bridges which the Engineers had built were washed out. In disgust Lawton wired Otis "Everything waterbound. Bridges constructed by our Engineers washed out. Young's advance will be delayed until water falls."

The inactivity of the situation reached a crisis on the following day. In a skirmish with some Insurgents Young's men captured a proclamation which had been issued by Aguinaldo at Tarlac a month previous. The proclamation read:[3]

"In view of the fact that Tarlac does not possess the hygenic and geographic conditions becoming for the numerous population of the Republic of the Philippines, the honorable President of the Republic and his council of the government have been pleased to order that the capital of the Republic be removed provisionally to Bayombong, the capital of Nueva Viscaya."

The receipt of this information made a quick movement to the north imperative if Aguinaldo was to be cut off from his new capital. The route to Bayombong, in the mountains some seventy-five miles north of Cabanatuan, led through passes which Lawton had intended to block. If Aguinaldo and his government reached these mountains one of the main purposes of the expedition had failed.

Young conferred with Lawton and proposed that he immediately move to the north regardless of the weather or conditions of the road. If the wagon train could not keep up, he would break away from them and live on the country. As he said:* "This month is the rainy season here and in the north. We cannot expect any complete success anchored to our wagons and carts. My people understand the hardship that we may undergo in any long separation from our train, but they are ready and willing to make the attempt and I am ready and willing to assume the responsibility whenever it may please you to give your approval."

Lawton hestitated because he knew that Otis would never approve of such a proposition. However, Young was under his direct command, and once he broke loose, Otis' constant supervision via telegraph would be eliminated. After consideration he decided to let Young go ahead with the hope that the mountain passes would be closed before Aguinaldo reached them. Young was authorized to take two squadrons of the 3rd Cavalry, one of the 4th, Ballance's battalion of the 22nd Infantry, Scott's artillery and Batson's battalion of Macabebe scouts, about 1000 men. The remainder of the division was to follow as soon as possible.

In order to make Young's column mobile, all wheeled transportation except four light ration carts per company were left behind. All cooking stoves, ovens, and other kitchen furniture were stored. Each man carried 120 rounds of ammunition on his person, with an extra 100 rounds being carried on the light company transportation. Nothing except the bare minimum in food supplies was taken. November 6 was devoted to preparation; the departure was planned for the early morning of the 7th.

At Cabanatuan the Rio Grande turns to the east. So at this point the expedition left the fickle stream which had been alternately a problem and a boon. Also at Cabanatuan the river was about 100 yards wide and of strong current. As neither a bridge nor a ferry suitable for transporting wagon transportation existed at this point, the 22nd Infantry hastily constructed a large raft and stretched a rope cable between the two banks to permit the ferrying of the troops.

Assembled on the south bank on the morning of the 7th, the command was treated to a parting slap by the malignant river. The first load consisted of two horses and fifteen men. Midway in the stream the swift current snapped the rope cable, setting the raft free and carrying it rapidly downstream. The frightened horses jumped overboard, careening the raft and spilling the men, arms, and equipment into the water. Lieutenant Thomas Hannay and three soldiers of the 22nd Infantry watching operations from the bank plunged into the river and at the imminent risk of their lives saved those who could not swim. The horses managed to gain the bank, but all equipment which had been on the raft was lost. The raft floated downstream for a mile and ran aground on a sand bar. After much tedious labor it was finally returned to the ferry, the tackle ropes replaced, and another attempt made. This was more successful, and bit by bit the command was slowly taken across. By 5:30 p. m. part of the command was still on the south bank. So General Young, impatient with the delay, mounted his horse and boldly swam the river with his heavily laden escort of thirty cavalrymen. Fortunately no one was drowned.

Anxious to accomplish more than a mere river crossing in one whole day, Young and a squadron of the 3rd Cavalry under the command of Lieutenant Colonel Henry W. Wessels pushed forward through the mud and late that night entered Talavera, nine miles to the north. The trains were unable to reach Talavera that night because of the miserable road. In some places the carts bogged down to their axles, and it was necessary to unload the ration carts and carry them by hand over bad stretches.

On the following morning, November 8, the 3rd Cavalry and the Macabebe scouts pushed forward and marched into the town of San Jose, capturing a large amount of Insurgent dispatches. Also seized were the personal effects, papers, and private cigar stock of the Insurgent General Llanera. A captured dispatch signed by Aguinaldo on November 8 directed the repair of a military road through Tayug towards Bayombong, indicating that Aguinaldo had not yet reached Bayombong, and that if Young moved quickly he might be able to block the passes.

Consequently Young determined to push forward immediately to Tayug. Colonel Hayes, with a squadron of the 4th Cavalry, was sent to Carranglen, a town in the mountains eighteen miles northeast of San Jose, while Young with one troop of cavalry and the Macabebe Battalion pushed forward towards Tayug. Orders were given to Colonel Wessels and his squadron of the 3rd Cavalry at Talavera and

Ballance's battalion of the 22nd Infantry to push forward as quickly as possible, if necessary abandoning their wheeled transportation north of San Jose.

Young's instructions to abandon wheeled traffic north of San Jose were not necessary. After a forty-eight hour rain, roads on which natives during the rainy season used primitive bamboo sledges instead of carts, were impassable to army wagons.

At a stretch where the road passed through a wood, the ration carts sank to the wagon bodies where virtually floating in the muck they fell apart under the strain of draft. As a further addition to the difficulties of the march, some forty abandoned native vehicles periodically blocked the path of the struggling column. The only ambulance in the column fell over on its side, and no one was interested enough to set it aright and take it along. After one artillery piece had virtually disappeared in the roadbed, a halt was called and a new road cut through the woods. But finally, with most of its wheeled transportation abandoned, the column emerged into the open road.

It might have been expected that from then on difficulties would disappear, but the reverse was true. At stretches where the occasional rainy-season sunshine had partially dried the road its composition merely changed from a thick, dirty soup to heavy, sticky mud. Large quantities of cogon grass which natives had thrown on the roadbed to improve traction, served only to make it a glutinous odorous mass. The troops had by this time been campaigning in the open for over a month and had been on half rations for two weeks. Wallowing through the hip-deep muck, lugging a ten-pound rifle and a belt filled with ammunition, drenched to the skin and with their feet becoming heavier with mud at each step, the infantry became discouraged. Some men simply cried, others slipped down in the mud and refused to rise. Threats and appeals by officers were of no avail. Only a promise of food in the next town and the fear that if they remained behind they would be butchered by marauding bands of Insurgents forced some to their feet to struggle on.

The road was difficult for mounted troops as well as those on foot. The slow-moving infantry column passed a troop of cavalry which had left San Jose twenty-four hours ahead. In the rain this troop had been able to make only two miles in thirty-six hours. When the column finally reached Lupao, ten miles from San Jose, virtually every wheeled vehicle had been abandoned. Henceforth the troops would be forced to live on the country.

Fortunately for Young's desire to rush through to Tayug, the battalion of Macabebe scouts and the main elements of the cavalry had passed the bad stretch of road before the forty-eight hour period of rain set in.

Reaching Lupao at 1:30 p. m. on November 10, these troops pushed on the following day to Humingen, which was captured after a fifteen minute fight with one hundred Insurgents. The 3rd Cavalry under Colonel Wessels then pushed on to Tayug, five miles distant.

The sudden thrust of the cavalry into the center of Insurgent territory had borne considerable fruit. As Wessels entered Tayug at 1:30 p. m. he captured Aguinaldo's main supply train marching to Bayombong. The booty included the printing press of the Insurgent *Herald of the Revolution,* 270,000 pounds of rice, 3000 pounds of sugar, 1000 pounds of coffee, 1000 Insurgent uniforms, 25,000 pounds of salt, 4000 ball cartridges, a large batch of Insurgent orders, and miscellaneous bits of Insurgent equipment and flags.[5]

After sending detachments into all passes in the vicinity, Young then pushed his cavalry forward towards San Manuel and Asignan in an effort to establish contact with Wheaton's force.

Within the past five days Young's force had, without supplies, marched more than fifty miles over the most difficult of roads. He had by necessity left garrisons in each town passed through, and his command was stretched to the limit. One squadron of the 4th Cavalry was in the mountains at Carranglen, one company of scouts and a cavalry guard for the trains was at San Jose; and Ballance's Battalion of the 22nd was at Lupao. The field artillery battery was stuck in the mud near Lupao. Two other squadrons of the 3rd Cavalry were escorting trains south of San Jose. The Macabebe scouts were at Humingen. One troop of cavalry was guarding the pass into the mountains at San Quentin, another at Santa Nicholas, another at San Manuel, and a fourth at Asignan. He had formed a veritable cordon around the mountain passes between Cabanatuan and San Manuel. However, as General Young said:[6] "Aguinaldo's chances of getting away west of us were good unless Wheaton connected with me."

Let us leave General Young with the advance elements of the cavalry for a moment and follow a rather interesting diversion by the infantry. The march through the mud from San Jose had nearly finished Ballance's battalion of the 22nd Infantry. By pushing every man to the limit, however, it had finally managed to get through to Humingen. There, on Young's orders, it had stopped. It was indeed in a poor plight, for blankets had been thrown away and there was no shelter at night. Many of the men's clothes had not been dry for two weeks. Constant wetness had rotted leather and stitching in shoes, and many of the men were barefoot. The majority were suffering from malarial fever and chills. Many faces were pale and emaciated, the indication of dysentery. Nearly everyone had dhobie itch in one form or another. Everyone was hungry.

On November 14 Ballance received orders to take his battalion on a flank march through Rosales, a town on the Agno River fourteen miles west of Humingen. Rosales was on the main road north from Tarlac and within fourteen miles of the Manila-Dagupan Railroad. They would very probably encounter detachments from the main Insurgent army and even possibly, as Major Ballance said, "Have to fight Aguinaldo's entire army of five or six thousand men with the three hundred in his battalion."

Shortly after the march started they found themselves opposed by Insurgent delaying forces, with the result that the column was deployed virtually the entire day. The going through the water-soaked rice fields was little better than on the San Jose-Lupao road. Moreover, the advance was held up at a small river until a bridge could be constructed for the battalion's attached artillery platoon to pass. The only available tools being a hatchet and an axe, American pioneering ingenuity was taxed to the extreme. Still, Rosales was reached that night and a large amount of rice, Insurgent uniforms and documents captured. For food the battalion was forced to eat rice and fresh carabao meat; the men slept in their wet, muddy clothes.

Rosales is situated on the Agno River, a wide unfordable stream with a swift current. In the face of numerous difficulties caused by a sudden rise in the water, Ballance managed to construct rafts and carry his troops across. Pushing on through the town of Villasis, the battalion reached Binalonan on the night of November 16. There, although ordered to push on to Porzorubio, the battalion was simply unable to make the objective as nearly all were in a state of collapse. Ballance "threw up the sponge," and then three hundred men, practically the entire strength of the battalion, went on sick report. Several were in such a bad state that they later died from the effects of the exposure to which they had been subjected. It was over a month before the battalion was available for further field service.

Returning to the cavalry, it may be recalled that Young's advance elements had reached San Manuel and Asignan on the 12th. These towns were only twenty miles from San Fabian. Word had been received via Manila that Wheaton had landed at San Fabian on the 7th, nearly a week previous, and Young felt certain that Wheaton's troops must be in the near vicinity. The cavalry had closed all passes to the mountains as far as they had come, but if access to the mountains was to be completely denied to the Insurgents, contact with Wheaton must be established. Despite the fact that his force was stretched to the limit, Young determined to push farther west.

Though he did not know where Aguinaldo was, Young's energy and initiative were rewarded by almost capturing the Insurgent President. Dr. Simeon Villa, a member of Aguinaldo's staff, kept a diary of the movements of the Insurgent presidential group and by comparison of this diary with Young's report, we are able to follow closely the movements of both elements, one attempting to escape, the other to capture.

On the night of November 13 Aguinaldo with a body guard of troops under the command of General Gregorio Del Pilar left Bayambang (not to be confused with Bayombong, his destination) by train, proceeding north. At Calasio the party detrained after having been joined by a brigade of Illocano Insurgents under the command of General Manuel Tinio. This party, which consisted of some 1500, started on foot, marched all night towards Manaog, which was reached at 4:00 the following afternoon. Aguinaldo, with his wife and sister, a small staff, and about 250 troops then continued the march towards Pozorrubio. To follow as a rear guard were about 1000 of Tinio's troops escorting the President's mother and son.

Meanwhile Young had sent on the 13th Lieutenant Thayer with a troop of cavalry west to Manaoag with orders to push through to San Fabian if such was necessary in order to establish contact with Wheaton. During the afternoon of the 13th, before Aguinaldo had left Bayambang, Thayer passed through Manaoag and continued west towards San Jacinto.

On the 14th, while Aguinaldo and his party were marching from Calasiao, Young pushed forward to Binalonan and directed Major Swigert with a squadron of the 3rd Cavalry to push on to Pozorrubio. He knew that control of Pozorrubio would block another pass north along the west side of the Benguet Mountains and might have reasonably assumed that Wheaton would have closed this pass. Swigert's guide, however, instead of heading the column to Pozorrubio followed the road to Manaoag, where at about 5:00 p. m. Swigert's column ran headlong into the head of Aguinaldo's rear guard which was moving from Manaoag to Pozorrubio. Both forces were surprised, Swigert's force was outnumbered by some 800 men, but because principally of the insistence of Lieutenant Colonel James Parker, one of Young's staff officers, the Insurgent force was charged and dispersed. Aguinaldo, meanwhile some distance ahead, was continuing on to Pozorrubio, unaware of the proximity of the American cavalry. When General Young arrived on the scene a short time later, he was disgusted to find his troops on the outskirts of Manaoag instead of Pozorrubio. As General Young said:[7] "The only reason that the guide who had led us to Manaoag instead of Pozorrubio was not shot was because he could not be found." Aguinaldo and his party proceeded to Pozorrubio where they spent the night. Early the next morning Swigert and his squadron were sent from Manaoag to Pozorrubio. After two short fights the squadron reached the outskirts of Pozorrubio about 9:00 a. m. Aguinaldo was still in the town. To quote from Dr. Villa's diary:[8]

> "At daylight it was raining. At 9:00 a. m. we received the news that the Americans were at the entrance to the town and as we had only a small force, our rear guard not having yet arrived, we at once took up the march for Alava."

Major Swigert held Aguinaldo within his grasp, but permitted the Insurgent President to leave the town and continue north. Reasons for Major Swigert's lack of energy are not particularly difficult to find. He was a graduate of West Point in the class of 1868 and after thirty years of commissioned service had reached only the grade of major. He had not received temporary advancement as had many officers by being given a volunteer commission. He was fifty-three years of age and possibly, shall we say, somewhat devoid of ambition. The day before he had engaged in a verbal altercation with Lieutenant Colonel Parker of Young's staff, who was eight years his junior in the regular army, but was temporarily senior to him by virtue of a volunteer commission. When Swigert's squadron had run headlong into Aguinaldo's rear guard, Parker had in a measure assumed command of the squadron and given the order to charge. He and Parker were at such swords' points that when his squadron was sent to Pozorrubio the following day, Parker, who was detailed to accompany it, begged off. Swigert entered Pozorrubio as Aguinaldo left, but made no effort to pursue and returned to Binalonan. Upon his return he was asked if he had heard anything about Aguinaldo and replied:[9]

"Oh yes, he was there. He left Pozorrubio as I entered."

"Why did you not pursue him?"

"I had no orders to pursue him."

General Young later told Parker that if he (Parker) had accompanied Swigert's squadron, Aguinaldo probably would have

SOLDIERS IN THE SUN

been captured. Young was bitterly disappointed and immediately issued orders for the pursuit.

Aguinaldo had escaped for the time being at least, and Otis' plan for "closing the circle" had gone awry. What had happened to Wheaton? Young's Cavalry had moved through terrain of the most difficult nature, some 120 miles, but still had not established contact with a force which had arrived at its base by boat and then apparently had not moved even ten miles away.

General Wheaton's lack of aggressiveness is difficult to understand. He had taken part in virtually every campaign since the Insurrection had commenced and had been prominent because of his aggressiveness, and even rashness. Lack of supplies was less of a problem to him than it was to Young. His troops were experienced and conditioned. Had he displayed even a modicum of initiative, Aguinaldo undoubtedly would have been captured, or at least kept out of the wild mountain regions to the north, and the pacification of the Islands with its attendant loss of both American and Filipino lives, to say nothing of the expense to the American government, would probably have been shortened by two years. The only explanation for his inaction is the possibility that he had been in contact with Otis for so long that, unlike Lawton, he had absorbed Otis' fear of any movement into hostile Insurgent country until the stage was completely set and ample supplies and troops assembled to insure methodical success. Wheaton's orders, given verbally by Otis,[10] contemplated that he would: "Sail to the Gulf of Lingayen and land at or north of San Favian, placing his command on the roads leading north and near the coast to prevent the retreat of the Insurgent army to the north along the roads or trails leading in that direction." Bare compliance with these orders indicated that Wheaton would have blocked the road leading north through Pozorrubio and Alava, but he appears to have contented himself with merely blocking the road through San Fabian. His negligence in this respect is directly responsible for Aguinaldo's escape to the north.

Wheaton's force consisted of the 13th Infantry, veterans of the debacle in Cavite in June, and the 33rd Infantry which had been recruited in Texas and was noted for the large number of expert riflemen it contained. In addition he had a platoon of artillery, a detachment of engineers, and some signal corps troops. He carried 100,000 rations, a supply sufficient to subsist his command of 2000 men for fifty days. Loaded into transports and conveyed by three navy cruisers and three gunboats, the expedition left Manila on

November 6. On November 7, while Young was leaving Cabanatuan, it arrived at Lingayen Gulf off San Fabian.

The transports anchored about a mile and a half off shore, while the three cruisers and three gunboats steamed inside the line of transports. A battalion of the 33rd and 13th Infantry each disembarked in cascos and started for the shore in the face of fire from entrenched Insurgents in front of San Fabian. The Navy ships opened up and swept the Insurgent line with a well-directed fire from their artillery pieces and automatic weapons. The two battalions landed on the flank of the entrenchments and drove the Insurgents into San Fabian without difficulty. The disembarkation of the entire command of some 2000 men was accomplished in less than two and a half hours.

On the following day reconnaissance was instituted towards Mangalden, Rosario and San Jacinto. Some 200 Insurgents near Mangalden were routed by a battalion of the 33rd Infantry under Major Peyton C. March, but except for this action no hostile groups were encountered, and upon Wheaton's orders the reconnaissance parties all returned to San Fabian. Had they occupied these towns, the story might have been different.

On the 10th Wheaton received word that some 1200 to 1600 Insurgents under the Illocano General Tinio were entrenching themselves at San Jacinto, six miles east of San Fabian. The 33rd Infantry was sent to disperse this force which it scattered at the cost of a battalion commander, Major John H. Logan and six enlisted men killed and fifteen others wounded. 134 Insurgents were killed. After the San Jacinto fight, the 33rd Infantry returned to San Fabian. Had it moved forward and occupied Manaoag two miles to the east, or even remained at San Jacinto, Aguinaldo would have had difficulty in slipping past them.

On November 14, still unaware, principally because of lack of enterprise, that Aguinaldo was evading him, Wheaton sent the 13th Infantry north to the town of Santo Tomas, with instructions to reconnoitre to Rosario. This force encountered opposition at the Rabon River and then proceeded to Santo Tomas, five miles north. Returning from Santo Tomas the following day, a battalion of the 13th Infantry was sent to reconnoitre Rosario. It left the road junction of the Santo Tomas-Rosario roads shortly past noon. It moved four miles in the direction of Rosario and then returned because Lieutenant H. T. Ferguson, in command of the battalion, "could see nothing but range after range of high hills beyond." According to the map, this battalion was within one mile of Rosario.

Had it continued into the town, it probably would have encountered Aguinaldo and his party which was moving north from Alava, and entered Rosario at 3:00 p. m.[11] that day.

And, considering the fact that Aguinaldo's wife had undergone a fainting spell and was necessarily being carried on a cot, it is very possible that had he encountered a battalion of American infantry, the Insurgent President would have very much inclined to surrender. Had Wheaton carried out his original mission of blocking the roads along the coast, Aguinaldo could not have got through. Ferguson returned to San Fabian with the remainder of the regiment that night, little knowing that Aguinaldo had been within his reach.

On the morning of the 14th Lieutenant Thayer, with twelve men of the 3rd Cavalry from Young's force, rode into San Fabian and acquainted Wheaton with the efforts which Young was making to connect with him. Two days later Wheaton took the 33rd Infantry to San Jacinto, one battalion marching via Alava and Pozorrubio. Had he made this movement on the same day that Thayer arrived at his headquarters, or even the following day, Aguinaldo would have been again blocked as he spent the night of the 14th at Pozorrubio and passed through Alava at noon of the 15th.

Wheaton's dilatoriness throughout the entire campaign appears to be inexcusable. On the 16th the 33rd Infantry clashed with the remnants of Aguinaldo's erstwhile army, which was fleeing before MacArthur's advance, and drove them toward Managaterem in the Zambales Mountains to the southwest. This force captured Felipe Buencamino, a member of Aguinaldo's cabinet, Aguinaldo's son, and his mother, all of whom had been in hiding since Young had dispersed Aguinaldo's rear guard on the 13th. Also captured were some 2000 dollars in specie. The Insurgent army was dispersed and scattered, but the big fish had escaped the net. Wheaton in a somewhat half-hearted manner permitted the troops of his brigade to be used in the pursuit of Aguinaldo, which General Young immediately instituted.

Let us turn momentarily and follow events in the front of MacArthur's division which had been pushing the main Insurgent army along the railroad. That force apparently did everything that was or could be expected of it. As with Lawton's division, the weather conspired to make the movement of supplies extremely difficult. However, since MacArthur's mission was not one of rapid movement, delays caused by bad weather and poor roads did not necessarily jeopardize the success of the combined movement of the three forces.

MacArthur's supply problem was theoretically simplified at the outset by the fact that he was moving along the railroad. This facility was, however, nullified by the Insurgent habit of destroying the railroad line as its army retreated. However, if having once started his advance, MacArthur could push them back rapidly and vigorously, they might not have time to destroy the line and the all-important bridges.

As to the date of his advance he was in no particular hurry. Both Lawton and Wheaton must be permitted to get in rear of the Insurgents before any advance could be initiated. Preparatory movements began on November 5, but the actual movement north did not commence until the 8th, the day after Young cut loose from his trains at San Jose and one day after Wheaton had landed at San Fabian.

It may be recalled that the Insurgent line ran from Porac through entrenched positions just north of Angeles, thence east about eight miles to the town of San Pedro Magalang. Magalang was situated at the foot of Mount Arayat, an extinct volcano which, like a lone sentinel, jutted 3500 feet up from the center of the comparatively flat Pampanga Plain.

Consequently, before the contemplated advance along the railroad could be safely made, the left flank of the Insurgent line at Magalang must be dispersed, if constant harassing of the American right flank was to be prevented. On November 5 a mixed force was sent to occupy Magalang. The 12th Infantry approached the town from Angeles and the 17th Infantry and two troops of the 4th Cavalry marched from Calulut. In the outskirts of the town a running fight ensued and about 1000 Insurgents under the command of General Concepcion were dispersed, some 100 being killed and wounded in the movement. Possession of Magalang by the Americans made Mabalacat the next town on the railroad to the north of Angeles decidedly vulnerable from a flanking attack.

In accordance with his plan of striking quick decisive blows once the advance had commenced, MacArthur directed that the 36th Infantry would, as soon as the town of Capas was taken, become a virtual "spearhead" of the advance with instructions to keep pushing forward and to maintain constant contact with the Insurgents.

The 36th Infantry was not picked for this mission at random. It was one of the newly constituted volunteer regiments which had been recruited in the Philippine Islands. Practically every member had belonged formerly to state volunteer regiments and had seen service against the Insurgents. In command was Colonel J. Franklin Bell, a most aggressive, enterprising officer. He had graduated from

West Point in 1878. After twenty years of commissioned service he had, because of the slow promotion system in the regular army, attained only the rank of 1st lieutenant of cavalry. In 1898, with a commission as major of volunteers, he arrived in the Philippines with Merritt's expedition. Intrepid, he had a few days after his arrival, crept to within 100 yards of the Spanish trenches on a reconnaissance and made a sketch of their position. Assigned as Division Intelligence Officer, he had repeatedly made bold and often rash reconnaissances into Insurgent territory for the purpose of obtaining information. With the formation of the 36th Infantry in July 1899 he had been given the volunteer rank of colonel and placed in command. In September, during an attack on Porac, he charged into the town in advance of his regiment and captured several Insurgents who had been too surprised to escape. A Congressional Medal of Honor had been his reward. Before the Islands were pacified, he attained the rank of major general and eventually became Chief of Staff of the Army.

From Porac, Bell's 36th Infantry, augmented by a troop of the 4th Cavalry, was to operate against the Insurgent right flank, converging towards the railroad at Capas. From San Pedro Magalang the 17th Infantry plus a platoon of field artillery and a troop of the 4th Cavalry, all under the command of Colonel Jacob Smith, was to operate against the Insurgent left flank, and from Angeles the 9th and 12th regular regiments of infantry, a battery and a half of field artillery and a company of engineers under the command of Brigadier General Joseph Wheeler were to move forward along the railroad. The 32nd Infantry, assigned to the division, was to remain in Angeles and guard the supply lines to the rear.

General Wheeler was an interesting character. A graduate of West Point in the class of 1859, he threw in his lot with the Confederate cause during the Civil War, eventually becoming the senior cavalry officer of Lee's armies. In 1881 he was elected to Congress from Alabama and held his seat until 1898. Then, the war urge coming over him, he managed to have himself appointed as Major General of Volunteers and placed in command of the dismounted Cavalry Division in the campaign in Cuba. At Las Guasimas, while Lawton's division was forming the advance guard for the movement on Santiago, he "had perceived that under cover of darkness, he could hurry his first brigade up, neatly outflank Lawton and by assaulting the Spanish position have the first battle all to himself, thus scoring a brilliant victory over the regular Infantry."[12] His premature attack caused sixty-eight American casualties and criticism of Wheeler by other officers. Later Lawton, so the story goes, flatly told Wheeler that "this was no political campaign but a military campaign."[13] The eagerness of "Fighting Joe," as he was called, to push rashly forward regardless of his orders or the military situation finally resulted in instructions from General Shafter, who commanded the expedition, to "stay where he was and attempt no more battles."[13] Following the Spanish-American War, Fighting Joe was recommissioned as a brigadier general of volunteers and sent to the Philippines. His reputation came with him, and despite the vicissitudes of MacArthur's advance to the north, the operations assume a seriocomic commentary on MacArthur's determination to keep "Fighting Joe" repressed.

The original advance on Mabalacat had been scheduled for November 8. Bell, while making a reconnaissance on the 7th, moved around the Insurgent right flank and walked into Mabalacat unopposed. He returned to Angeles that night with the information. The Insurgents north of Angeles having withdrawn during the night, the "attack" the division made the next day, November 8, consisted principally of a road march along the destroyed railroad between Angeles and Mabalacat. Wheeler's Brigade entered Mabalacat at 9:00 a. m.

Though it started so auspiciously, the advance of the division was threatened by two unforeseen obstacles. The first was a series of heavy rains, unprecedented for that period of the year, and which turned normally fordable streams into raging torrents, washed away river banks and even the railroad track. The second was a rather efficient bit of bridge destruction which the Insurgents had accomplished over the Paruao River, just south of Bamban, a town four miles north of Mabalacat. This railroad bridge was some thirty feet high and contained four seventy-foot spans. The bridge piers were metal tubes filled with concrete. One span and its piers had been blown down and were resting on the river bed, one other pier was destroyed, and a third had fallen about two feet. To complicate the situation, the Insurgents had run seven locomotives and seventeen cars from the destroyed abutments on the north bank of the river into the river twenty feet below. An eighth engine had run off the track on the partially destroyed bridge and was lodged there.

The repair of this bridge, normally within the abilities of the engineers, was rendered particularly difficult by lack of suitable repair material. Large timbers which were necessary for the construction of temporary piers were simply not available in that part of the country. If the division was forced to stop while the bridge was being repaired, the purpose of the whole campaign would be destroyed. Consequently MacArthur accepted the fact that there would be a break in the railroad at this point and made plans to ferry supplies over the normally fordable Paruao River.

He stopped at Mabalacat two days, moving supplies forward and reconnoitering to the north and on both flanks. On the left, near what is today the Fort Stotsenburg artillery range, Bell and a reconnaissance group of eighteen men met and charged 100 entrenched Insurgents, killing and wounding twenty-nine, capturing six prisoners and thirty rifles. On the right flank Colonel Jacob Smith and the 17th Infantry reconnoitered the muddy roads towards Capas, fourteen miles north of Mabalacat.

On the 11th the Paruao River had fallen sufficiently to be fordable and the advance was resumed, the next immediate object being the town of Capas.

MacArthur had planned to have Bell and Smith, moving along the flanks of the division, enter Capas from the west and east respectively. Wheeler was directed to "demonstrate" along the railroad with the hope that the Insurgents would not retreat so fast that their force would melt away completely.

A "demonstration" was not "Fighting Joe's" idea of the mission to be assigned his brigade. He thought that he should be permitted to "attack"[14] and so advised MacArthur. The suggestion was adamantly refused by the division commander.

On the 11th Smith and the 17th Infantry moving through the town of Concepcion and Bell advancing through the hills to the west, entered Capas without difficulty. Their worst obstacles had been the swollen streams and wretched roads.

In Wheeler's brigade more interesting events occurred. In accordance with division orders, the brigade moved forward from Mabalacat with three battalions of the 9th and 12th Infantry in advance. On the north bank of the Paruao River the Insurgents had constructed a strong line of entrenchments, and again "Fighting Joe's" impetuousness got him into difficulty with the division commander.[15]

MacArthur had directed Wheeler to demonstrate only towards the Insurgent trenches. However, when his advance elements came under fire, Wheeler deployed his brigade and ordered it to charge. Seeing the situation, MacArthur sent a messenger to Wheeler directing him that he report to him in person immediately. Wheeler rode at a dead gallop to the division command post, where MacArthur told him to recall the line of skirmishers and send only a few scouts up to the river bank. Wheeler saluted, mounted his horse, and galloped back to the firing line. There, despite the definite instructions he had just received, he ordered his entire line forward across the river. The brigade became disorganized in the crossing and, as it followed the retreating Insurgents through the town of Bamban, became more scattered and disorganized. Out of hand entirely, Wheeler and his brigade had advanced two miles before another messenger from the division commander could locate him and again direct him to report to General MacArthur in person.

What MacArthur said to Wheeler in this instance is not recorded; doubtless it was uncomplimentary. Probably had not the Federal administration been sponsoring a "boys of the blue and gray fighting under the same flag" idea, Wheeler would have been relieved of his command. The brigade was finally rounded up and marched back into Bamban; the remainder of the division marched on into Capas. On the following day "Fighting Joe" was directed to keep his brigade in the rear and supervise the movement of the supply trains.

On November 12, despite a heavy rain which immobilized the supply trains, Bell's 36th Infantry was sent forward to Tarlac. Pushing through the mud, Bell's force entered the town the same night, only to find it deserted and, better yet, the railroad line from Capas north, intact. Also, in Tarlac Bell's men had found forty partially burned freight cars and 2500 rails. Two miles to the north reconnaissance groups located four disabled locomotives.

Unknown to MacArthur, Aguinaldo and his few remaining loyal commanders had on this date held a council of war at Bayambang, a town on the railroad some twenty-six miles north of Tarlac. There they decided that further united Insurgent resistance was useless, and the only alternative was to break up into small bodies and engage in the guerrilla warfare which had been their last resort in the Insurrection of 1896. Aguinaldo, with a small group of followers, moved towards the mountains to the north where, as has been related, he was nearly captured by Young's troops. Generals Concepcion and Alexandrino, who had been opposing MacArthur's advance, moved into the Zambales Mountains to the west. From this time on MacArthur encountered no Insurgent resistance.

The wagon road between Capas and Tarlac was, to quote MacArthur, "Indescribably bad," in fact so bad that despite the fact that he possessed no engines which would function, the railroad was resorted to as the only means of supplying the division. As a substitute for locomotives he organized a "pusher train" consisting of relays of natives, 100 in a group, spread along the track. These groups pushed the cars and thus formed the supply link between Capas and Tarlac.

Despite the disappearance of Insurgent opposition, it appeared as though nature was once again conspiring with the Insurgents to delay the advance of the American troops. On November 15 ten inches of rain fell within twenty-four hours. So sudden and violent was the storm that the Tarlac River, three miles north of the town, overflowed its banks and actually cut a new channel, half a mile wide.

About 2000 feet of railroad track was submerged under two to three feet of water and, at the north end of the washout, 250 feet of track and roadbed were completely gone. It was impossible to ford either men or pack animals. This condition effectively blocked further advance until the flood should recede. On the same day that Young was stepping on Aguinaldo's heels some sixty miles north, MacArthur wired Otis:[16]

"It seems to me this washout here is a crisis in the campaign, and if this problem can be successfully solved we will stand a very good chance of finishing the war within a week as far as the organized forces are concerned north of the Pasig."

Fortunately the rains stopped the following day and on the 17th six hundred picked men of the 36th Infantry, two hundred and fifty of the 17th, fifty cavalrymen, and a pack train carrying six days rations were able to cross the washout in improvised rafts. Gerona was entered that day while the cavalry, under Lieutenant Slavens, pushed forward to Paniqui, fourteen miles north of Tarlac.

At Paniqui four locomotives were found collided on the railroad track, and thirteen cars in good condition were secured. Information was also received that Bayambang thirteen miles further along the railroad had been occupied by American troops, probably from Lawton's command. A native scout sent forward reported the railroad intact into Bayambang.

The battalion of infantry which was loaded on the train found at Paniqui entered Bayambang on the 19th and continued to Calasiao seventeen miles further that night. At Calasiao it was determined that the track was destroyed to its terminus at Dagupan, five miles further. Insurgent resistance along the railroad had died.

Back with the supply trains at Bamban, "Fighting Joe" was champing at the bit. On November 11 MacArthur had directed that the trains be moved to Capas on the following day, adding "an unusually early start is not necessary as the artillery is stalled by an impassable stream." Exactly what an "unusually early start" in the morning might be is not clear. At any rate, under "Fighting Joe's" orders, the brigade and the drivers of the supply wagons stood reveille at 3:30 a. m. and moved out at 4:30, only to be stopped by the exasperated MacArthur and forced to stand fast until 9:00 a. m.

On the following day the "pusher" railroad train having been organized between Capas and Tarlac, "Fighting Joe" was authorized to march his brigade into the latter town. Unrepressed, Lee's ex-cavalry leader marched his infantry brigade into Tarlac with a speed which would have been creditable for mounted troops. Despite his sixty-one years, "Fighting Joe" gave his horse to a sick man, carried the rifle of another sick man, and, marching at the head of the column, made the twelve and one-half mud-heavy miles to Tarlac in four hours. Arriving there he begged MacArthur to let him push on and attack an Insurgent force reported at Gerona. MacArthur told him he would stay at Tarlac and assist in getting supplies over the Tarlac River washout.

"Fighting Joe's" energy is to be applauded. The following day he and a staff officer waded through the washout for a distance of over a mile. There, encountering a place where a bridge was submerged under eight feet of water, this brigadier general took off his clothes and dove in in order to "personally determine whether the iron rails still adhered to the stringers of the bridge." From this point, for a distance of 250 feet, the washout was unwadable. Wheeler personally directed the construction of an improvised bamboo bridge over the gap and then, working his infantrymen all night, pushed 25,000 rations across the washout in fourteen hours.

Feeling that he had done his duty in the rear areas, the following day Wheeler addressed a message to MacArthur, intimating that if he was being held back from "active service" because he was an ex-Confederate such was not the idea of the President of the United States.[17] MacArthur replied:[18] "Do not attempt to move forward until further orders. No enemy in front between here and Bayambong and none in that town." Joe was henceforth doomed to inactivity.

On the 20th MacArthur, who had moved forward to Bayambang,

received information that the remnant of the Insurgent force which had opposed him had retreated to the west into the Zambales Mountains, intending there to institute a system of guerrilla warfare. The same day, Dagupan, the terminus of the railroad was reached and occupied by American troops, thus placing the entire line of the road in American hands. It had taken the American troops ten months to secure control of the 120 miles of railroad line stretching from Manila to Dagupan.

On November 23 MacArthur sent this wire to Otis:[19]

"The so-called Filipino Republic is destroyed. The congress has dissolved. The President of the so-called republic is a fugitive as are all his cabinet officers, except one who is in our hands. The Army itself as an organization has disappeared. . . . . In this view how would it do to issue a proclamation at an early date, offering complete amnesty to all who surrender within a stated time, with a payment of 30 pesos to every soldier who gives up a rifle and declaring with emphasis that after the date fixed, the killing of American soldiers will be regarded as murder and that all persons concerned therein would be regarded as murderers and treated accordingly. Such a proclamation would have the effect of forcing the generals to consider the expediency of continuing a hopeless struggle which would commit them irrevocably to death or to lifelong expatriation and I think would have a powerful influence at a time when it is apparent that most if not all of the leaders are more or less doubtful of what course to pursue."

MacArthur hoped that if the killing of an American soldier made the perpetrators guilty of the crime of murder, it would prevent the guerrilla warfare which was in the offing. But Otis decided that the time was not ripe for an amnesty. As he said:[20] "The enemy had a formidable army in southern Luzon and maintained many strong armed organizations in the immediate neighborhood of Manila and in the southern Islands. Besides the Insurgents at this time had in captivity some twenty American soldiers and more than 5000 Spanish subjects, upon whom they would retaliate should we publicly proclaim an intended enforcement of the law in all its rigor." However it was agreed that the matter of paying $30 (Mex.) for each rifle surrendered should be urgently pressed.

Meanwhile MacArthur's troops were still busy. On November 28 Bell, with the 36th Infantry reconnoitering in the Zambales Mountains near the town of Managataem about ten miles west of Bayambong, surprised the last remnants of the Insurgent Army, remnants that had assembled there under Generals San Miguel and Alexandrino for the purpose of establishing a base for guerrilla raids into the Pampanga Valley. Bell scattered them in all directions and captured what few "war" materials still remained in their hands. The captured supplies included several quick-firing modern Krupp cannon, thousands of pounds of lead and copper sheeting, large supplies of clothing, engineering tools, and food supplies.[21] Bell then continued west and occupied the town of Santa Cruz on the west coast of Luzon.

"Fighting Joe" who, with his brigade, had been forced to "cool his heels" south of Paniqui, was finally permitted to make a reconnaissance of the mountains to the west. He failed to encounter hostility from the apparently peaceful natives.

The effects of the guerrilla warfare being instituted by the Filipinos manifested itself immediately. At Mabalacat, only ten days after MacArthur's division had passed through, four soldiers of the 9th Infantry, which was garrisoning the town, wandered into the surrounding barrios in "search of some chickens." When about four miles from the town they were suddenly surrounded by some fifty or sixty armed Filipinos who commenced to fire on them. In the ensuing fight three Filipinos were killed, four wounded and one American soldier killed and the other three captured. The dead American was mutilated by bolos and the three prisoners hurried off to a small barrio on the slope of Mount Arayat. There for six weeks they were subjected to numerous indignities by the Insurgents. A favorite amusement of the Filipinos appeared to be to step up to a prisoner and snap a cocked pistol in his face, the prisoner not knowing whether or not it was loaded. A Macabebe prisoner had his throat cut before their eyes. Their sole diet was rice, sometimes interspersed with a small amount of salmon. In a short time they became so weak and emaciated that they could barely stand. In January the camp which was occupied by some 600 Insurgents was attacked by a detachment of the 25th Infantry. As the American troops approached the camp the prisoners were lined up, forced to kneel, and shot by a Filipino firing squad. As the Americans entered the camp the Insurgents hacked the wounded Americans with bolos as a parting gesture. Strange to say two of the Americans survived the horrible incident, though critically injured, and were able to give an account of their ordeal.[22]

As far as MacArthurs' division was concerned, the active insurrection was ended and the pacification of the Islands became a problem of occupation. The situation is perhaps best summed by MacArthur, who sent the following message to Otis:[23]

> "The time has arrived for the movement of several columns west from the railroad to the China Sea. . . . . I would proceed rapidly to a general cleanup of Zambales and Bataan wherein are now located the fragments of that part of the Insurgent army which was formerly in my immediate front. In the first place I should start a column from O'Donnel (seven miles west of Capas) to move directly west to Botolon or Iba, the movement to be connected by water through a small ship to arrive at designated point, simultaneously with the troops. . . . . Another column not to exceed 500 men to be assembled at Florida Blanca (about twenty miles west of San Fernando) from thence to pass into Bataan as far south as Balanga and therefrom returning to Llana Hermosa and from thence to Subig. For purpose of cooperation, communication and supply another ship should be placed in the vicinity of Orani and Balanga and proceed at the proper time to Subig and meet the column at that place."

Otis approved and during December the proposed march was made under the command of Brigadier General F. D. Grant, detachments from the 3rd and 32nd Infantry marching from Florida Blanca and 400 men of the 25th Infantry (colored) marching across the Zambales Mountains from O'Donnel. Although on one occasion the 25th Infantry became so short of food that it was forced to shoot wild monkeys for meat, the supply situation was generally ably solved by having naval vessels touch at the various towns along the coast of Zambales province. Frequent skirmishes resulted in the death of twenty Insurgents, the wounding of twenty-one, the capture of fifty-two prisoners, sixty-five rifles, over 8,000 rounds of ammunition, one hundred cattle, twenty-five ponies, and the release of several Spanish prisoners held by the Insurgents. The provinces of Zambales and Bataan were occupied and, nominally at least, brought under American control.

4

Let us return to General Young, whom we left at Binalonan on November 14, having just missed capturing Aguinaldo. Young's troops were scattered from Cabanatuan to San Fabian. His cavalry was exhausted, and the majority of the horses were unshod. Anxious, however, to take up the quick pursuit of Aguinaldo, he rushed couriers to Colonel Wessels at Tayug directing him to send all cavalry capable of movement to Binalonan immediately. Another message was sent to Major Ballance and Major Batson, who were at Villasis, each with a battalion of the 22nd Infantry and the Macabebe scouts, respectively, to come forward as soon as possible. The Macabebes responded instantly and on the 16th pushed on to Pozorrubio, seventy-four hours behind Aguinaldo. Ballance's battalion reached Binalonan but simply could not go any farther and was ordered to San Fabian, where practically the entire command collapsed. On the 17th Young and Captain Chase's troop of the 3rd Cavalry following the Macabebes, received definite information that Aguinaldo had moved north through Alava and Rosario. Young determined to follow if for no other reason than to "prevent the uniting of the scattered commands and follow up those having prisoners in their charge and to release all of them."

Leaving Chase at Pozorrubio to obtain sugar, coffee and salt, Young and the battalion of Macabebes pushed north to Alava and Rosario. Young's temerity must be admired. He was some 142 miles north of Manila with a lone battalion of about 300 native troops. He was advancing without any arrangements being made for supplies into an unknown country never before occupied by the Americans. The troops accompanying him had for the past month been engaged almost daily in skirmishes with Insurgents and had moved over the most difficult of roads without adequate food supplies. Certainly the Macabebes were well repaying the confidences which the Americans had reposed in them. Before leaving on the venture, Young sent the following message to Otis, perhaps with a grim bit of satisfaction:[24]

> "Aguinaldo is now a fugitive and an outlaw, seeking security in escape to the mountains or by sea. My cavalry has ridden down his forces wherever found utterly routing them in every instance, capturing and liberating many prisoners and destroying arms, ammunition, and other war impedimenta. Aguinaldo is accompanied by his wife and several other women, also by Generals Pilar and Tinio with about 150 soldiers. I shall renew pursuit with Chase's troop and the Macabebes. The route of the fugitives is through Alava, Rosario and probably through Tubao to Benguet province. My men have had no supplies from the government for the past five days. Many of them are barefooted, hatless and coatless, but their hearts are all right. The Navy should examine all ports from San Fernando (Province of La Union) northward. Please inform Major General Lawton, as floods prevent my communicating with him by courier."

Unquestionably Otis never would have sanctioned such an expedition, but Young was completely out of control by telegraph.

On November 18 Young and the Macabebes pushed north to Rosario, sixty hours after Aguinaldo's departure, and there found some of Aguinaldo's abandoned carts. Then they pushed on to

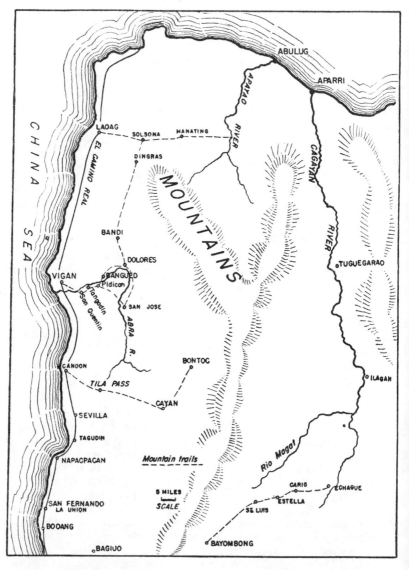

Tubao, following such a difficult mountain trail that two horses and one man were disabled.

On the 19th, feeling that his force "was too small to allow any

concentration of the enemy," Young sent this message to Lawton: "I need additional forces but cannot wait. A battalion of light Infantry which can march rapidly without impedimenta should follow on my trail, with an officer in command who will push for all he is worth."

From Tubao Young followed the trail for Aringay, a coastal town some eight miles distant, and at dusk was forced to disperse Insurgents entrenched on the outskirts of the town. Lieutenant Batson in command of the Macabebes was wounded and one Macabebe soldier killed in the engagement. Lieutenant Dennis Quinlan, in command of a Macabebe company, was hit over the heart by a bullet and his life saved by a plug of chewing tobacco which he carried there.

On the 20th, leaving a small party at Aringay to guard the sick and wounded which were perforce left behind, the small command pushed up the Camino Real towards San Fernando La Union, capital of La Union Province and a seaport of some importance. Near the town of Booang, Young was able to establish flag communication with the U. S. Navy gunboat *Samar*. The boat was requested to assist in the attack on San Fernando, which it did effectively, permitting Young's troops to disperse some 300 Insurgents there with little difficulty. From San Fernando reconnaissance was initiated towards Naguillian, a town in the mountains some six miles east. Information was received that Aguinaldo had left Naguillian two nights previously. Actually, as indicated in Dr. Villa's diary, Aguinaldo had left Naguillian at midnight of the 19th and had passed through San Fernando on the morning of the 20th. He then proceeded north along the coast to the vicinity of Napacpacan, twenty miles distant, where he remained until the 21st. Young, at San Fernando, was closer to his quarry than he realized.

Meanwhile, to quote Young:[25] "The situation was perplexing; my cavalry was crippled for want of shoes; the Macabebes were disheartened at the loss of their beloved leader Batson, and many were sick and footsore."

Hearing that a battalion of the 33rd Infantry from Wheaton's force had entered Aringay, eight miles in his rear, Young sent orders for this battalion to follow in his trail in the quickest possible manner. This battalion started to follow him but was intercepted at Booang, and upon Wheaton's orders returned to San Fabian.

Young had received information that Aguinaldo intended to continue up the coast into Abra Province, where it was intimated that the American prisoners in the hands of the Insurgents, as well as some 4000 Spanish prisoners, were being held.

On November 21 Young sent the following message to Wheaton, who was still at San Fabian:[26]

"My forces are much depleted and worn out. Aguinaldo has been playing hide and seek. One day in the mountains, the next day he or some of his generals on the coast road. . . . . Am sorry that you found it necessary to recall Faison. The Infantry force promised has not arrived. . . . . Aguinaldo is an outlaw and fugitive in the Mountains and can be caught with fresh troops. If you can assist me in this matter, I don't see how he can escape."

In another effort to cut off Aguinaldo's escape from the rear, Young sent Colonel Parker of his staff aboard the gunboat *Samar* to proceed to San Fabian and attempt to obtain at least a company of infantry which could be taken to Vigan on the coast some ninety miles north of San Fernando. If this force were landed at Vigan it could operate from the north and possibly cut Aguinaldo off from that direction. Parker went to San Fabian on the *Samar* and there found that a battalion of the 33rd Infantry under Major March was already enroute to San Fernando.

Wheaton refused to release any more troops. Disheartened, Parker noticed that the U. S. battleship *Oregon* lay at anchor off San Fabian. He paid Commander Wilde of the *Oregon* a courtesy call and in the course of the conversation suggested that she accompany the *Samar* back to San Fernando. Wilde consented and Parker decided that if the army refused to furnish soldiers for the venture to Vigan, he would call upon the navy for assistance.

Upon his return to San Fernando, accompanied by the *Oregon* and the gunboat *Callao,* Parker found March's battalion already there. Although armed with instructions from Young that he would assume command of whatever troops he was able to obtain, either in direct command if he were senior or as a staff officer giving orders in Young's name if he were junior, he found Major March unsympathetic to the proposed expedition to Vigan. Parker was March's senior by some twelve years in the regular army and held higher rank by virtue of his commission in the volunteers. However, March flatly refused to follow Parker's orders on the basis that his organization was a part of Wheaton's command and therefore not subject to the orders of General Young. After what Parker called a "sharp discussion" a written demand by Parker was answered by a written refusal on March's part and Parker was forced to leave on his expedition without any troops. Professional jealousy is the only answer to March's attitude, for when he established contact with General Young's forces the following day he obeyed Young's orders with alacrity.

Undiscouraged, Parker boarded the *Samar* and accompanied by the *Callao* and the *Oregon,* steamed towards Vigan.

The capture of Vigan, 213 miles from Manila, by the navy under Parker's auspices was both amusing and interesting. Until Young had started his rapid march north, no Americans except prisoners had been within 150 miles of the place. On the morning of November 26 the *Samar* approached the shore opposite the town and received fire from Insurgent entrenchments. This was the provocation the navy sought. The *Oregon* opened up on Vigan with one of her 13-inch guns and several "six-inchers." The *Callao* and *Samar* fired their 3-inch and Gatling guns. One of the navy officers remarked to Parker that "he guessed the old man will shoot until he has used up his annual allowance. He hasn't had any target practice this year."[27]

The effect of this bombardment is vividly described by an American prisoner who was in Vigan at the time:[28]

"We had been conversing when suddenly a loud report startled us all. Again it came and then boom—boom—boom. Rushing to the balcony we saw soldiers flying helter skelter up the street. Suddenly there came a report that shook the building and a shell hissed over the town, exploding in the jungle between Bantay and Vigan. A second explosion seemed to rend the universe to pieces and again a terrific whirling and screeching overhead brought a shriek from a hundred voices outside. In a group stood all the civil officials, both Provincial and municipal, the local president, the governor, the chief justice, the tax collector and the chief of police. A third shell was fired over the town causing the governor and all his councilmen apparently to leap several feet in the air. Just then the earth again seemed to split under us and the limb of a large tree growing within two hundred yards of us was neatly cut off, the shell burying itself six feet in the ground without exploding fortunately. . . . . As we learned later in the day, three persons were killed."

With due credit to the navy it should be said that Commander Wilde had no intention of bombarding the non-combatant inhabitants of Vigan. The shells which were fired were purposely laid at what was intended to be harmless ranges.

Following the "bombardment" a detachment of sailors and marines landed on the beach and proceeded towards the town, two miles distant. Parker had also managed to get ashore and, following up the landing party, found it halted while its commander gave instructions in advance-guard and patrol duty. Accompanied only by four sailors, Parker went on ahead and entered the town, being received with cheers and the ringing of bells. Native explanation of the friendly reception was that Illocanos were glad to be freed from Insurgent domination. Perhaps the big guns of the *Oregon* had prompted the attitude. At any rate, the navy took over formal occupation. Two days later a company of the 33rd Infantry, which General Young had dug up at San Fernando, arrived on the gunboat *Callao* and took over from the navy. A few days later 113 more men under the command of Major Marcus Cronin also arrived. After an argument with Cronin as to who was in command, culminating in the threat by Parker to place Cronin in irons,[29] Parker took charge of the prosperous city of 20,000 inhabitants.

Returning to General Young whom we left at San Fernando, we find that he was joined by Major Swigert, who marched along the coast road after having had his horses re-shod at San Fabian. On the 23rd, with three troops of cavalry and the 75 remaining effective Macabebes, he marched to Napacpacan, twenty-five miles to the north. There he received information that the Insurgent General Tinio had gathered together a force of some 1700 men for the purpose of opposing further movement north. Young sent another urgent message to Wheaton asking him to send troops to his assistance. As we know, Major March's battalion of the 33rd Infantry had already been sent.

On November 26 March's battalion joined Young and was sent forward to garrison the town of Tagudin, four miles further along the coast. Young and the cavalry moved six miles north to Sevilla and on the 28th to Candon. Young had found that the mass of people along his route of advance showed strong demonstrations of friendship and welcome to the American troops. Their attitude was the same as that of the inhabitants of Vigan. They stated that they had been robbed by the Insurgent troops and welcomed occupation of the country by the Americans.

On November 28 Young obtained a captured letter which indicated that Aguinaldo was at Anagui and that Tinio, who held twenty American and some 4000 Spanish prisoners in the mountains of Abra Province, was fortifying a position in the rugged hills at Tangadin.

Being reinforced on December 1 by a battalion of the 34th Infantry under Colonel Howze, Young decided to send March's battalion into the mountains towards Anagui in the trail of Aguinaldo and to continue north himself along the coast road, destroy Tinio's force at Tangadin, and effect, if possible, the release of the prisoners which Tinio held.

Moving into the mountains November 30 March's battalion passed through Concepcion and marched to Tila Pass, where it exterminated Aguinaldo's Tagalog bodyguard and nearly captured the Insurgent President. To quote from March's report:[30]

"The trail was very narrow, the entire command having to proceed in single file up the mountains. Tila Pass is 4400 feet high and the rise is extremely rapid. The enemy had constructed a stone barricade across the trail where it commands the turns of the zigzag for a considerable distance. The advance was checked by heavy fire from this barricade which killed and wounded several men. It was evident that the position could not be taken by a frontal attack, when the trail only allowed the men to pass one at a time. On the left of the barricade was a gorge several hundred feet deep. On its right was a precipitous mountain which rose 1500 feet above the trail. I ordered Lieutenant Tompkins to take his company, move along a slight ridge which struck the face of the mountain about 150 feet from the summit. From there he had a straight up climb to the top where the men pulled themselves up by twigs and by hand. The ascent took two hours during which time the enemy kept up an incessant and accurate fire which they varied by rolling down stones on our heads. When Tompkins appeared upon the crest of the hills above their heads, I charged the barricade and rushed the enemy over the hill. We found eight bodies on the trail among which was that of General Gregorio Del Pilar, Commanding General of the Insurgent forces. The Insurgent loss was 52. My loss was two killed and nine wounded. I reached the summit at 4:30 p. m. and camped there for the night, finding at that point a large amount of rice, etc."

From their positions in the mountains, the Insurgents had watched the American advance since it had left Concepcion. General Gregorio Del Pilar, a youth of 22 years, who was killed in this fight, became a hero to many Filipinos and a large monument has been erected to his memory at Calumpit.

Aguinaldo, who had been resting at Cervantes, about fifteen miles southeast of Tila Pass, received word of Del Pilar's defeat and death at 5:00 the same afternoon. He immediately decamped and set out for the village of Cayan farther east in the mountains. He reached there at midnight and continued his hegira northeast towards Bontoc.

On the morning following his fight at Tila Pass, March heard that Aguinaldo was at Cervantes (Cayan) and continued on. Let Major March tell the story:[31]

"Aguinaldo was reported at Cervantes so I made a forced

march to that place 28 kilometers from the summit, arriving at Cervantes at 6:30 p. m. (Aguinaldo had left the place nearly twenty-fours hours previous). I spent the 4th resting and sifting evidence of his whereabouts. All large numbers of Spanish prisoners were abandoned and from their tales, I located him as passing through Cayan at 2:00 a. m. on the 3rd. I set out on the 5th for Cayan with a picked force of 100 men and officers who were the least exhausted from their long march and the fighting. The road immediately begins to ascend and goes straight up until a height of 9000 feet is reached. Upon arriving at Cayan, General Venancio Concepcion, Aguinaldo's Chief of Staff surrendered and was sent back to Cervantes. A number of the men were now exhausted by the climb to Cayan so I weeded out the command again and set out after Aguinaldo with eighty-six men. I had been living off the country and now got into a country which produces very little besides yams and in which the marching was extremely severe. However, I pushed on to near Bontoc where I learned that Aguinaldo had gone through three days before. He was gaining on me with fresh ponies and bearers and with his party unencumbered. I therefore rounded up the Spanish prisoners throughout the region and returned to Cervantes. The number of prisoners released was 575, including 150 friars."

March's expedition had destroyed the last vestige of Aguinaldo's Tagalog Army and had sent him dashing through the mountains like a hunted animal. The expedition indicated the difficulties that would be encountered in playing a game of hide and seek with the erstwhile Insurgent President in the Benguet Mountains.

Returning to Young, who was determined to destroy Tinio's force and effect the release of the American prisoners, we see that by December 3 he had been re-inforced by Penn's battalion of the 34th Infantry and had moved along the coast road to Narvacan, some twelve miles south of Vigan. On the same day, Otis had relieved Lawton of the command of the troops in the north and sent him on an expedition against the Insurgents, who had again assembled southeast of San Miguel de Mayumo. On that date Lawton sent the following message to Young:

"Wheaton has relieved me at Tayug; you must look out for yourself from this time. Hope you will find as good a chief quartermaster as I have been. Good luck and best wishes for you and your command."

When Lawton left, Young lost a most loyal and sympathetic superior.

Young's fighting force now consisted of 145 infantrymen and 115 cavalrymen. At midnight of December 3 he received definite information from a native that Tinio with 1200 men was building an elaborate system of defensive works at Tangadin, a narrow pass in the gorge of the Abra River, about six miles east of Figan. It was rumored that the prisoners were being kept at Bangued, five miles beyond this pass. Despite the inequality in numbers Young decided to attack Tinio immediately.

The idea of 260 weary and poorly equipped troops, over eighty miles from the nearest reinforcements, attacking 1200 securely entrenched Insurgents in a difficult mountain defile would have given Otis a nightmare had he been conversant with the situation. However, Young went on and marched towards Tangadin.

The Illocano, General Manual Tinio, was of different stamp than the majority of Insurgent generals. He knew that Young was marching towards him with the intent of releasing the prisoners. He had, as reported, built a strongly fortified position at Tangadin. Knowing that the American garrison at Vigan consisted of Colonel Parker with about 100 effectives, he decided to make a night raid on that town before Young could either attack him or reinforce the small garrison at Vigan.

On the night of December 3 while Young was marching on Tinio's defenses at Tangadin, Tinio sent 400 men on boats down the Abra River to attack Vigan. The Americans quartered in public buildings facing the main plaza of the town, awoke to find that Insurgents were pouring a hot fire on their quarters, Parker's men fell out of their beds, grabbed their rifles, and returned the fire. In a short time the city plaza was swept with a storm of bullets from both sides. After two hours the Americans located their assailants' exact positions in the darkness and prepared to rush the buildings they occupied. The charge of Parker's men was repulsed, and the attackers were forced to take cover in shrubbery only thirty-five yards from the muzzles of hostile rifles. As dawn broke the fight developed into a sniping contest, and with daylight the Insurgents became discouraged and melted away. The Americans had held the town, but at a cost of eight killed and three wounded. Sixty-five Insurgent dead were found in the plaza, their wounded as usual being carried away. Colonel Parker later recommended that every member of the command be awarded a Congressional Medal, but actual awards were limited to himself and Private James B. McConnell.

While Colonel Parker was chasing the raiding force out of Vigan, General Young's small group reached Tinio's fortified position at Tangadin. As he approached the position Young realized that it was indeed a strong one. Located on the slope of a bald knob, it contained line after line of entrenchments. Midway up the hill was an earthen redoubt of the Vauban type, containing lunettes and covered ways. On the summit of the knob was another redoubt, flanked by trenches. Had Young possessed artillery his attack would have been simplified. With only a small force of infantry and cavalry, however, he realized that a direct attack on the position would have been disastrous. The only solution was to "flank the Insurgents out." To the north of the defenses was another hill, the crest of which was somewhat higher than the summit of the knob. Young sent two companies of the 34th Infantry on a flank march with instructions to climb the hill and attack the Insurgents from that direction. The remainder of the force sat down and waited for the flanking party to reach its position.

The march of the two companies of the 34th Infantry to the top of the hill was replete with difficulties. No trail up the steep incline existed and the men were forced to cut their way through the thick tropical underbrush. After four hours of exhausting effort, the group was still far from the top and men began falling out from exhaustion. The entire group then worked its way down several hundred feet to a small canyon where they obtained water. Finally at sundown, after eight hours of weary effort, the group reached the summit. There, though separated from the Insurgents by an impassable gorge, they were about 1000 yards away from the Insurgent position, and could look down into the Insurgent trenches.

Meanwhile General Young had became worried as to the condition of the flanking force and sent a dismounted troop of cavalry to ascertain its situation. His force was now split in half and had the 1000 odd Insurgents in the entrenched position attacked the group in their front they would have been opposed only by about 125 men. Young realized this and was therefore much relieved when he was joined at 4:00 in the afternoon by a battalion of the 33rd Infantry which had made a forced march from Candon to join his force.

When the flanking force began firing from above and slightly to their rear the Insurgents began to evacuate the trenches and when Young's main force charged up the slope another "impregnable" position was taken without a casualty.

On the following morning a battalion of the 34th Infantry under the command of Lieutenant Colonel Robert Howze and Lieutenant Colonel Luther Hare's battalion of the 33rd Infantry were assigned the mission of following up Tinio's retreating forces and to effect if possible the release of the American prisoners. General Young and the cavalry marched to Vigan.

5

The march of the two battalions of infantry through the wild Benguet Mountains on the trail of the American prisoners is one of the outstanding feats of American arms. Under the command of Colonel Hare the column proceeded to San Quentin, where 50,000 pounds of Insurgent rice were found and destroyed. Also a report was received that the American prisoners were at Bangued, five miles further in the mountains. Hare rested his command and then, leaving his fires burning as a ruse, left for Bangued at 2:00 a. m. The town of Pidican was reached at 6:00 in the morning and Hare received information from the 800 odd Spanish prisoners, who found their way to this camp, that the Insurgents were moving south to the town of San Jose. Howze and the battalion of the 34th were sent on to Bangued, and Hare, with the battalion of the 33rd, moved southeast towards San Jose, thirty-eight miles distant.

Covering the thirty-eight hilly miles to San Jose in two marches, Hare to his disappointment learned that the trail had been false and that the Insurgents had moved north through the mountains rather than south. He immediately turned north and moved along the Abra River, intending to catch Howze's battalion if possible. At the town of Dolores he received a message from Howze that he was on the trail of the Insurgents and that they had the American prisoners with them. Taking 100 picked men, Hare moved north with all possible dispatch through the mountain villages of Bandi, Dingras, and Solsona following Howze's trail. On the 13th he managed to catch up with Howze's column.

Comparing notes with Colonel Hare, Howze reported that he had entered Bangued on December 6 where he had received information that the American prisoners had left Bangued two days previous and had been taken to either the town of Dolores or La Paz. Howze followed a hunch and took the mountain trail to La Paz where he was rewarded by meeting three Americans who had escaped in the confusion incident to the flight of Tinio's force. These three were L. R. Edwards, a U. S. Navy landsman who had been captured with Lieutenant Gillmore's landing party at Baler the previous April; William Bruce of the 1st Nevada Cavalry who wandering away from Manila on a pay-day pass in February, 1899, had been arrested by the Insurgents and detained until after the battle of Manila at which time he became the Insurgents' "Exhibit A" as an "American prisoner of War"; and an English civilian, J. O'Brien, whose persistence in attempting to extort a gold mining concession from the Insurgent

Government had been rewarded by arrest as a spy and incarceration with other prisoners of war. The three Americans thought that they had escaped at the town of Dunlass and offered to guide Howze's battalion to that place.

The trail to Dunlass was narrow, steep, and impassable for carts. Howze was now moving through a wild and unsettled part of the Benguet Mountains. The inhabitants of the area were Tinguines, a wild, primitive tribe, illiterate and crude. Howze impressed two Tinguines into service as guides and pushed on, following closely the trail of Tinio's dwindling force. Lining the trail, the battalion found seven cannons, several hundred rifles and thousands of rounds of ammunition. Near the village of Bandi Tino's rear guard of about 100 men made a short stand. Howze's battalion destroyed the force, and henceforth Tinio's "retreat" became a rout. Dunlass was reached on December 9, but the quarry had flown, following a trail further into the mountains. Howze followed.

At the town of Dingras Howze forced Tinio to drop 800 Spanish prisoners, 500 of whom were officers. Continuing the chase, the Americans entered the town of Solsona, and then pushed on to Manating, where the trail entered a canyon leading into the wild country around the head of the Apayao River.

At this time Howze had to make a decision. He had little food. The trail led through mountains, absolutely impassable for even pack animals or ponies. Among the 120 men of his command there were only twelve pairs of shoes. In six days his force had marched one hundred miles over mountain trails, engaging in a skirmish practically every day. Howze, deciding that he must stop to wait for shoes, sent a message to General Young to that effect. Two days later Hare with his 100 picked men joined Howze at the mouth of the canyon.

Hare decided to take his battalion of the 33rd Infantry and follow up the canyon immediately. Weeding out his command until it consisted of seventy enlisted men and twelve officers, he left Manating the same night.

The ever active Young, meanwhile, had proceeded by navy boat up the coast to the town of Laoag, which was nearly due east of Manating and about twenty miles distant. Receiving Howze's message as to the condition of his troops, he immediately dispatched to Manating a troop of cavalry with supplies and shoes borrowed from the navy. This force arrived on the 14th, and Howze, his men refreshed by their two days' rest, immediately followed Hare up the canyon. He overtook Hare at 8:30 that night. The following day the command, now consisting of 17 officers and 133 men, continued the march over the wild mountain trails. On the 16th three more escaped Americans joined the column. They consisted of two more sailors, Norman Fitzgerald and John Burke, and Sergeant Frank McDonald of the 21st Infantry. Fitzgerald had been a seaman aboard the USS *Baltimore* and had been captured at San Fabian on November 8; Farley, a fireman on the battleship *Oregon* had been captured at Orani on September 8. McDonald had been captured at Imus, Cavite. It was a commentary on the Insurgents' "underground railroad system" that McDonald had been spirited from Imus, a town fifteen miles south of Manila, through the American lines and into the mountains 150 miles north, without recapture.

On the 17th the column reached the headwaters of the Apayao River which, pursuing a tortuous course through the mountains, eventually empties into the China Sea at the northern tip of Luzon.

On the 17th, moving down the river on a trail which crossed the river frequently and necessitated the construction of rafts for crossing, the pursuing party found a note in the sand from the fourteen remaining American prisoners stating "Here we are but God knows where."

The following morning the prisoners, who had been abandoned by the fleeing Insurgents two days previous, were located. The meeting is described by Major Penn of the 34th Infantry:[32]

"The prisoners dazed for a moment rushed to meet us and commenced to embrace the first men. It took some minutes to make us understand that they had been abandoned two days before by the Insurgent guard and left to their fate in a wild unknown land, filled with savage tribes, left without arms, without food, nearly starved, almost naked, footsore, weak, emaciated. The Lieutenant in charge of the prisoners told Lieutenant Gillmore that his orders from General Tinio were to take the prisoners into the mountains and kill them. He told Lieutenant Gillmore that his conscience would not permit him to carry out the orders that he had received, that he would not kill them but would abandon them to their fate."

Those rescued consisted of Lieutenant J. C. Gillmore, Chief Quartermaster, W. Walton, Coxswain, J. Ellsworth, Sailmakers Mate, Paul Vandvit, Seaman, Albert Peterson, Silvio Brisolese, and Samuel J. Herbert, Landsman, Fred Anderson, Privates Elmer Honeymen of the 1st Nevada Cavalry, Selan S. Smith and Frank Stone of the Signal Corps, Harry F. Huber of the Hospital Corps, Albert Bishop of the 3rd Artillery, George T. Sackett and Archie H. Gordon of the

3rd Infantry, James P. Curran and Martin Brennan of the 16th Infantry, and civilians F. W. Langford and David Brown.

The prisoners rescued, Colonel Hare's party had to make another decision. Should they return to safety via Manating or go on down the river to the sea? The trip to Manating meant four days or probably longer without food as the march with the enfeebled prisoners would be slow. Hare decided to take his chance on the river.

The trip by water proved to be more arduous and dangerous than was anticipated. The river was full of rapids, and rafts were destroyed by the angry current almost as quickly as they were constructed. The emaciated condition of the prisoners made short marches a necessity, and on several days only two miles were covered. Christmas and New Year's Day passed, both days finding the benighted force hungry and staggering over the countryside in search of food. One soldier contracted measles and died. Finally on January 2, virtually in a state of collapse, the group arrived at Abulug, a town at the mouth of the river and on the northern tip of Luzon. Succor was received from navy ships stationed at Aparri, a city on the coast ten miles east of Abulug. The weary and footsore veterans were taken by boat from Aparri to Vigan and the released prisoners taken on to Manila. The expedition had released some 1500 Spanish prisoners, twelve American sailors including an officer, Lieutenant Gillmore, ten soldiers and three civilians, all of whom had suffered untold hardships while in the hands of the Insurgents.

General Young had every reason to be proud of the accomplishments of his brigade. True, he had not captured Aguinaldo, but he had chased the Insurgent President into hiding. On January 1, Aguinaldo's wife and sister, finding the rigors of the mountain traveling too great, surrendered to Major March, as did several of Aguinaldo's staff officers. The President himself remained in hiding.

To quote the accomplishments of the brigade in General Young's words:[33]

> "The endurance of the men of my command surpasses the belief of a non-participant and is beyond any ever encountered by an American army. It traveled over miles of road which were always wet and muddy, sometimes only a few inches deep, at other places two feet; sometimes covered with a little water, at other times waist deep, and at others the bed of a torrent; wading, swimming, rafting and bridging innumerable streams, torrents, rivers and lagoons. Poorly clad and shod and generally hungry. After leaving San Jose, all issues of rations ceased and the men had to live on what they could find in the country

which had been largely desolated by the Insurgents. The officers and men of my command are entitled to the best and highest substantial recognition that it is possible to give them who have given to their country's cause the best that is in them regardless of life, health, food and shelter."

General Young might have expected that the smallest recognition which would be given for his services would be to place him in command of the division which Lawton had vacated. Despite Wheaton's inactivity and lack of cooperation, Young had turned the campaign into a brilliant maneuver and a most creditable feat of American arms. However, General Otis had not forgotten the letter that Young had written to the War Department, and besides was not particularly pleased with the way that Young had broken away from the telegraph line and gotten out of control. Brigadier General R. H. Hall, junior to Young, was given command of the division, and the brave, energetic cavalryman was relieved and given another assignment. When the smoke of the Insurrection had cleared away Young's services were recognized. In 1903 he was promoted to the rank of lieutenant general in the regular army and made Chief of Staff, the highest rank to which an army officer can aspire.

6

It would be a culpable omission not to describe what might be considered a side trip, made by a company of native scouts under the command of Lieutenant Joseph Castner and a battalion of the 24th Infantry (colored) under the command of Captain Joseph B. Batchelor. It was the type of operation which was a complete anathema to Otis, who undoubtedly must have squirmed at his desk in Manila while reports of the movement came in.

Young's pursuit of Aguinaldo had led him up the Benguet Mountains on the northwest coast of Luzon. Just east of this range, through the provinces of Nueva Viscaya, Isabella, and Cagayan, ran the fertile tobacco-growing Cagayan Valley, split through the middle by the large, gentle-flowing Cagayan River.

In order to follow the movements of Batchelor's little expedition, the clock should be turned back to November of 1899, shortly after Young had cut loose from his supplies at San Jose, Nueva Ecija. On November 23, Batchelor's battalion of the 24th Infantry (colored) reached Tayug, where General Lawton called Captain Batchelor to his headquarters and directed him to march over the mountains to Bayombong, the town which Aguinaldo had intended to use for the next Insurgent capital and which could be reached only by mountain trails. After Young had shunted Aguinaldo into the mountains further west, the military importance of Bayombong ceased, but Lawton thought that it would be a good idea to garrison the town anyway. Batchelor was authorized to live off the country, giving receipts for whatever he found it necessary to take.

His orders were quite vague as to his movements after he reached Bayombong, and possibly Lawton desired them to be so. It appears that a few days previously Young had proposed that an expedition be sent over the mountains to enter the fertile Cagayan Valley. Lawton knew that Otis would never consent to an unsupplied expedition moving through an area far beyond which any American troops had penetrated, and perhaps even Lawton himself was dubious of the efficacy of such a march. However, since Bayombong had at the time been already occupied by a troop of the 4th Cavalry and a company of native scouts, Batchelor had some grounds for believing that whether specifically mentioned or not he was authorized by General Lawton to operate further north if he felt able.

Loading his men with as much salt as they could carry, Batchelor started out for Bayombong on November 24. The route he was to follow over the mountains was known as the "infernal trail," apparently well named. It led in zigzags up hill and down caverns, over and around mountain streams. It was only eighteen inches wide and at places bordered precipices 300 feet high. At other places tall grass hid from view sheer drops of hundreds of feet. The pack animals could not follow because of abrupt turns overlooking steep cliffs. The second day the battalion was without food, except what wild animals they could shoot. Wearing light clothing, carrying no blankets, the men were unable to sleep during the cold nights in the mountains. The command had already been marching through the mud for a month before the trip started and the rocky trail put the finishing touches on the almost rotted shoes, causing lacerated feet among the already suffering soldiers. Dragging themselves forward, the battalion managed to cover the twenty-eight miles to Bayombong in six days. There the whole command was forced to stop and recuperate.

At Bayombong, Batchelor received information that Insurgent forces in the Cagayan Valley numbered about 1100 and that Aguinaldo was making preparations to enter the valley. Then "in order to carry out the spirit of his orders" Batchelor conceived the idea of moving across the mountains to the Cagayan River and following the river to its mouth at Aparri. He sent a message back to Lawton, advising him of the move and requesting that transportation and rations be sent by boat from Aparri, up the Cagayan River to meet him as he marched down. With his force consisting of 300 negro soldiers and fifty native scouts of Castner's force, he struck out from Bayombong on December 1.

The distance across the mountains from Bayombong to the Cagayan River was some forty miles over difficult mountain trails. After he reached the river, he would still be 135 miles from Aparri. Bayombong itself was 160 miles from Manila, and American troops had never been near the area. Everyone who heard about the proposed march shuddered.

When Lawton heard that Batchelor had struck out from Bayombong he remarked: "If successful, good results will follow to the probable credit of the officer, but very different if a failure." He immediately rushed a battalion of the 22nd Infantry under the command of Major Baldwin to Bayombong with instructions to stop Batchelor if possible. Baldwin's men hurried over the "infernal trail" to Bayombong as fast as they could, but reached the place one day after Batchelor had set out.

Rushing a courier forward to Batchelor, who was then only twenty miles away, Baldwin transmitted the order to return to Bayombong. Batchelor refused to obey the order stating that he was "acting under the direct orders of General Lawton and besides he was pursuing an Insurrecto force." Three days later when Baldwin reached Batchelor with another message directing that he return, the message was ignored. Batchelor could not be stopped.

On December 9, Lawton the alleged sponsor of the expedition, wired to Otis:[34]

"Batchelor had no instructions to go farther than Bayombong and vicinity. His departure for Aparri was as much a surprise as though he had started for San Francisco. A message was sent with all haste with orders to him to remain at Bayombong. The enthusiasm and desire on the part of all officers to do something has led them to unauthorized conduct, which has embarrassed me greatly."

Catching up with Batchelor, we see that the first day out he routed some 250 entrenched Insurgents at San Luis and marched into the settlement of Estella, where he found that the people were more afraid of marauding Igorot headhunters who lived in the nearby mountains than they were of the Americans. He then continued to the town of Carig, where he was met by the local brass band, and informed that the Insurgents had collected a large force at Echague.

Echague was a town twenty-seven miles beyond, where the trail he was following met the Cagayan River. Arriving at Echague during the morning of December 5 he was "disappointed" to find that the Insurgents had evacuated the town.

Resting for a day there and hiring carts to carry his sick, he continued on the 6th twenty-one miles down the river to Cagayan, where he received information that the Insurgents were entrenched at the junction of the Cagayan and the Rio Magat, seven miles further on.

Forced to fight at this point, he was able to rout the Insurgents on the opposite bank only after a raft had been constructed by tying bamboo poles together with canteen straps and shelter tents torn into strips. Under a protecting fire nine naked men crossed the river on a raft and drove the Insurgents away from the opposite bank, killing nine and wounding eight. Batchelor had suffered the loss of one man who was drowned while trying to cross the river and three slightly wounded. The only cause of anxiety to Batchelor was his ammunition supply, which was growing short. On the 8th his command marched into Illagan, a prosperous town of 13,000 inhabitants, and was met by the municipal authorities with the "keys of the city."

Batchelor was now sixty miles from Bayombong, nearest supporting American troops. His force at this time consisted of only 300 men, some sixty disabled by sickness and many without clothing. Only sixty cartridges per man remained. He was particularly relieved when the next day he received a communication from General Daniel Tirona, the Insurgent commander of all Insurgent forces in the Cagayan Valley, offering to surrender and submit to the United States. Batchelor accepted the surrender with alacrity.

At Illagan, he borrowed cascos from a Spanish tobacco company and placing his command in the boats, floated down the Cagayan River in comfort. At Tuguegarao, the capital of Cagayan province, twenty miles further on, he was met at the dock by city officials with carriages and the province formally turned over to him. Four hundred and twenty Spanish prisoners were released.

On the 13th, he was met at Tuguegarao by navy officers who had steamed the sixty miles up the river from Aparri. Leaving one company to garrison Tuguegarao, he and the remainder of his command were then transported on boats down the river to Aparri, where on the 21st he was taken to Manila on the navy gunboat *Helena*. Despite the shudders evinced when he started on the daring march, it had been amazingly successful. To sum them up as reported by Batchelor:[35]

"A force of about 350 men, insufficiently clothed, marched without guides into an unknown country; following trails, just passable, through chilling nights and sweltering days. Made 123 deep fords. Crossed eighty miles of precipitous mountains in five days where the daily average ascent and descent was not less than 8000 feet. Lived three weeks on unaccustomed and insufficient food; twice drove the enemy from strong positions. In twenty-four days turned over to the United States three provinces, said to contain seventy towns. Liberated more than 400 prisoners. Forced the surrender of the General commanding the Insurrecto forces in its front, with one large seagoing steamer, one river steamer, one steam launch, more than 100 cascos, four modern field guns, 800 rifles and 1100 men; restored and continued order and neither maltreating men nor insulting women, left people of the valley enthusiastic advocates of American supremacy."

As an aftermath of Batchelor's march, one might expect that he would have been decorated. But such was hardly the case. General Otis was annoyed no end. As he later said in his report:[36]

"Captain Batchelor conceived the idea of proceeding northward by the Magat and Cagayan Rivers to Aparri, which he proceeded to do without any definite knowledge of the country over which he intended to pass or the force with which he might be obliged to contend. Every possible effort was made to arrest him but without avail. He proceeded on this perilous journey, short of rations, clothing and ammunition, after having sent back a request to have the navy supply at the headwaters of Launch Navigation on the Cagayan River. This movement necessitated the holding at Bayombong of the battalion of the 22nd Infantry (Baldwin) which was needed at other points and gave great concern for the safety of Batchelor's men who could hardly escape destruction if the Insurgents in the Cagayan valley should press hostilities."

Instead of Batchelor returning to Manila a conquering hero, the story goes that upon his return, "Otis abused him like a pickpocket."[37]

NOTES ON CHAPTER IX

1 Brigadier General (then Captain) Ernest D. Scott
2 cf HD No. 2 Vol. 7 56th 2nd p. 123
3 cf Ibid p. 110
4 cf Ibid p. 272
5 cf Ibid p. 275
6 cf Ibid p. 276

[7] *cf* Ibid p. 278
[9] *cf* Parker *op. cit.* p. 266
[8] *cf* Hearings Part III p. 1987
[10] *cf* HD No. 2 Vol. 7 56th 2nd p. 529
[11] *cf* Hearings Vol. III p. 1988
[12] *cf* Millis "The Martial Spirit" p. 270
[13] *cf* Ibid p. 275
[14] *cf* HD No. 2 Vol. 9 56th 2nd p. 242
[15] *cf* Ibid p. 243
[16] *cf* Ibid p. 54
[17] *cf* Ibid p. 229
[18] *cf* Ibid p. 254
[19] *cf* Ibid p. 59
[20] *cf* HD No. 2 Vol. 5 56th 2nd p. 286
[21] *cf* HD No. 2 Vol. 9 56th 2nd p. 67
[22] *cf* Ibid p. 286 *et. seq.*
[23] *cf* Ibid p. 63
[24] *cf* HD No. 2 Vol. 7 56th 2nd p. 318
[25] *cf* Ibid p. 280
[26] *cf* Ibid p. 281
[27] *cf* Parker *op. cit.* p. 277
[28] *cf* Sonnichsen *op. cit.* p. 352 ff
[29] *cf* Parker *op. cit.* p. 281
[30] *cf* HD No. 2 Vol. 7 56th 2nd p. 331
[31] *cf* Ibid p. 332
[32] Penn, "A Narrative of the Campaign in Northern Luzon" p. 31 by the 2nd Bn. 34th Infantry
[33] *cf* HD No. 2 Vol. 7 56th 2nd p. 287
[34] *cf* Ibid p. 240
[35] *cf* Ibid p. 378 *et. seq.*
[36] *cf* HD No. 2. Vol. 5 56th 2nd p. 309
[37] Parker *op. cit.* p. 303

Chapter X

JANUARY AND FEBRUARY of 1900 witnessed the dying gasp of organized military resistance in the Philippines. American troops marched over Luzon from one end to the other. What few organized bodies of Insurgent troops remained were either scattered into the hills or captured. Areas and provinces which had caused the Spanish no end of trouble were occupied in a comparatively peaceful manner. During the months of March, April and May, virtually every island of consequence in the Archipelago was occupied and the inhabitants permitted to return to their normal pursuits. It appeared as though the United States had finally obtained control over the island group which she had purchased from Spain for twenty million dollars.

The military operations during these months were montonously similar to those that had taken place during the past eleven months. The Insurgents entrenched themselves; the Americans attacked; and the Insurgents retired. The so-called cool season, which made campaigning and marching a comparatively simple matter, was at hand. As usual, supply trains experienced their customary difficulties in crossing unbridged streams, but taking it all in all operations were simple when compared to what Lawton's and MacArthur's divisions had gone through during November and December.

To pick up the thread of the story, let us return to General Lawton who, late in December, had been recalled from northern Luzon and had been directed by Otis to clear a force of Insurgents that had assembled in the vicinity of Baliuag and San Miguel de Mayumo. Lawton accomplished this assignment without difficulty and then evolved a plan for delivering a *coup de grace* to the Insurgents in the southern part of the Island.

For all practical purposes the Island of Luzon is divided into two parts. About a hundred miles southeast of Manila in the vicinity of the town of Antimonan, the island narrows down to a slender isthmus. Farther south it again broadens out, but the isthmus is separated from the southern portion by a mountain range inaccessible to wheeled vehicles and impracticable to any kind of traffic. Consequently all traffic from Manila to the southern portion of the island moved by water. Isolated though it was from the remainder of the island, this southern portion was rich and fertile, particularly in the production of the commerically valuable abaca, more generally known as Manila hemp.

General Lawton intended to make a bold move into the provinces south of Manila, quickly occupy the Antimonan Isthmus, and cut off all Insurgents in that area from possible escape to the south except by boat. His detailed plans included taking one regiment of infantry and one of cavalry, moving around the east shore of Laguna de Bay, and reoccupying Santa Cruz, Laguna. (It may be remembered that he had led a "sightseeing expedition" to Santa Cruz the previous April.) He then intended to swing south through the provinces of Laguna and Tayabas and herd all Insurgents in the area towards Manila, where capture would be easy. His swinging movement would have extended to the west coast of Luzon and have included the province and city of Batangas. He was interrupted in the midst of his preparations by preemptory orders to return to Manila. If the plan were ever presented to Otis, it was apparently not approved, for Lawton was forced to cool his heels at Manila for two weeks and then given command of a comparatively minor expedition against a small Insurgent group at San Mateo, eighteen miles northeast of Manila.

Good soldier that he was, Lawton, a major general and division commander, accepted command of the San Mateo expedition without a murmur. Consisting of but two battalions of infantry and two squadrons of cavalry, the command hardly justified the services of an officer of his rank.

During the month of December 1899, more rain had fallen in Manila and vicinity than during any December in thirty-three years. On the night of December 18 a typhoon struck Manila, during which six inches of rain fell within twenty-four hours. The San Mateo expedition was slated for that night, and despite rain, wind, and mud, Lawton determined to go ahead with it.

The troops assembled at La Loma church and started shortly after dark on the eighteen mile march to San Mateo. Stopping by Otis' quarters in the Governor General's Palace at 7:00 p. m. to ascertain if Otis had any last minute instructions, Lawton found the Military Governor and his staff enjoying dinner in well-furnished, well-lighted luxury. When Lawton appeared, his yellow slicker and white cork hemlet dripping from the drenching downpour outside, Otis suggested that in view of the weather, the expedition be called off. Lawton replied that the troops were already on the march and begged that the orders not be changed at their present stage of execution. Otis finally consented, and Lawton mounted his horse and trotted off into the darkness.

The expedition arrived near San Mateo at dawn and found that the Mariquina River, which must be crossed in order to occupy the town, was a raging torrent. Lawton sent the two cavalry squadrons to the north to find a ford and with further instructions to prevent the escape of the Insurgents to the north. The two infantry battalions were then deployed opposite the town, and in the face of an intense fire from the Insurgents entrenched on the opposite bank, worked their way towards a ford known to exist at that point.

From a hill a short distance in rear of the infantry line, Lawton, conspicuous in his yellow raincoat and white helmet, watched the advance of the two infantry battalions. About 9:00 one of his aides, Lieutenant Breckenridge, was wounded. Lawton personally helped carry Breckenridge to cover and in reply to a question said that Breckenridge was not seriously wounded because a mortally wounded man had a peculiar ashiness which Breckenridge did not have. His aide placed as comfortably as possible, Lawton returned to the firing line. Standing there with his other aide, Captain E. L. King, he suddenly waved his hand before his face in a peculiar manner. Captain King asked, "What's the matter, General?" Lawton replied, "I'm shot." King asked, "Where?" Lawton replied, "Through the lungs."

The staff gathered around the stricken general, who was gritting his teeth, apparently attempting to overcome increasing faintness. Then he lay down, and after he turned his head to one side, blood gushed from his mouth. He said nothing more but died in about three minutes with his head on one of his officer's knees. Thus was lost one of the few major generals who, in modern warfare, has been killed in battle—the man who should have been in Otis' place, and in that position would have made the Insurrection of much shorter duration. People who knew Lawton intimately say that a kinder, braver, more tolerant, more understanding officer never lived.

The San Mateo expedition itself was of minor importance. The town was taken and as usual the Insurgents scattered. The troops who returned to Manila in the rain the following day were not a victorious procession. It was a funeral cortege carrying the body of a soldier who died exactly as he would have wanted to die. Lawton's body was shipped to the United States where it was laid to rest with great reverence in Arlington Cemetery at Washington. A floral wreath which friends sent to his funeral expressed the feeling that all felt who had known him. It simply said, "Duty Done Rest Won."

Two weeks after Lawton's death Otis authorized the execution on a more conservative scale of Lawton's plan for dealing with the Insurgents in the area to the south of Manila.

It may be recalled that prior to this time two expeditions had gone out from Manila and toured through the Province of Cavite. Although these expeditions had penetrated as far west as Rosario, on the China Sea, and as far south as Dasmarinas, about twenty-six miles south of Manila, Otis' policy of a thrust followed by a withdrawal had made the net result of these expeditions nil. The retirements invariably increased Insurgent morale and gave them the belief that the Americans were actually weaker than they were. The most distant American outpost in Cavite province was at Imus, about thirteen miles south of Manila. On the southern shore of Laguna de Bay the towns of Calamba and Los Banos had been occupied by American troops moving via boat. However, since the intervening territory was in Insurgent hands, the posts at Calamba and Los Banos were necessarily supplied by boat.

The command of Lawton's division was given to Major General John C. Bates. General Bates had served throughout the Civil War as had most of his contemporaries, but having been commissioned originally in the regular army, did not receive the phenomenal promotion accorded the officers holding volunteer commissions. However, he had come out of the Civil War with a bona fide captain's commission in the regular army, which placed him fairly high on the promotion list. By 1898 he was the fourth ranking colonel in the regular army. At the beginning of the Spanish-American War he was commissioned as a brigadier general, then a major general of volunteers and given the command of a division in the Cuban expedition. The Spanish War over, he was sent to the Philippines where he succeeded to Lawton's command on the latter's death. More will be heard of General Bates in connection with his dealings with the Moros of Mindinao.

Bate's division was divided into two brigades which throughout the campaign operated virtually independently of each other. One, placed under the command of Otis' Chief of Staff, General Theodore Schwann, and officially labled "Schwann's Expeditionary Brigade" consisted of the 20th and 46th Infantry regiments, a squadron of the 4th and a squadron of the 11th Cavalry, a detachment of the 6th Artillery, two companies of Macabebe scouts and a company of engineers. The other brigade, placed under the command of General Wheaton and dubbed "Wheaton's Expeditionary Brigade," consisted of the 4th, 28th, 38th, and 45th Infantry regiments, companies G and H of the 37th Infantry, detachments of the 4th Artillery, engineers, and signal corps.

The general plan was for Wheaton's brigade to contain the Insurgent forces in the vicinity of Imus until Schwann's brigade, marching along the west shore of Laguna de Bay, could establish a line running from the town of Binan (on the Lake) to Naic on the west coast of Luzon. Then as Wheaton's force attacked, the Insurgents would be pushed into the waiting arms of Schwann's brigade.

Schwann's brigade left San Pedro Macati on January 4 and marched the twenty miles to Muntilupa. On the following day Binan was taken, after a short engagement with about 300 Insurgents. Supplies for the brigade were sent by boat to Binan, and the 6th was spent in preparing for the movement west towards Naic. On the 7th, with the cavalry in front and a battalion of the 46th Infantry left to garrison Binan, Schwann's force moved southwest towards Silang, about fifteen miles distant. On the same day a battalion of the 4th Infantry (part of Wheaton's force) reconnoitering from Imus towards Dasmarinas, defeated a force of some 500 Insurgents in the vicinity of the latter place. The same day a battalion of the 28th Infantry (Wheaton's force) reconnoitering towards Cavite encountered opposition at Putol and in the ensuing fight 74 Insurgents were killed and eleven Americans wounded.

Reilly's battery of the 4th Artillery suffered one fourth of the American casualties in this fight, having been brought to within 250 yards of the entrenched Insurgents. Not long afterwards this same battery of Reilly's would be blasting at the gates of the Forbidden City at Peking and its intrepid battery commander killed.

The two engagements in which the elements of Wheaton's brigade had become involved were a bit in advance of the contemplated time. Schwann's brigade had not reached Naic, and since the Insurgents in both encounters with Wheaton had been sent in flight towards the south, it was feared that they would filter through Schwann's barrier, before it could be completely established. Consequently Bates sent word to Schwann to move on Naic as fast as possible. Schwann sent Colonel Hayes and the cavalry on ahead of his column with instructions to push through to Naic with utmost speed.

Hurrying on towards Silang, Hayes found the roads four miles out of Binan impassable for wagons. Pushing on with his mounted men, however, he caught up with the Insurgent force retreating from Binan. So close did Hayes press the Insurgents that he found the road strewn with household goods, rice, chickens, bull carts, ammunition, and records, which the Insurgents abandoned in the hasty flight. About five miles east of Silang a rugged gorge, over which mounted men and pack animals could cross only with difficulty, barred the road completely for wheeled transportation. The 30th Infantry following close in Hayes' rear, from necessity abandoned their wagons at the gorge, pushed on behind the cavalry and arrived at Silang during the evening of the 7th. Hayes had meanwhile marched towards Indang, eight miles further west where he routed 200 Insurgents on the same evening. At Indang he captured 62 rifles, 4000 rounds of ammunition, $7000 in Insurgent funds, and found a well-equipped Insurgent hospital containing many sick and wounded Insurgents.

On January 8 and 9, while the leading elements of Schwann's brigade were approaching Naic, Wheaton's brigade attacked the Insurgents at San Francisco de Malabon and drove them to the south. Bates advised Schwann to watch for this force and not let it through his lines. On the same day Hayes' cavalry reached Naic and the barrier line was complete. Hayes encountered the main body of Insurgent force, which was retreating from Wheaton's front, and in a sharp skirmish fought in rice fields knee deep in mud and water, scattered them. With Schwann's line now established from Binan to Naic, the escape of large bodies of Insurgents to the rear was cut off; in fact the Insurgent force of General Trias, which had been composed of some 1500 men, was scattered not to be reassembled. Small bodies of Insurgents unquestionably did sift through Schwann's lines, but owing to the nature of the country such escapes could not be prevented. The Province of Cavite, home of Aguinaldo, birthplace of the revolt, and the province which had for a hundred years been a thorn in the sides of the Spanish, was finally in American possession.

The next phase in the operations which Lawton would have accomplished in one fell swoop was the conquest of the Province of Batangas. It was a prosperous territory, with its capital city situated on the easily navigable Batangas Bay, which had been the seat of Insurgent activity in the unloading of imported arms and ammunition. In the center of the province was the large Taal Lake, which contained on an island in its center the periodically active Taal volcano.

On January 10 the 39th Infantry operating from Calamba, under

the command of Colonel Robert L. Bullard, defeated a force of Insurgents at the town of Santo Tomas, about fifteen miles to the
south. Bates feared that this force uniting with the scattered remnants of Trias' forces from Cavite province would cause sizable opposition in the future. Therefore he rushed the 38th Infantry to
Bullard's assistance with instructions that the movement south be
continued towards the town of Lipa, in contemplation of Schwann's
brigade eventually moving around the south shore of Lake Taal and
enclosing the Insurgents within the Province of Batangas.

After a brisk fight in which the artillery figured prominently on
January 15, the 38th and 39th Infantry regiments moved south and
occupied Lipa. Of the Lieutenant in command of this artillery
Colonel Bullard later reported:[1]

> "Too high praise cannot be given Lieutenant Summerall and
> his battery. His judgment was ever sound; he was full of vigor
> and activity and as cool and brave as anyone I ever saw. He
> should receive some reward."

Nearly thirty years later, after a brilliant World War record,
Lieutenant Summerall did receive his reward. He was appointed
Chief of Staff of the entire army with the rank of general.

An hour after the capture of Lipa, Colonels Bullard and Anderson, commanding the two infantry regiments heard that American
prisoners were being held in the town of Rosario about eight miles
to the southeast. Acting on an impulse, the two colonels, accompanied by a lieutenant colonel, a major, a captain, two lieutenants
and four enlisted men mounted their horses and moved down the
road to Rosario. It is difficult to figure their line of reasoning, for if
American prisoners were being held at Rosario, undoubtedly a sizable band of Insurgents would have been there also, and it was un-
reasonable to expect that eleven Americans, brave as they might be,
could disperse any large band of Insurgents and take the prisoners.
At any rate, the group topheavy with rank and armed with rifles,
started for Rosario at 2:30 in the afternoon. As Colonel Anderson
reported:[2]

> "We saw the road full of flying people, some of them in uni-
> forms, and some armed, but most of them were men, women
> and children moving their household goods. On arriving at
> Rosario, we cleared the town by a few pistol shots. Here we
> found and liberated 70 prisoners. . . . . ."

American prisoners were not found, but acting on the information
of a Spanish officer they had relieved, the group located $20,000 in

Insurgent funds and carried the booty back to Lipa the same after-noon.

Brilliant an exploit as it was, General Bates was not particularly pleased. As he said later in his report, in referring to the event:[3]

"This exploit in which two colonels left their regiments in violation of their responsibilities as commanders, in obedience to an impulse of enterprising courage, is so peculiar that it is impossible to praise it without combining rebuke with appro-bation or to censure it without expression of admiration for the dash and gallantry displayed."

Perhaps it was while these officers were absent that their regiments in violation of all orders looted the town of Lipa. Colonel Cornelius Gardner of the 30th Infantry reported one battalion of the 39th Infantry as being "loaded down" with articles looted at Lipa.[4]

On January 16 Schwann's brigade, moving along three parallel roads, advanced on Batangas, arriving there the same day after a couple of minor skirmishes. Schwann immediately issued the follow-ing proclamation:[5]

"The authority of the Government of the United States has come to you not in the spirit of ruthless invasion but in the spirit of peace and good will to all citizens and with the object of establishing good government among you, which will secure to individuals the protection of their persons and the peaceful pursuit of industry and happiness. It is enjoined upon all citi-zens to continue in or to return to their homes and to pursue their peaceful avocations in which they will not be molested.

"The Commanding General or in his absence the local com-mander will be glad to receive the peoples' representatives for the purpose of advising with them as to the measures necessary to promote prosperity and contentment under the authority of the United States government."

Garrisons were then established in the principal towns of Batangas province, and with Wheaton's brigade left in Cavite and Batangas provinces, Schwann's brigade was swung about and set to the task of occupying the provinces of Laguna and Tayabas.

With his headquarters established at Lipa, Schwann was directed to make the next objective the large town of Santa Cruz, Laguna, which had already been occupied on one occasion by Lawton on a "sightseeing tour" in April.

Santa Cruz was about thirty miles northeast of Lipa. The territory to the direct east which included the sizable towns of Candelaria, Lucena, and Tayabas was virgin as far as the Americans were concerned. In order to take the entire area in one movement and prevent the escape of Insurgent bodies through the Antimonan Isthmus to the wild country on its south, it was directed that the infantry make a direct movement on Santa Cruz while the cavalry make a wide sweeping movement to the southeast, going as far south as Lucena and as far east as the town of Tayabas.

Very little Insurgent opposition was expected or received. It became evident however that harassing operations from small Insurgent bands might be expected at any time. On January 17 a pack train guarded by twenty-one recruits and accompanied by fifty-three convalescent soldiers was attacked by 150 Insurgents near the town of Alaminos. The recruits went into a panic with the result that the Insurgents captured the pack train and killed two and captured eight Americans. Lieutenant Ralston, the commander of the pack train, came very close to being tried by a court martial. On the following day a reconnaissance party from the 30th Infantry permitted itself to be surprised while eating dinner and beat off the attack with difficulty. The commanding officer of this detachment actually was tried by a court martial but was eventually acquitted.

The infantry elements of Schwann's brigade encountered little difficulty in advancing. Having been concentrated at San Pablo on January 20, they commenced the march towards Santa Cruz. At the town of San Diego they ran into a strong Insurgent position. The Insurgents were entrenched on a high hill which commanded all approaches. After a short fight in which one American and thirty-seven Insurgents were killed, the position was taken.

On the 22nd, the town of Narcarlang was occupied without opposition, but from an escaped Spanish prisoner, Schwann received information of an allegedly impregnable position held by some 3000 Insurgents at the town of Mayjayjay about five miles further on. Reconnoitering the enemy position he found it to be indeed strong. Entrenched on the opposite side of a thirty-foot gorge was a large group of Insurgents apparently well armed and well supplied with ammunition. The only apparent means of crossing the gorge was a narrow foot bridge which was flanked for 250 yards on either side by trenches. Fearing an excessive number of casualties if the bridge were rushed, Schwann halted and looked for another place to cross, with the idea of attacking the Insurgents from flank. After several hours of reconnaissance, a battalion of the 39th Infantry under the command of Major Mulford was able to find a place where by lowering troops about thirty feet on ropes they were able to scale the bluff on the opposite side of the gorge. Two companies were crossed in this manner, and when they presented themselves on the Insurgent flank the entire position was abandoned without further ado. The command then marched to Santa Cruz, thirteen miles to the north, arriving there on the 23rd.

Swinging around the right (south) flank, the cavalry had not experienced such easy going. Near Candelaria a skirmish cost the lives of three Americans. Sariaya was entered without opposition on January 20. The unit splitting into two groups, one column moved on Tayabas by the main road while another swung south through Lucena and approached Tayabas from the south. Tayabas was occupied with little difficulty, Insurgent trenches and earthworks along the road having been found abandoned. Hayes' orders had then contemplated that he swing north through Lucban and Luisiana to Santa Cruz and there unite with the remainder of the brigade. From Tayabas, reconnaissance north indicated that the road to Santa Cruz via Lucban was, considering the condition of his command, entirely impracticable. The cavalry had been the spearhead of advance all the way from Binan to Naic, then to Batangas. Twenty percent of the command was on sick report and the horses were shoeless. Consequently Hayes gave up the maneuver and marched to Santa Cruz via Tiaong and San Pablo, arriving there on the 25th. His movement had scared all Insurgents out of the Province of Tayabas and very probably the knowledge that he was in their rear was one reason why the Insurgents at Mayjayjay had evacuated as suddenly as they did.

Persistent rumors that American prisoners were being hustled towards the Camarines' provinces to the south of Antimonan caused Schwann to send a battalion to that place on January 26. It was also anticipated that this force might be able to cut off the retreat of Insurgents who had been pushed east of Santa Cruz. The march was made and Antimonan occupied, but the American prisoners were not located. The march to Antimonan was over mountain trails most difficult of access. When one battalion returned to Tayabas early in February, of the 240 men in the battalion 230 were shoeless.

Strategic towns in Tayabas were garrisoned, and except for minor attacks by roving Insurgent bands, the province was under control of the American forces. Lawton's plan had been sound. Within three weeks the bold entry of Insurgent territory had caused three provinces to be occupied with negligible losses to American troops. And as General Bates said in his report:[6]

"Now it became evident to the natives that the Americans had come to stay and those who felt well disposed towards our rule felt a sense of protection that had been formerly lacking. The result was apparent in the labor and building of new houses in the conquered provinces and only the lingering fear of robber bands seems to stand in the way of peace and contentent."

As will later be seen, Schwann's estimate of the conditions in the provinces proved to be a bit optimistic. Total American casualties in Schwann's brigade during these entire operations amounted to six killed and five wounded. Forty-five Insurgents were known to have been killed. Eighty-seven rifles and 4500 rounds of ammunition, and $27,000 in Insurgent funds had been captured. The conquest of three rich Insurgent provinces had been cheap.

3

Except for the so-called "hemp provinces" on the southern end of Luzon, the entire island was now occupied. Strange to say, pressure on Otis for the occupation of the hemp provinces came from Washington. It seems that the insurrection was blocking the source of materials for the American rope and twine industry. As a result of the price of rope and twine in the United States going up, Otis received orders from Washington to open the hemp ports as soon as possible.

While Bate's division was clearing out the provinces south of Manila, Otis organized an expedition under the command of Brigadier General William Kobbe to move by boat to the hemp ports and try to get the hemp industry on a paying basis again.

General Kobbe had enlisted in the 178th New York Volunteers as a private in 1862 and had ended the war as a brevet colonel. In 1866 he was commissioned a 2nd lieutenant in the regular army. By 1898 he had attained only the rank of major in the artillery and had gone to the Philippines in command of the 3rd Artillery. His regiment was a part of MacArthur's division, and with it he fought his way up the railroad to San Fernando. When the new volunteer regiments were organized, he was rewarded with a promotion to brigadier general of volunteers.

The expedition consisted of the 43rd and 47th Infantry regiments and one battery of field artillery. Accompanying the transports conveying Kobbe's troops were the navy cruiser *Nashville* and the gunboats *Helena* and *Merivales*. As General Kobbe later reported, the cooperation that he received from the navy on the expedition was "not only valuable but indispensable."

On January 20, the expedition arrived off the port of Sorgoson, capital of the province of the same name. No evidences of hostility being present, a party landed and the American flag was raised. It appeared that the Insurgent governor of the town with 300 armed men had fled at the approach of the transports. Leaving a battalion of the 47th Infantry equipped with custom blanks and stamps, the expedition sailed south to the Port of Bulan. The place was also occupied without incident, the inhabitants appearing to be friendly. Continuing around the southern tip of Luzon through the San Bernardino straits, the expedition landed at Donsol, where it found the town deserted. Shortly after its occupation, long-range fire was received from Insurgents in the surrounding hills. Leaving a battalion at Donsol, the expedition proceeded north to the large port of Legaspi. There it was found that the planking from the wharves had been removed and well-constructed trenches manned by 800 armed natives lined the shore. Anticipating a dispute of the landing, Kobbe granted permission to the commanding officer of the British gunboat *Plover* which had accompanied the expedition, to go ashore and remove British residents from the town. The Insurgents refused to allow the British citizens to leave, näively stating that as long as they were in the town it would probably not be bombarded.

The situation placed Kobbe in a quandary. There were so few boats available for landing troops that not more than seventy-five could be put ashore at once. He feared that the concentrated fire of the 800 Insurgents on such a small group would cause an unnecessarily large amount of casualties. Further, he hesitated to bombard the town. A request to the captain of the transport *Venus*, to steam right alongside of one of the dismantled wharves, where troops could fire from her decks upon the trenches, was refused with the excuse that the steering gear would not work.

He finally decided that a bombardment of some sort would be necessary and set about to force the landing. Seventy-five men of the 47th Infantry were loaded into small boats and pushed towards shore near the flank of the Insurgent trenches. The *Nashville* opened up on the Insurgent trenches with its four-inch guns and automatic weapons. This fusillade kept Insurgent heads below the parapets until enough troops could be landed to attack safely. Then the Americans moving on the trenches from the flank, drove out the Insurgents after a resistance which, as Kobbe said, "was so stubborn either from ignorance or indifference to consequences that many were killed or wounded at hand to hand range without giving any sign of surrender." The American casualties in the attack amounted to six wounded, while those of the Insurgents totaled 100. The remainder of the day and that night was spent in bringing troops and supplies ashore.

On January 24 the town of Virac on the small Island of Catanduanes was occupied without incident. The expedition then moved south to the Island of Samar where the town of Kalbyok was occupied. Moving around Samar to the port of Catbalogan the Insurgent troops of General Lucban did not oppose the landing, but did attempt to burn the town as the Americans landed. Laborious efforts of the American troops, assisted by fire-fighting parties of bluejackets finally managed to save the majority of the permanent buildings. Moving to the port of Tacloban on the Island of Leyte, the expedition occupied that town without difficulty.

There still remained the two provinces of North and South Camarines to be occupied before Luzon would be entirely in American hands. The capture was accomplished by two battalions of the 40th Infantry on February 13. They moved by boat to the Port of Barcelonetta on the southeastern coast of Luzon, the landing sharply disputed by a large body of Insurgents. In the ensuing fight at the town of Libmanan one American officer was killed and ten enlisted men wounded. The Americans buried sixty-four Insurgents after the battle. In a march through the provinces on February 24, sixty Spanish prisoners were released. American garrisons were established in the principal towns. The occupation of Luzon was complete. Eventually some 1000 prisoners of the Insurgents, many of them Spanish friars, were released by the Americans. Many of those released showed evidences of having been slashed with bolos and were in a pitiful condition.

The principal ports of the hemp provinces had been occupied, but what of the Insurgent bodies which had fled into the surrounding territory upon the approach of the Americans? It appeared that the majority of the natives living in and near the ports welcomed the arrival of the Americans because of the protection which the presence of American troops gave them in following their normal pursuits. In the thickets outside of the towns, however, small groups of recalcitrant Insurgents still remained. These groups not only threatened the lives of natives who accepted the American rule, but in many cases actually attacked the American garrisons. An Insurgent group in the vicinity of the town of Donsol was particularly active. The battalion of the 47th Infantry garrisoning the place was attacked time after time. Attempt after attempt to burn the town was made. Wily natives would slip through the American outposts and set fire to nipa houses. Small groups sent on reconnaissance were constantly attacked by bands armed with bows and arrows and spears. It appeared that though the occupation of all Insurgent territory in Luzon had been effected, the pacification still remained to be accomplished.

The occupation of the other islands of the Archipelago went on apace. In March a battalion of the 44th Infantry peacefully occupied the Island of Bohol. By the end of May American troops controlled Marinduque and Masbate, Calamianes, the Cuyos group and Paragua. In the majority of the southern Islands the dissident influence of the Luzon Tagalogs had not made itself felt, and the occupation was accomplished peacefully.

The occupation of Mindanao deserves more space. This large island, second in size to Luzon, was inhabited except for a few Visayan and Spanish settlements on the coasts, by Mohammedan Filipinos known as Moros. In encountering them, the Americans ran into an entirely new type of opponent. In the first place, the Moro was a religious fanatic. He believed that the more Christians he killed, the more houris he would have in paradise after his death. Also he was adept not only with a bolo but with a long, curved, well-balanced knife known as the barong. In the hands of a trained wielder a barong could take a man's head off as easily as a sharp knife cuts bread. Periodically a Moro would work himself into a religious frenzy and start through a barrio to cut and kill everything he met. On such occasions the only thing which would stop him was a bullet, and on occasions the Americans found that a "juramentado" (as the frenzied individual was called) would continue to fight and slash long after he had been mortally wounded. One eye-witness of such a fight saw one man receive fourteen wounds in five minutes, three of which penetrated the brain, and yet the man still fought on. If the Moro-inhabited portions of the Archipelago had to be occupied by force, American troops would find the fighting of a nature entirely different from that which had occurred in Luzon.

For centuries the Moros had followed customs, many of which were revolting to Americans. By the Koran they were authorized to practice polygamy. Many exceeded the quota of wives authorized by the Koran and others kept a large number of concubines. It was known that for years they had practiced slavery and even in 1900 raided villages of weaker tribes for captives. People who well knew the Moros stated that Moro slavery was not the same type as that practised in the United States prior to the Civil War, but was a form of serfdom; that the slaves were well treated and enjoyed the status of unpaid retainers rather than slaves. Any slave could buy his freedom for twenty dollars. However, the fact that polygamy and "slavery" were thriving under the American Flag was an anathema to the various "anti" societies in the United States. Otis realized that "hostilities with the Moros would be unfortunate for all parties concerned and would be expensive to the United States in men and money." So despite the fact that he represented a democracy, where monogamy and liberty were watchwords, he decided that the Moros would have to be handled with kid gloves, particularly in regard to their customs.

Residing on the Island of Jolo, just south of Mindanao, was the so-called Sultan of Jolo. This man was not only recognized as the spiritual head of all Moros in the Philippines, but was politically respected as a sort of super tribal chieftan (Datu). His influence extended to large numbers of Moros living in the British owned portions of Borneo.

The Spanish had never successfully brought the Moro tribes completely under control. In 1857 they had made a treaty with the Sultan of Sulu under which Spanish sovereignty of the Islands was accepted, but the Moros were permitted to continue living under their old customs.

During the early part of 1899 emissaries of Aguinaldo had set up Insurgent governments on the Filipino inhabited coastal cities of Mindanao. However, Otis at once recognized that the real problem of Mindanao and Jolo would be that of maintaining friendly relations with the Moros.

Upon the evacuation of the Moro Islands by the Spanish garrisons following the Treaty of Paris, General Bates was sent by Otis to negotiate an understanding with the Sultan of Sulu. He had a difficult task to perform and executed it with tact and ability. Going to Jolo in July of 1899 he found the Sultan aloof and expecting to receive large annual payments from the United States in the same fashion he was receiving them from the British in North Borneo. Negotiations lagged for two months.

Bates used every tactful artifice of which he could think. He got leading Datus aboard the cruiser *Charleston* and showed them the marvels of American science. He fired the *Charleston's* 8-inch guns. He allowed one Datu to pull the trigger of a Colt automatic. To their delight he gave the Datus mild electric shocks. He showed them how the Americans were able to press a button and "kindle a light on the masthead." The Moros stared at the mysterious box that produced the wind. At length one Datu admitted, "What could an ignorant people like the Moros do against you?"

Possibly it was the big guns on the *Charleston*. At any rate Bates was finally able to make a favorable treaty with the Sultan concerning the Moro-inhabited islands. In brief, the Sultan recognized the sovereignty of the United States and agreed to fly the American flag throughout the area. The Moros were permitted to retain their own customs, including that of slavery, and were allowed a sort of extraterritoriality in regard to the trials and punishments among themselves. The Sultan agreed to cooperate heartily in the suppression of piracy which had been one of the bugbears of the entire area during the Spanish regime. For maintaining order among the Moros the United States agreed to pay certain Moro Datus' salaries, ranging from 250 dollars (gold) per month for the Sultan, to fifteen dollars a month for the minor Datu Serif Saguin. The agreement was made with the understanding that it must be approved by the President of the United States.

With the Moros on the American side, so to speak, the handling of the Tagalog Insurgents became simple. They quarreled among themselves, and when Otis sent expeditions to occupy the principal ports early in 1900 the Insurgent groups either surrendered or moved into the hills. The ports of Zamboanga, Cottabato, Pollack, Parang Parang, Davao, Surigao, Cagayan, Iligan, Misamis and Dapitan were all occupied without firing a shot.

The Moro problem was not entirely solved, as shall be seen, but for the time being it looked as though the United States had peacefully acquired possession of a potential scene of trouble.

NOTES ON CHAPTER X

1 *cf* HD No. 2 Vol. 5 56th 2nd p. 523
2 *cf* Ibid
3 *cf* HD No. 2 Vol. 7 56th 2nd p. 649
4 *cf* HD No. 2 Vol. 6 56th 2nd p. 453
5 *cf* Ibid p. 425
6 *cf* HD No. 2 Vol. 7 56th 2nd p. 656

Chapter XI

W HEN THE Insurgent army was dissipated, Aguinaldo chased into the Benguet Mountains, and the inhabited parts of the Archipelago occupied by American troops, Otis believed that the Insurrection was virtually ended. His error arose from the fact that he thought that mere occupation meant pacification. In fact, the hardest job of the American Army was yet ahead. It had taken eleven months to disperse the Insurgent Army. It was to take two years and a half to pacify the Islands.

In May of 1900 Otis said in an article in *Leslie's Weekly*:[1]

> "You ask me to say when the war in the Philippines will be over and to set a limit to the men and treasure necessary to bring affairs to a satisfactory conclusion. That is impossible for the war in the Philippines is already over. The Insurrection ended some months ago; and all we have to do now is to protect the Filipinos against themselves and to give protection to those natives who are begging for it.
>
> "There will be no more real fighting in the Philippines . . . . of course the Islands must be thoroughly policed and it will take a good many men to do it. . . . .
>
> "Since peace was practically restored throughout the Archipelago, many towns have appealed to us for protection. Luzon is pacified and there are only a few outlying districts where the natives are still terrified by the ladrones into a show of opposition to us. You will see that there will be no more fighting of any moment. What there is will be but little skirmishes which amount to nothing. . . . ."

It is somewhat shocking to find that an officer in as high and responsible a position as General Otis occupied should have mistaken conditions so thoroughly. How thoroughly they were misjudged is indicated by the following figures. During the last four months of 1899, during which the Insurgent Army was giving its death groans, the American casualties amounted in 229 engagements, to 69 killed and 302 wounded. During the first four months of January 1900 at the beginning of the so-called guerrilla warfare period which Otis had characterized as one of "little skirmishes which amount to nothing," the Americans had 442 encounters with the Insurgents in which 130 were killed and 325 wounded.

After the so-called end of the war, the American casualties doubled.

The number of wounded remained about the same. The increase in the number of fatalities brings up the point as to why the number killed should jump so much higher than the number merely wounded. The answer is given in the new type of fighting during the guerrilla period. The American casualties were caused by ambushes, with firing at close range, or by sudden attacks on small parties of American soldiers who, actually believing that the war was over, ventured away from villages. Most casualties were caused by soldiers being hacked to death by bolos instead of being wounded by merciful Mauser bullets. The Americans were not fighting a uniformed army. They were fighting determined groups of men who tilled the fields by day and stalked outposts by night. The new type of warfare was infinitely more dangerous.

Despite the fact that General Otis thought that the Insurrection was over, the War Department found it necessary to increase the strength of the army in the Philippines to two-thirds of the armed forces of the United States. It was to take ten thousand more American troops to pacify the Islands than it had taken to beat the Insurgent army. The strength of the army in the Philippines had increased from 15,000 troops, which defended Manila in February of 1899, to 59,722 by December of the same year. By December of 1900, when the Insurrection was really at its height, the United States forces in the Philippines numbered 69,420 officers and men.[2] On November 1, 1899, fifty-three stations were occupied by American troops. By September 1, 1900, the number of occupied stations had risen to 413.[3]

The duties of the troops were in no sense merely that of police, for as General MacArthur said,[3] "Each little command has had to provide its own service of security and information by never ceasing patrols, explorations, outposts, escorts and regular guards." Troops had to march farther under more difficult conditions than during the so-called organized Insurrection. It is true that few of the hundreds of engagements with the Insurgents, or guerrillas as they should be called, involved a sufficient number of combatants on either side to merit the dignity of being called a battle. However, walking through jungles with the possibility of being cut by a bolo or shot by a rifle is as dangerous and enervating as a battle on an open field . . . ."

2

Credit must be given to Aguinaldo's devoted subordinate leaders for their persistence, and recognition must be given them for the efficient way in which the guerrilla warfare was conducted. Backed possibly by the 10,000 odd rifles still in their possession, they were for a time at least able to dominate completely the Filipino civilians. While American troops were occupying towns and establishing municipal governments with the natives holding offices, the Insurgents arranged a parallel organization, in many cases employing the same natives who held office under the Americans. The towns were taxed, contributions and supplies collected, and recruits for the guerrilla forces enlisted right under the noses of the unsuspecting Americans.

Their method of conducting warfare under the guerrilla system is perhaps indicated in a pamphlet with instructions for guerrilla tactics, printed in Madrid, Spain, by an Insurgent revolutionary Junta there. Parts of the pamphlet appear to have been copied from a drill manual of a foreign army, possibly the Spanish. Some excerpts give an idea of the proposed method of conducting the warfare:[4]

> "The purpose of the guerrilla will be to constantly worry the Yankees in the Pueblos occupied by them, to cut off their convoys, to cause all possible harm to their patrols, their spies and their scouts, to surprise their detachments, to crush their columns if they should pass favorable places and to exterminate all traitors, to prevent natives to (from) vilely selling themselves for the invader's gold.
>
> "The guerrillas shall make up for their small numbers by their ceaseless activity and their daring. They shall hide in the woods and in distant barrios and when least expected shall fall upon the enemy. . . . . but they shall be careful to never rob their countrymen.
>
> "We repeat that we must not give or accept combats with such a powerful foe if we have not the greatest chance of success . . . even as should we rout him three times or five times, the question of our independence would not be solved. Let us wait for the deadly climate to decimate his files and never forget that our object is only to protract the state of war. . . . ."

The success of the system of course depended on the loyalty of the townspeople who furnished the supplies, and could, if they dared, advise the American authorities that the leader of the band which had attacked an outpost was the town presidente. To prevent such exposure, dire threats were made by the guerrilla leaders to anyone who divulged information to the Americans. These threats were issued in the form of proclamations with death as the penalty for violations of their provisions.

It is a commentary on the character of the Filipino that the vast majority, even though they were sick of the war, were pro-American and favored American sovereignty, refused to divulge the names of Insurgents who lived in the towns or the hiding places of rifles. General MacArthur said: "This characteristic reluctance of everybody even among the most active pro-Americans to give any information of military value is one of the greatest difficulties of the existing system."

The few Filipinos who divulged information concerning the activities of guerrillas suffered heavily at the hands of their own countrymen. Instances occurred where women, children, sick or weak men, were beaten to death with clubs or stones. Others were conducted to some spot beyond the sight of passers-by and killed with a bolo. When it was particularly desired to inspire terror in a community, a bound and helpless victim was buried alive in a grave usually dug in his presence. It is small wonder that the natives were reluctant to divulge information.

On their part, the Americans were equally eager to pry information out of the natives. In the numerous small barrios occupied by American troops, any native in them could probably recite the names of every Insurgent living there. As a result the average native found himself ground between two millstones and living in a constant state of terror, his life, property and family never secure.

Much has been written and said about the many "cruelties" practiced by American soldiers on Filipino natives. In 1902 the Senate Committee on the Philippines, investigating the conduct of the army, found plenty of witnesses who had seen what were termed atrocious practices.

In defense of the soldiers, who were later pilloried for alleged cruel treatment of Filipino natives, it should be borne in mind that the situation had developed into a case of dog eat dog. The Insurgents possessed rifles which were hidden. As long as these weapons were in hostile hands, they represented a potential threat to lives of American soldiers. The Americans did not torture natives for sport. It was a matter of self-defense. In view of the type of warfare or mass assassination which the Insurgents were conducting anything was considered fair. The so-called tortures were invariably used only to force natives to divulge the hiding place of arms or the hiding places of Insurgent bands. And as the casualty list was constantly mounting under the methods employed by the Insurgents, a tolerant view would indicate that under the circumstances the end justified the means.

The most common torture used by the American soldiers was the so-called "water cure." This treatment consisted of laying a native flat on his back, his mouth pried open with a stick, bayonet, or even a cartridge case. Large quantities of water, sometimes salty, sometimes dirty, were then poured down the victim's throat until his stomach became distended. When the stomach became so filled that no more water could enter, someone sat or stood on the victim's stomach until the water was disgorged, and the process was repeated. Never having received the treatment, the writer cannot adequately describe the sensations of the victim. That they were painful is indicated by the fact that one native flattened out a brass cartridge case, attempting to close his mouth while water was being poured in. Apparently the water cure was efficacious, however, for the American troops employed it to a great extent.

The so-called "rope cure," which appears to have been used rarely, consisted in wrapping rope around the victim's neck and torso two or three times until it formed a sort of girdle. A stick was then placed between the ropes and twisted until a combination of smothering and garroting effect was created.

Sometimes the treatment consisted simply in giving an Insurgent a good "beating up." This method was not particularly effective. One soldier who was an ex-policeman on a large city force testified before the Senate Committee that he had never seen anything in the Philippines which would compare with the "third degree" methods used by American police departments in dealing with criminals.

During the Insurrection several officers of the American Army were tried by courts martial for alleged cruelty to natives. It was generally assumed that the soldiers involved were acting under orders and the responsibility rested with the officer in charge.

Lieutenant Bissell Thomas of the 35th Infantry was convicted of "striking native prisoners and using threatening language towards them and striking one while lying on the floor in a helpless condition, bleeding at nose and mouth." The court fined Lieutenant Thomas $300 and gave him a reprimand, which in the case of an officer is more serious than it appears.

Lieutenant Preston Brown was charged with "the murder of an unarmed, unresisting prisoner of war." The court found him guilty of manslaughter and sentenced him to dismissal from the army and five years in the penitentiary. President Roosevelt commuted the sentence to a reduction of thirty files on the promotion list and placed him on half-pay for nine months.

Two officers in the 27th Infantry, Captain George Brandle and Lieutenant Alva Perkins, were tried for "wilfully and cruelly causing six Filipinos to be hung by the neck for a period of ten seconds, causing them to suffer great bodily pain." The court found the two officers guilty but changed "great bodily pain" to "mental anguish" and sentenced both to reprimands. Apparently General MacArthur thought the sentence too light, for he denounced the court for its findings.

The 9th Cavalry (colored) used a rather unique and harmless method. A native whom it was desired to "interrogate," was taken into a semi-dark room and securely bound. Then a huge black, dressed only in a loin cloth and carrying a cavalry sabre, entered and danced around the victim making threatening gesticulations with the sabre. To an ignorant Filipino he undoubtedly looked like the devil incarnate. Quite often the method made the victim talk. [5]

Other methods were unquestionably used. As a rule a medical officer was present to prevent vital injury.

3.

During 1900, acting on the assumption that the Insurrection was over, the actual divisional tactical organization of troops was dropped and a geographical occupation system adopted. The entire Archipelago was divided into four departments, each subdivided into from three to six districts. The Department of Northern Luzon, placed under the command of General Wheaton, consisted of all of the island north of the Pasig River. The Department of Southern Luzon, placed under the command of General Bates, took in the part of Luzon south of the Pasig River. The Department of the Visayas, placed under the command of General Hughes, consisted of the Islands of Panay, Leyte, Bohol, Cebu and Negros. The Department of Mindanao and Jolo, under the command of General Kobbe, took in Mindanao, Jolo, and the small islands in that area. Each departmental district was placed under the command of a brigadier general or colonel, who was directly responsible to his department commander. The City of Manila was organized as a separate command, something similar to the District of Columbia, and placed under the command of General J. F. Bell. At the top of the pyramid formed by the districts and departments was General Otis, the Military Governor of the Philippines. In each district were garrisons of troops who were supposed to keep that area pacified.

During 1900 the Insurgents were eminently successful with their guerrilla warfare. Mobilizing the native population as they did, Aguinaldo's henchmen were able to harass the American garrisons to distraction. On several occasions small bodies of American troops were roughly handled.

An incident at the town of Tinuba, near Tarlac, Luzon, on March 4, 1900 gave an indication as to what could be expected. Two companies of the 9th Infantry marched to the town of Tinuba to round up a force of Insurgents reported there. They took with them two natives, former Insurgents who purported to be able to identify the Insurgents living in the town. Arriving at Tinuba the infantrymen lined up all male residents for identification. Twenty-nine men were identified as active Insurgents and told to divulge the hiding place of their rifles. Let Captain John Sigworth, in command of the expedition, tell the rest:[6]

"They led the guards in various directions in and out of the barrios but persisted in disclaiming the knowledge of the whereabouts of any rifles, stating that all had been taken to the mountains. Three Insurgents were then taken some distance away and informed that they would be harshly dealt with unless they divulged where their rifles were hidden. One of these three men then announced to Lieutenant Koehler that he would show where his rifle was hidden and started out in a southwesterly direction. Lieutenants Koehler and Wallace followed him on a trail which led into a forest. They followed him about a half a mile from the barrio when they came to a bend in the trail. At this point the Insurrecto jumped to one side and escaped. This was immediately followed by some rifle shots fired from a short distance in front. Lieutenant Koehler fell on his face and and although mortally wounded raised himself and emptied his revolver at the Insurgents. Lieutenant Wallace fired away all his ammunition and then being unable to see anyone, pulled Lieutenant Koehler off the trail, made him as comfortable as possible and ran down the trail to inform me what had happened. The mounted detachment galloped to the rescue of Lieutenant Koehler, who was found still alive, but unable to speak. In the meantime barracks were discovered about 100 yards from the trail. These were all burned and Lieutenant Koehler was brought to the barrio, dying just as the barrio was reached.

"Just after the firing had been heard in the direction Lieutenants Koehler and Wallace had gone the Insurgent prisoners under guard made a break to escape. I ordered my company to fire on them which they did, killing twenty-seven men."

Captain Sigworth then relates how the town was burned, the inhabitants first being permitted to remove their belongings. The net results of the expedition were that no rifles were found, but one American officer and twenty-seven Insurgents were killed. The question runs through this writer's mind as to whether the Insurgents actually made a bona fide "break for it" or whether Sigworth applied the "Ley de Fuga" so efficacious in Mexico. Twenty-nine Insurgents had been found in the town and twenty-seven were shot, the other two escaping.

On May 14 the barracks of a detachment of the 40th Infantry at Loculan, Mindanao, were rushed by 300 Insurgents armed with bolos. The American guard detail of four men on the first floor of the barracks were killed before the remainder of the detachment could obtain their rifles and fire on the Insurgents from the second story windows of the building. The Insurgents were finally driven from the town, but not before they had killed seven Americans. The commanding officer of the detachment, Captain Lamdin, reported[7] that the Insurgents had approached the barracks dressed as ordinary civilians and on a given signal had attacked the guard.

At the isolated town of Catubig on the Island of Samar, a detachment of thirty-one men of the 43rd Infantry came very close to being massacred.[8] At daybreak of April 15 the detachment which was quartered in the town convent, received a heavy fire from some 600 Insurgents located on a nearby hill. Taking refuge in the convent, the detachment returned the fire, which continued during that entire day and night. On the following morning a large number of Insurgents gained access to the town church which joined the convent, and attempted to set fire to the convent by throwing lighted bundles of kerosene-saturated hemp. An attempt by the Americans to drive the Insurgents out of the church was repulsed. On the following morning the Insurgents managed to set the convent on fire and the beleaguered detachment, which up to this time had only suffered one casualty, was forced to leave its shelter. Loaded down with ammunition, the Americans attempted to move down a street but were driven back by a heavy fire. They then started towards the river on which the town was located, but were forced back by Insurgents blocking that exit. The detachment then appears to have become panic stricken, for it broke into two groups, one rushing for some boats on the river bank and the other for a clump of grass in rear of the convent. The group of fifteen odd men who ran to the river were annihilated as they attempted to enter the boats. The other group reached the clump of grass where they hastily entrenched themselves. There, these fifteen men held some 200 Insurgents at bay for two days until another American detachment making a routine visit to the village relieved them. Of the garrison of thirty-one men, eighteen had been killed and three wounded. One hundred fifty dead Insurgents were found on the streets of the town by the relieving force.

In the Province of Illocos Norte, the Insurgents were so active that within a period of six weeks the telegraph line was cut twenty-three times, fifteen American soldiers had been killed in ambushes, and fifteen native policemen had been kidnapped from towns and assassinated.

In the town of Tarlac Insurgents entered the American camp while the troops were at dress parade and carried off thirty-two rifles stored in one of the company kitchens. The Insurgents had actually driven a bull cart into the camp and with the connivance of a native cook carried the arms off in the cart.

The situation was plainly out of control. The surest way for an American soldier or a native policeman to commit suicide was to wander away from a town alone. The situation became so bad that in June General MacArthur issued an order authorizing the native police of trusted loyalty to be armed with American revolvers to enable them to protect themselves from their countrymen.

In the midst of these conditions General Otis wired for his relief as Military Governor of the Philippines. His official reasons were "private interests require my return to the States; absent from family and business attention to which important since November 1, 1897 except for a few days." Some people believed that he asked for relief because of the new Philippine Commission which had been appointed and was enroute for the Islands.[9] The instructions which this commission had received from the President contemplated that inasmuch as Otis has reported "the Insurrection was over" that the military governor would be relieved of some of his authority in favor of the civil commission. At any rate Otis received his relief and departed from the Islands on May 5, a few days before the commission arrived.

In bidding adieu to General Otis, perhaps it is only fair to temper our criticism of his administration with a few words of appreciation of his accomplishments. He was faced with a problem entirely unique to an army officer. He was not only 7000 miles from his next immediate superior, but was constantly forced to make decisions with no precedents as a guide. The adaptations of Spanish law worked out under his direction to meet the new conditions, still stand as the basis of Philippine administration. He was a civil administrator par excellence and not only made the transition from Spanish to American regime in an efficient manner but also gained the respect of the Filipinos in so doing. His interference in the operations of the troops in the field was only one phase of his multifarious duties and was unquestionably motivated only by a super sense of responsibility. Apparently his administration of the Philippine Islands was eminently satisfactory to President McKinley, for shortly after his return to the United States he was promoted to the rank of major general in the regular army.

The new Philippine Commission was headed by William Howard Taft, at that time the senior Federal Circuit Court Judge of the United States. As members were Bernard Moses, Professor of Political Economy at the University of California; Luke E. Wright of Tennessee, a Democrat and considered one of the ablest jurists in the South, Henry C. Ives, a prominent Vermont Republican who had acted as American Commissioner in settling with the Germans and British the land troubles which had arisen in Samoa; and Dean C. Worcester, a member of the former Philippine Commission, who was regarded as a walking encyclopedia of information concerning the Philippines.

The commission was placed under the supervision of the Secretary of War and directed to proceed to the Philippines for the purpose of "continuing and perfecting the work of establishing civil government already commenced by the military authority."[10]

It was contemplated that after the commission had familiarized itself with conditions in the Philippines it would set up municipal codes throughout the Islands "in which the natives both in the cities and rural communities shall be afforded the opportunity to manage their own local and provincial affairs to the fullest extent of which they are capable." The commission was to advise the Secretary of War whenever it felt that the central administration could be safely transferred from the military governor of the Islands to civil authority. To give the commission some actual authority in the Islands it was further provided that on September 1, 1900 it would assume direction of the legislative phase of the government of the Islands, as distinguished from the executive which was to be retained by the military. This "legislative authority" included the passing of laws for the raising of revenue, the appropriation and expenditure of insular funds, the establishment of an educational system, and the organization and establishment of civil courts. Until the complete transfer of control the military governor was to remain the chief executive head of the Islands. It is beyond the scope of this book to go into the accomplishments of the Taft Commission. Needless to say, the members carried out their instructions to the letter and within one year after its arrival, Mr. Taft had been installed as

Civil Governor of the Islands. And considering that for the first time in the history of the United States the military was not subordinated to the civil, for a period at least, the executive and legislative branches of the government got along quite famously.

4

General MacArthur succeeded General Otis as military governor, and a new regime came into effect. MacArthur had campaigned in the field and was much better qualified to estimate the true situation in the Islands. He realized that until the native civilian population of the towns became pro-American, the guerrilla warfare would continue. As he said at the time:[11]

> "The Filipinos are not a warlike people. Left to themselves a large number (perhaps a considerable majority) would accept American supremacy. The people of the Islands, however, during the past five years, have been maddened by rhetorical sophistry and stimulants applied to national pride until the power of discrimination in matters of public concern has for the time being been almost entirely suspended . . . . . The truth is, the real effective opposition to pacification comes from the towns. The 'skulking bands of Guerrilla' as the remnants of the Insurgent army have been called, are mere expression of loyalty of the towns. They could not exist for a month without urban support . . . . . Intimidation has undoubtedly accomplished much to this end, but it is more probable that the adhesive principle comes from ethnological homogeneity which induces men to respond for a time to the appeals of consanguineous leadership, even when such action is opposed to their own interests . . . . . ."

As a trial balloon, MacArthur, six weeks after he became Military Governor, issued a proclamation of amnesty.[12] In this proclamation he unreservedly stated that all Insurrectos (except those who had "violated the laws of war," meaning those who were charged with murder) would, if they surrendered themselves and took an oath of allegiance to the United States within ninety days, be given complete amnesty without fear for the future. As a further inducement, Insurgents who surrendered rifles, would be paid the usual bonus of thirty pesos.

As a result of the proclamation, 5,022 people, including 115 Insurgent officers, came in and took the oath. In Manila, Aguinaldo's Chief of Staff Pantaleon Garcia and Generals Concepcion and Soliman, who had been captured, took the oath of allegiance, as did Pedro Paterno, former President of the Philippine Cabinet, However, when it is considered that the population of the Archipelago was some ten million the results were disappointing. Only 140 rifles were surrendered, and of these 130 came from one small area in the vicinity of Tarlac. The proclamation had not affected the pacification of the Islands to a marked degree.

Meanwhile, the guerrilla warfare broke out in renewed intensity. In a report signed August 1, 1900, General Bates, who was in command of the Department of Southern Luzon, stated:[13]

> "I regret that I cannot recommend the reduction of the forces in this Department by so much as a single soldier. The duty of occupation in fact renders necessary a larger number of troops than would be needed in conducting a campaign against armed forces . . . . . A single battalion can today march from one end of this Department to the other without encountering enough resistance from the enemy to seriously impede its progress, but small parties of troops cannot leave the garrisoned posts without incurring the danger of attack. The Insurrectos, after making an attack, disperse, assume civilian garb and conceal themselves among the peaceable inhabitants by threatening punishment to those who display friendship towards the Americans."

Major Mulford, in command at Calamba, complained that the town Presidente was an Insurrecto and while professing friendship for the Americans was giving information and assistance to the Insurgents in the neighborhood. Major Mulford added:[14]

> "The people say that conditions are worse here than when the Spanish ruled; that they were told that the Americans would protect them but instead that they allowed them to be robbed and do nothing to stop it."

On the Island of Bohol, which had been peaceably occupied, not a shot had been fired until August, 1900. Then, under the leadership of Pedro Samson, guerrillas attacked an American patrol, killed one American and wounded six by bolos, with a loss of 100 of the natives.

The district commander in Abra province reported:[15]

> "The insurrection has assumed such proportions in Abra that I do not consider it advisable to send a detachment out with less than 100 rifles. To abandon any territory that we are now occupying would be delivering up to the Insurgents all natives that have shown themselves friendly to us. If it is not considered advisable to send all the troops recommended, I request that two regiments be sent here to relieve the strain on the troops in this district so as to give them a rest."

From the town of Donsol in the southern part of Luzon, Major
Wise of the 47th Infantry reported:[16]

"This seems a critical time. This command has averaged
about 300 miles a month to break up the Insurgents in this
neighborhood . . . and I therefore request that the question
of more troops to garrison Pilar and Banaguran be considered."

From the Province of Nueva Ecija, General Funston reported:[17]

"Everything possible is being done to locate the Insurgent
bands in this vicinity, but so far without success. Indications
are that the greater part of them have hidden their guns and returned to the barrios, though they will no doubt concentrate
somewhere again before long."

In the Province of Cavite it developed that 375 armed Insurgents under the command of General Manual Trias were quartered
in the town of San Francisco de Malabon while the town was occupied by an American garrison.

On September 17, 1900, occurred what might be called a disaster
to the American troops. On the northeast corner of the Laguna de
Bay rested the town of Sinaloan. West of Sinaloan and separated by
a wide but shallow estuary of the Laguna was situated the small
barrio of Mabitac. Sinaloan and Mabitac were connected by a narrow
causeway. In Mabitac, the Insurgent leader, Juan Cailles, had raised
an Insurgent flag and sent an insolent message to Colonel Cheatham
in command of the American troops at Santa Cruz. Colonel Cheatham decided to send a company of the 37th and 15th Infantry regiments to make Cailles "eat his words." Command of the expedition
was given to Captain David Mitchell of the 15th Infantry. The general plan agreed upon had been for Mitchell's company of the 15th
Infantry to move around the east side of the estuary and attack
Mabitac from that direction, while Company L of the 37th was to
approach it in boats from the west and wade across the shallow bay.
On September 17, when the attack was made, Colonel Cheatham
watching operations from a launch, was horrified to see Mitchell's
company of the 15th Infantry approaching Mabitac not from the
east but directly across the narrow causeway. As the advance elements
of the company came under the fire of the entrenched Insurgents in
Mabitac, one officer, the first sergeant, and the entire advance party
were killed. The remainder of the company deployed in the estuary
where they became excellent targets and sure fatalities from drown-
ing if struck by a bullet. In attempting to rally his men, none of
whom had ever been under fire before and who refused to advance

further, Mitchell himself was killed. Finally some troops of the 37th Infantry, which were being held in reserve, were pushed into the action and forced the Insurgents from their trenches, but not until after the American casualties had mounted to twenty killed, twenty-four wounded, and thirty rifles lost. The entire command then withdrew and the Insurgents reoccupied Mabitac immediately. It was a testimony to the high character of the Insurgent General Juan Cailles, that on the following day he returned to the Americans the bodies of eight American soldiers killed in the engagement with all personal property remaining on their persons, a rare occurrence. Cailles claimed to have had only ten casualties in the engagement.

Successes like this emboldened the Insurgents to an extreme degree. On the following day the American garrison at Novaliches, a town within ten miles of Manila, was attacked by Insurgents and one American was killed.

The crowning blow came the same month on the Island of Marinduque. About twenty by thirty miles in length and breadth and just east of Luzon, this Island was mountainous and contained few roads. It had been garrisoned without difficulty since April of 1900 by two companies of the 29th Infantry, another regiment the majority of whose members had never been under fire. On September 11, Captain Shields, the company commander of Company F, which had been garrisoning the town of Santa Cruz on the north side of the Island, took fifty-one men of the company by boat to the town of Torrijos on the southern side, with the intent of marching back across the Island on the only trail between the two towns. A garrison consisting of a lieutenant and thirty-nine men was left at Santa Cruz.

At 2:00 a. m. on September 13 Captain Shields' column started its return march to Santa Cruz. Not anticipating trouble, the company carried little ammunition and when it was unexpectedly attacked at daybreak, Shields decided to push on towards Santa Cruz as rapidly as possible, rather than stop and fight. After the column had marched four miles under incessant Insurgent fire, Shields was severely wounded in the neck and halted his company to take stock of the situation. Helpless himself and fearing that if the company exhausted its ammunition supply the entire group would be massacred, he then sent orders to his senior sergeant for the company to leave him and cut its way back to Santa Cruz. Then, fearing that the men who were attending him would be boloed, Shields directed that they raise a white flag over his helpless body. Either the sergeant who was directed to take command and cut his way back to Santa Cruz, became panic stricken or never received the order, for when the white flag was raised the entire company surrendered to the Insurgents. The casualties so far had only been four killed and six wounded. Eight of the men in the company refused to surrender and attempted to reach the sea but were captured that evening. Besides, the wholesale surrender of the greater part of a company, the Insurgents obtained fifty-one Krag Jorgensen rifles with 800 rounds of ammunition. The next day the pro-American presidente of Santa Cruz was assassinated in the main street of the town, and the small garrison left behind was forced to take refuge in the convent while the remainder of the town was burned. The garrison managed to hold out until assistance arrived four days later, but the smirch of Shields' surrender was long remembered.

The number of engagements between Insurgents and Americans was so great that continual repetitious descriptions are apt to be boring. Possibly the extent of the situation can be summed up in the statement that a chronological list of brief descriptions of military events between May 1900, and June 1901, consumed 734 typewritten pages[18] in mentioning 1026 contacts between Americans and Insurgents. In the same period 245 Americans had been killed, 490 wounded and 118 captured; 3854 Insurgents were killed, 1193 wounded and 6,572 captured. The situation was so chaotic that the irrepressible soldiers coined a song, * the words of which implied that the actual Governor of the Islands was not General MacArthur but Aguinaldo. Truly the Insurrection was not ended when Aguinaldo's army was dispersed in January of 1900.

5.

However, after November of 1900 there was noticeable a definite if gradual cessation of Insurgent activities. The reasons may be ascribed to four causes: the adoption of sterner repressive measures by the Americans; the result of the presidential election of 1900 in the United States; the formation of the Filipino Federalist Party, and the capture of Emilio Aguinaldo. Each of these four causes is worthy of a brief discussion.

The guerrilla situation had become so bad that from Northern Luzon General Young proposed that "European methods with re-

---

* Oh is Mac the boss or is Mac the tool? Is Mac the governor general or a hobo? I'd like to know who'll be boss of this show—Will it be Mac or Emilio Aguinaldo?

bellious Asiatics"[19] be instituted. By that he meant the establishment of a virtual military dictatorship throughout the Islands. He advocated the summary punishment by death of all persons caught with arms after having taken the oath of allegiance to the United States and the confiscation of all property owned by Insurgent leaders. He proposed to remove all native office holders and replace them with the American military; to lay waste all parts of the country used by Insurgents as hiding places; to deport all persons whose presence in the country was deemed prejudicial to the interests of the United States; he proposed strict censorship of the press; the concentration of people living in rebellious zones into circumscribed zones; in other words, the institution of a virtual reign of terror.

General MacArthur thought that these measures were a bit too stringent, and that the freedom-loving American people would not stand for them. However, he did take steps to tighten the reins of government. On December 20, 1900 he issued a proclamation[20] placing the Islands under martial law. He directed that Insurgents who alternately took to the field and then returned to their barrios in civilian garbs would, if captured, be subject to trial for murder; he directed that known Insurgents be sent to Manila and imprisoned; he advised the civilian population that hereafter fear of Insurgents would not be accepted as a legitimate excuse for failure to give full cooperation and loyalty to the American authorities; that civilians who were not by overt acts loyal to American authority would be considered as being against the government; permission was also secured from Washington to deport to the Island of Guam certain Insurgent leaders who were recognized as irreconcilables.

The proclamation produced a signal effect in some parts of the Islands. In the province of Illocos Sur 2000 natives took the oath of allegiance. As a result of the punitive provisions some seventy-nine Insurgents were tried for murder and hanged; thirty-two irreconcilables, including the paralytic, Mabini, were deported to the Island of Guam. It is difficult to judge accurately the practical effects of the proclamation, since the presidential election in the United States was also exercising its effect during this period. However, in commenting on the proclamation later, General MacArthur stated:[21]

"As an educational document, the effect was immediate and far reaching. From the date of its issue secret resistance and apathy began to diminish and kidnapping and assassination were much abated. In a very short time these malign influences were to a great extent superseded by cooperation and active interest in American affairs. Rarely in war has a single document been so instrumental in influencing ultimate results."

Turning to a brief discussion of the effect of the presidential election in the United States upon the Insurrection, it may be recalled that the acquisition of the Philippine Islands had been a bitterly fought matter before the United States Senate. The issue had been so hotly contested that the two-thirds majority necessary for the ratification of the Treaty with Spain had been gained by only one vote. Greatest opposition came from members of the Democratic party who seriously questioned the advisability of the United States putting an iron in a fire so distant, particularly in view of a traditional isolationist policy. Despite the fact that ratification of the Treaty with Spain settled the matter of acquiring the Philippines, certain well-educated, prominent, and politically powerful citizens belonging to both political parties insisted on regarding the issue as not closed.

Although Senator Lodge, the senior Senator from Massachusetts and chairman of the Senate Foreign Relations Committee, strongly favored the acquisition of the Philippines, his colleague from the same state, Senator Hoar, bitterly opposed the idea.

During the early part of 1899 the so-called Anti-Imperialist Society was founded in Boston. It launched its campaign with a so-called "Address to the People of the United States." The aims of the society as expressed in the address were reasonable enough, since they urged all Americans only to disregard party affiliations and co-operate with the society in accomplishing the following ends:[22]

> "First—That our government shall take immediate steps toward a suspension of hostilities in the Philippines and a conference with the Philippine leaders with a view to preventing further bloodshed upon the basis of a recognition of their freedom and independence as soon as proper guarantees can be had of order and protection to property.
> "Second—That the Government of the United States shall tender an official assurance to the inhabitants of the Philippine Islands that they will encourage and assist in the organization of such a government in the Islands as the people thereof shall prefer and that upon its organization in a stable manner the United States in accordance with its traditional and prescriptive policy in such cases will recognize the independence of the Philippines and its equality among nations and gradually withdraw all military and naval forces."

Also, the following announced means by which the Anti-Imperialists intended to accomplish their aims were reasonable:
> ". . . . . . to continue the circulation of literature, to assist in the formation of leagues, and by public meetings and every

means known to a free people, to agitate for the revival in the land of the spirit of Washington and Lincoln; to protest against a spirit of militarism and force; to oppose the colonial idea and a permanently large standing army and to assert the vital truths of the Declaration of Independence embodied in the Constitution and indissolubly connected with the welfare of this Republic."

The anti-imperialist "address" was signed by twenty-nine eminent citizens. It contained such formidable names as Andrew Carnegie, multi-millionaire steel manufacturer and philanthropist; Samuel Gompers, President of the American Federation of Labor; David Starr Jordan, President of Leland Stanford University; and Charles F. Adams, former President of the Union Pacific Railroad. Three of the signers were ex-United States Senators, four were former members of the House of Representatives, four were ex-cabinet members, three were eminent writers or editors, three were prominent clergymen, two were what might be termed professional reformers, and eight were educators of a varying degree of prominence. Twenty-six of the twenty-nine signers were listed in the American "Who's Who" for 1899.

Regardless of the announced purposes of the society, altruistic as they purported to be, the methods employed and the effect of its propaganda lay it open to heavy condemnation. One of the society's most enthusiastic adherents, Edward Atkinson, a Boston insurance underwriter, edited a magazine known as the "American Anti-Imperialist." The periodical deplored the cost of the Insurrection to the United States; gloomily predicted that the tropical climate and prevalence of venereal disease in the Philippines would ruin the American youth sent to the Philippines to quell the Insurrection. One issue stated:[23]

> "If the regular army of the United States is stationed in the Philippine Islands and kept there six months, it is pratically certain that after that term had elapsed there will be no regular army of the United States in existence capable of any effectual service even on the part of the survivors."

The biggest crime of the Anti-Imperialist Society was not propaganda among the Americans, however, but the assistance and false hopes it gave the Filipinos. The society believed that if the Insurrection persisted until the presidential election of 1900 that the American voters, tired of a war 7000 miles away, would return an anti-imperialist,—the Democrat William Jennings Bryan—to the White House and thereby change the policy of the United States in regard to the retention of the Islands. The idea was built up to the extent that Aguinaldo and his adherents honestly believed that the election of Mr. Bryan to the presidency would mean independence for them. After Aguinaldo was forced to take to the mountains, the guerrilla warfare was continued mainly with the hope that it would have a definite influence on the American election. On November 4, 1900, election day, a prayer appeared in a pro-independence Manila newspaper, which ran something as follows:[24]

"On this day there is a struggle indeed in America: On this day is decided our life. . . . . .

"Glory to Bryan, Glory to America, Glory to the Fostering Fatherland, Glory to the sons of the nation . . . . . .

"Grief to Imperialism, grief to McKinley, Grief to the hated . . . .

"Mother Philippines—Blessed be Thou

"Mr. Bryan—triumphant be Thou

"Our independence may we win thee

"The life of Aguinaldo may it be for a thousand years

"Our army be thou great

"By this mercy, Lord curse those who watch over us. Do so then Lord all this, Lord, So be it."

It has never been definitely established that the Anti-Imperialistic Society actually aided the Insurgents with money and arms. The story goes, however, that many of its members were in constant correspondence with Aguinaldo and his aides, giving them advice and moral support. When Aguinaldo was captured, papers found in his possession revealed the extent of his correspondence with American citizens.

The influence which this anti-imperialistic influence exerted throughout the country is indicated by the fact that in January of 1901, while the guerrilla warfare was at its height and American soldiers were being attacked and killed daily, the Missouri House of Representatives passed the following resolution:[25]

"Whereas the sympathies of the American people go out to all nations and all peoples struggling for liberty; therefore be it

"Resolved, that the House of Representatives of the Forty-first General Assembly of Missouri extend sympathy to the people of the Philippine Archipelago, in their heroic struggle for freedom."

It was common talk in the Philippines that every anti-imperialistic speech of any importance made in the United States caused a corresponding attack by guerrillas on some tired and harassed American garrison stationed in the Philippine bosque.

Of course the members of the army in the Philippines realized that they were receiving a blow in the back from home and were justly indignant. A document captured at Tarlac revealed a communication from the United States advising Aguinaldo of banquets and meetings being held in his honor in this country. Any American soldier who was daily risking his life suppressing an Insurrection which unsympathetic fellow countrymen were deliberately encouraging had every right to be indignant. Most of the military personnel in the Philippines believed that the Anti-Imperialist Society was furnishing the Insurgents with money and arms. This belief was substantiated in August of 1899 when several Insurgent artillery "duds," falling into the town of Angeles, indicated that the shells had been manufactured in the United States.

General Lawton felt so strongly on the subject that a short time before his death he wrote to a friend:[26]

> "I wish to God that this whole Philippine situation could be known to everyone in America as I know it. If the real history, inspiration, and conditions of this Insurrection and the influences local and external that now encourage the enemy could be understood at home, we would hear no talk of unjust "shooting of government" into the Filipinos or hauling down our flag in the Philippines. If the so-called anti-imperialists in Boston would honestly ascertain the truth on the ground and not in distant America, they whom I believe to be honest men misinformed would be convinced of the error of their statements and conclusions and of the unfortunate effect of their publications here. If I am shot by a Filipino bullet it might just as well come from one of my own men.
>
> "These are strong words and Yet I say them because I know from my own observation confirmed by stories of captured Filipino prisoners that the continuance of the fighting is chiefly due to reports that are sent out from America and circulated among these ignorant natives by the leaders who know better."

Possibly fate had given Lawton a premonition of the future, for he was killed two months after the above letter was written.

The retention of the Philippines was a major issue in the presidential election of 1900. Anti-imperialist league notwithstanding, the American people gave their verdict and Mr. McKinley was re-elected President.

The outcome of the election had an immediate repercussion in the Philippines. Within three weeks after the issue was decided, another 2000 Insurgents in the Island of Luzon had surrendered and taken the oath of allegiance to the United States.

Early in January General Delgado led the Insurgents on the Island of Panay into the capital where 30 officers and 140 men surrendered their rifles and equipment. General Delgado had been a thorn in the side of the Americans since the occupation of Iloilo in February of 1899. His surrender was to mark the definite pacification of Panay.

The effect of the election is further indicated in the decrease of engagements with the Insurgents immediately following November 4.

During September and October of 1900 the Americans and Insurgents had 241 clashes in which 52 were aggressive on the part of the Insurgents. During November and December the number of contacts was cut down to 198 in which 27 were aggressive on the part of the Insurgents. In other words, Insurgents aggressiveness was reduced by 50% in the two months immediately following the election. During September and October, 54 Insurgents surrendered; during November and December the number rose to 2,534. A consideration of the number of arms surrendered, however, throws a new light on the subject. During September and October 18 rifles had been surrendered, and during November and December the number jumped only to 47. This would indicate that the Insurgents who surrendered as a result of the election were (possibly with the exception of Delgado's force) not the rifle-toting variety. The majority were bolo men who, not being equipped as soldiers, were awaiting the result of the election to see which way to jump. It would appear that the real Insurgents were still at large.

Another factor which exercised a decisive influence on the pacification of the Islands was the formation of the so-called Federal Party among the Filipinos. Its organization might be said to have been a direct result of the presidential election of 1900, combined with MacArthur's proclamation of December 21.

There were held in Manila at this time under what might be called "protective custody" a few well-educated Filipinos who had filled cabinet positions under Aguinaldo's government. When the Insurgent army had been scattered in November of 1899, the majority of these Insurrecto politicos had been captured and taken to Manila. One small group headed by Felipe Buencamino and Pedro Paterno had represented the pro-American elements (if such a group could have been considered as existing) in Aguinaldo's cabinet. It had been this group which had proposed peace during April of 1899 and had formed a commission to go to Manila and confer with Otis. It may be recalled that the commission was arrested by Luna, the Commanding General of the Insurgent Army at the time, and its members imprisoned.

At any rate, contact with the Americans in Manila, perhaps the friendly, lenient way in which they were treated, swung over a number of these former cabinet members to the idea of accepting American sovereignty as outlined in the proclamation issued by the Schurman Commission.

On December 23, 1900, a group of Filipinos issued a so-called manifesto for the formation of the "Federal Party" which included the party plank. The platform [27] advocated the immediate acceptance of the sovereignty of the United States by all Filipinos. It proposed a form of government as promised in the proclamation of the Schurman commission, which in many respects was the form finally adopted,—that is, government of the Islands by a civil governor general, Filipino representatives to be stationed in Washington, an elected Filipino House of Representatives and Senate, complete autonomy in respect to municipal and provincial governments, restriction of veto power to the President of the United States or the Governor General. The only aspiration of the party which the American authorities frowned on at the time was the announced hope to have the Philippines eventually admitted to the Union as a state.

With the assistance of the military and civil authorities, the party extended its influence throughout the Islands. Members from Manila traveled among the barrios making speeches, forming local groups, enjoining the people and Insurrectos to come in under the American fold. Its methods are perhaps best explained by an excerpt of a report by an American military commander in the Province of Sorgoson.[28] Lieutenant Disque stated at the time:

"I arrived at Irocin with twenty-two members of Company B and four members of the Federal Party. Soon after arriving there I instructed the presidente of the town to call all his people into the convent for the purposes of listening to speeches by the four members of the Federal Party. At the same time I sent a communication prepared by the members of the Federal Party to all leaders of the Insurgent forces located in the Province . . . . . . Soon after these letters were dispatched a large crowd of natives had assembled in the convent and the members of the Federal Party talked to them until 4:00 p. m. endeavoring to show them the uselessness of further resistance and the benefits they would derive from immediate peace . . . . After the members of the Federal Party had finished I told the people through an interpreter that all who wished to, could take the oath of allegiance to the United States . . . . . before 9:00 p. m. that night over 800 males all over 18 years of age had taken the oath. During the next two days, large numbers of natives, many of whom were recognized as Insurgents, came in from the surrounding countryside and surrendered . . . . . ."

Lieutenant Disque then goes on to cite how the members of the Federal Party actually went into the "bosque" surrounding the town and after talking to the "Insurgent Governor" of the province brought him in to surrender with his troops.

Probably the outstanding benefit of the Federal Party was to cause the surrender of General Mariano Trias in the province of Cavite. Trias, who was a Robin Hood sort of individual, was actually held in high esteem by the majority of the natives in the province and had been operating successfully a parallel government to that established by the Americans. The surrender of Trias not only brought an eminent Insurrecto into the American fold, but also insured the whole-hearted cooperation of the people living in the province. Trias' influence extended throughout several nearby provinces, and his surrender was followed by a marked cessation of activities outside of his native province. The organizers and promoters of the Federal Party received their reward from the Americans by being given high positions in the civil government of the Philippines which was established shortly thereafter.

In March of 1901 there occurred an event which was not only as romantic as any event ever taking place in the annals of American history, but also had a definite effect on the course of the Insurrection. This event was the capture of the erstwhile Insurgent President, Emilio Aguinaldo.

Otis had minimized the influence which Aguinaldo, from his hideout in the Benguet Mountains, was exercising on the Insurrection, as he said shortly after his return to the United States:[29]

> "Aguinaldo is merely a figurehead. His power was gone when we broke up his government and captured his advisors and friends . . . . what difference does it make whether Aguinaldo is dead or not when we know that if he is not dead he is a refugee in the mountains where he can do no one any harm."

MacArthur's attitude was just the opposite. He not only believed that Aguinaldo should be captured, but captured alive. As he said in referring to the capture:[30]

> "It dispelled the growing tendency to idealize his personality and to surround him with mythical legends of invincibility which millions of natives believed to be true and which they also believed would ultimately insure the success of the revolution.

Aguinaldo was the incarnation of the Insurrection and as such his death would have magnified the legend . . . . . Accordingly his capture alive by legitimate military methods, or his surrender . . . . . . became a prominent feature of the military administration of the Islands . . . ."

Credit for the capture of Aguinaldo must go to General Frederick Funston. As a brigadier general of volunteers, Funston had been placed in command of the military district which embraced the territory in the vicinity of Nueva Ecija Province.

On January 8 an Insurgent named Cecilio Sigismundo presented himself to Lieutenant J. D. Taylor, in command of the American garrison in the town of Pantabangan. This Insurgent, Sigismundo, was a courier for Aguinaldo, who was hiding in the town of Palanan, an isolated locality in the northeast part of Luzon. Sigismundo carried some twenty letters from Aguinaldo to guerrilla commanders scattered throughout Luzon. Near Pantabangan his escort of twelve Insurgents had encountered American troops and been dispersed. As was customary, Sigismundo appealed sub rosa to the native Presidente of Pantabangan for assistance in getting through the American lines. By mere chance the Presidente actually was loyal to the Americans and convinced Sigismundo that his best bet was to surrender and forget about his mission from Aguinaldo. After some negotiations with Lieutenant Taylor, he did come in and surrendered not only himself but all his dispatches. Taylor sent the prisoner with the papers to district headquarters at San Isidro. There, while looking over the captured dispatches, one in particular germinated a plan in Funston's mind for capturing the Insurgent President. This one dispatch was addressed to Baldomero Aguinaldo, the cousin of the Insurgent President, and directed him to send 400 armed Insurgents to Aguinaldo's mountain hideout using the courier Sigismundo as a guide. The dispatch had been in cipher and was decoded only with great difficulty. As General Funston later said:[31]

> "The cipher completely balked us for several hours. They seemed to be made up of a jumble of letters of the alphabet making words in no particular language. Captain Smith (Funston's adjutant) Lazaro Segovia, the versatile and courageous Spaniard, who for nearly a year had done such excellent secret service work for me, and I stripped off our coats, and even other things in fact, and with pencils and pads of paper seated ourselves around a table and racked our brains. . . . . daylight became darkness and dawn was at hand before the peerless Segovia, whose knowledge of both Spanish and Tagalog now stood us in such good stead, found the key word of the cipher,

having done it by ransacking his brain for every word in the Malay dialect that he had ever heard of."

On interviewing the defaulter Sigismundo, Funston ascertained that Aguinaldo, with an armed escort, was living in the small town of Palanan, Isabella, about due east of Illagan and about ten miles from the coast. Sigismundo stated that the only trail to Palanan from the coast was carefully watched and any attempt to capture Aguinaldo by ordinary methods would surely fail, since the Insurgent President was certain to receive warning of the approach of a hostile force in ample time to move back into the wild mountain fastness in the vicinity.

Funston conceived the plan of having a force of Macabebes disguise themselves as Tagalogs and represent the force of 400 men which Aguinaldo had directed his cousin to send to Palanan. Sigismundo came wholeheartedly over to the American side and agreed to guide such an expedition to Palanan. Despite its unorthodoxy, MacArthur approved the plan and Funston went to Manila where final preparations were made.

Out of the Macabebe troops eighty were selected who spoke Tagalog language fluently and could be reasonably expected to pass for Tagalogs. In order that a plausible reason for American officers accompanying the expedition could be made, it was decided the officers would pose as soldiers who had been captured by the column en route to Palanan. Five officers went along, Funston, Captain R. T. Hazzard and Lieutenant O.P.M. Hazzard, brothers who had been on duty with the Macabebe scouts, Funston's Aide-de-Camp, Lieutenant B. J. Mitchell, and Captain H. W. Newton, who was selected because he had at one time been in Palanan.

Feeling it necessary to have a few bona fide Tagalogs to act as Insurgent officers, Funston dug up four whom he considered unquestionably loyal. The Spaniard, Segovia, who had helped unravel the cipher, completed the complement for the expedition.

Greatest secrecy and detailed precautions accompanied the preparations. The Macabebes were clothed in nondescript Insurgent uniforms and armed with Mauser and Remington rifles. They were carefully rehearsed in the story of the "march" north, the fight with the Americans and the capture of the American prisoners. They were instructed that the American officers must be treated like prisoners and not like officers. The Macabebes fell into the plan wholeheartedly.

To make the deception complete, it was decided that the force would not make an overland march to Palanan, where daily contacts with Tagalogs might expose the real purpose of the expedition, but be taken by boat around the southern tip of Luzon and landed on the east coast on an isolated spot and make the march to Palanan from there. That part of the Island was so isolated from the central plain that an Insurgent force might appear there as out of nowhere without causing undue questioning.

The expedition left Manila on March 6 on the gunboat *Vicksburg*. The arrangements had been kept so secret that even the captain of the *Vicksburg* did not know the purpose of the expedition until it was well out to sea. The town of Casiguran, in a bay by the same name, had been picked as a landing place. It was over one hundred miles from Palanan, but Funston feared that if an American gunboat approached too close to Palanan, Aguinaldo's suspicions would be aroused. After a turbulent trip through the San Bernardino straits, the *Vicksburg* arrived in the vicinity of Casiguran on March 13 and in the dead of night landed the adventurous expedition about ten miles from the town. The five American officers, eighty Macabebes, one Spaniard, and four Tagalogs were left entirely on their own resources in a part of Luzon which had never before been occupied by American troops. One defaulter would ruin the whole plan, possibly cause a wholesale massacre. It was arranged that the *Vicksburg* would contact the coast near Palanan Bay on the 25th.

To allay suspicion on the part of the natives in Casiguran, Funston sent couriers ahead with a message for the town Presidente, stating that the force was enroute for Palanan with reinforcements for Aguinaldo and asking that in view of their "difficult march over the mountains" that quarters and rations be furnished the group. The inhabitants of Casiguran were completely hoodwinked as General Funston said:[32]

> "There was much excitement in the little town of Casiguran and crowds of people came to greet us. Of course they thought that they were greeting some of their own victorious soldiers bringing prisoners that they had captured. The village band was pressed into service and we entered the town in great style. Of course we were a great show, being the first Americans they had ever seen. They crowded around us and there were some black looks and some remarks not of a complimentary nature, but in general there was nothing in their conduct to criticize."

The expedition remained in Casiguran two days, assembling food for the one-hundred mile march to Palanan. Funston took advantage of the delay to send forward by two native couriers forged messages to Aguinaldo stating that the expedition was on its way to join him. To further confuse the Insurgent Presidente, Funston had prepared these messages before he left Manila, using stationery captured from the Insurgent General Lacuna. Lacuna was known to be loyal to Aguinaldo and his signature was cleverly forged by the adept Segovia. Aguinaldo later admitted that it was this forged letter which completely allayed any suspicion he might have had.

Leaving Casiguran, the expedition made a most difficult journey north following the irregular coast line. As General Funston said:[33]

> "The rain never ceased pouring and from the morning we left Casiguran we were drenched to the skin for a week. We waded more than sixty streams, some of them mere brooks but others so deep and swift that we had to put our hands on each others shoulders and go in up to our armpits. The food soaked through and through and became a soggy fermenting mass. From the start we went on half rations and in a few days were ravenous with hunger. Of sleep we could get very little as our bed was the bare ground and we were exposed without shelter to the never ending torrents of rain. To eke out our food supply a few small fish were caught in their hands by the Macabebes and they scraped limpets from the rocks and gathered snails. The snails, limpets and small fish were stewed up with corn and made a revolting mess. . . . . Segovia had developed a terrible abscess on one of his feet. . . .all day of the 22nd we stumbled along in a half dazed condition, our men were scattered for a mile along the beach, some of them so weak they reeled as they walked. . . . . It seemed impossible that the madcap enterprise could succeed and I began to have regrets that I had led all these men to such a finish."

In the evening of the 22nd the persevering band reached the town of Dinudungan, where the trail started to Palanan, ten miles distant.

There it was met by a messenger from Aguinaldo, who directed that the American prisoners be left on the coast and not brought to Palanan. Exhausted, the expedition sent word back to Aguinaldo to send them some food, which he did. Fearing that the absence of the American officers might make the whole plan go awry when Palanan was reached, Funston decided to disregard Aguinaldo's instructions about leaving the "American prisoners" on the coast and to march up to Palanan with the Macabebes. En route to the town the Americans had to dive into the brush and hide while an Insurgent patrol sent from Palanan for the purpose of guarding them met and passed the column on the trail.

The actual capture of the Insurgent President was accomplished without the American officers being present. Knowing that if they appeared in Palanan with the column of Macabebes Aguinaldo would sense something wrong immediately, Funston sent the Maca- bebes with the purported Insurgent officers ahead into the town. The 22nd of March had been Aguinaldo's birthday and Palanan was bedecked in festive colors. As the column of Macabebes marched into the town plaza, Aguinaldo's bodyguard of some fifty men was lined up at present arms, with the band playing. The Macabebes swung into line opposite Aguinaldo's troops. In the second story of the municipal building overlooking the Plaza was Aguinaldo with several aides. Segovia and Tal Pacido, one of the Tagalogs who had accompanied the expedition, walked upstairs to report to Aguinaldo. After receiving a few congratulatory words from the Insurgent Presi- dent for making the difficult march, Segovia walked to a window and gave the signal to the Macabebes below. The deception had been perfect and the surprise was complete. Without further ado, the Macabebes raised their rifles and opened fire on the Insurgents lined up a few yards away. Exhausted and nervous as they were, the volley only resulted in three casualties, one being the band leader. How- ever, its effect was sufficient to cause the bodyguard to scatter and disappear in the nearby woods. In the municipal building, Segovia drew his pistol and fired at Aguinaldo's aides, who either escaped by jumping out of the window or were shot. Tel Pacido tackled Agui- naldo and threw him under a table saying, "You are a prisoner of the Americans." When Funston and the other Americans entered the town a few moments later, the situation was well in hand.

The return to Manila was uneventful. The expedition rested at Palanan for one day and on the 25th marched to the coast where it was picked up by the *Vicksburg*. On the morning of the 28th the *Vicksburg* reached Manila. Funston took his prisoner ashore and presented him to MacArthur, who was astonished at the successful outcome of the wild venture.

A few days later, as a reward, Funston was made a brigadier general in the regular army. A rank which few officers attain in forty years of service, he had attained in three. The Macabebes and Tagalogs on the expedition were liberally rewarded by cash pay- ments for their part in the capture.

MacArthur treated Aguinaldo with extreme consideration. He installed the Insurgent President in a spacious house near to the Malacanan and sent for his family. The ever-present guard held over him was as unobtrusive as possible. In short time Aguinaldo recip- rocated by issuing a proclamation advising his followers to come in under the American flag. He said in part:[34]

"The country has declared unmistakably for peace; so be it. Enough of blood; enough of tears and desolation . . . . after mature deliberation I cannot refuse to heed the voice of a people longing for peace. . . . . By acknowledging and accepting the sovereignty of the United States throughout the entire Archipelago, as I do now without any reservation whatsoever, I believe that I am serving thee, my beloved country. May happiness be thine. . . . . ."

And henceforth Emilio Aguinaldo, the *bete noir* of the American sovereignty in the Philippines, ceased to be a problem. Perhaps it is only in the interests of a generous appraisal of an honorable opponent to quote the eulogy printed in the anti-imperialistic magazine *Nation* in its issue of April 4, 1901, shortly after Aguinaldo had been captured. Said *Nation:*

"Whatever fate may be in reserve for him (Aguinaldo) he will be known to history only as a defender of liberty under desperate circumstances and against terrible odds. With little money and scant resources in arms, ammunition and supplies, he has maintained the fight for more than two years against an organized army of more than 65,000 men, possessing every appliance of modern warfare and having entire command of the sea. That in this heroic endeavor he was moved solely by patriotism and that his character was above reproach is the testimony of officers of our own both military and civil. Nor has his career been stained by any act of cruelty. At the time when these great responsibilities were thrown upon him he was only twenty-seven years of age. History can show few brighter examples of patient endurance, intellectual resource and high principle. We feel sure that such virtues will stir the admiration of every lover of liberty in the world and that the name of Aguinaldo will find a place eventually in all American hearts. . . . ."

General Aguinaldo later received a pension from the Insular Government and settled down to complacent farming and acting as the head of the Philippine Veterans' Association.

The proclamation was issued on April 19. Its practical effect was immediate. Five days later over 1500 Insurgents in the vicinity of Manila surrendered. On May 1st General Manuel Tinio, the soul of the Insurrection in the Illocano provinces of northern Luzon, surrendered with thirty-six of his officers, admitting that his surrender was a result of Aguinaldo's proclamation. As a gracious gesture for Tinios' surrender. MacArthur directed that 1000 Insurgent prisoners be released. In central Luzon Generals Mascardo Alexandrino and Lucuna surrendered, after which 500 Insurgent prisoners were released. In June General Juan Cailles, who had been a thorn in the American side in southern Luzon, surrendered and another 1000 prisoners were released. Within a comparatively short time virtually every Insurgent of importance in Luzon had, with one exception, surrendered. The exception was General Miguel Malvar, in the Province of Batangas. Except for General Lucban on the Island of Samar, the Insurgents in the other Islands came in and laid down their arms. Between June and September of 1901, besides the numerous leaders, over 4000 Insurgents surrendered, bringing in with them 1363 rifles.[35] Those who refused to accept American sovereignty were rapidly assuming the status, not of Insurrectos, but of bandits. Funston's venture had been well worth while.

The operation of these above factors towards pacification permitted the gradual transition from military to civil government in the Islands. In January of 1901 Manila was taken from the direct jurisdiction of a military provost guard and given to a civilian police force. Within the next few months nine companies of native police were organized and distributed throughout Luzon. In February of 1900, the Philippine Scouts, a native military unit built around the Macabebe Scouts, was organized and distributed throughout the Archipelago. Today these "Philippine Scouts" numbering some 5000, form the nucleus of the American armed forces stationed in the Philippines. In February of 1901 the Taft Commission authorized the establishment of provincial civil governments, provincial governors to be elected by the natives; municipal codes and native councils were set up in barrios which were felt to be loyal to the United States. As fast as pacified provinces could be organized and civil governments established, they were removed from the jurisdiction of the military authorities and placed under the supervision of the Civil Commission headed by Mr. Taft. It was true that throughout the Archipelago the number of American troops under arms had decreased but little, They were still forced to make night marches in attempts to capture minor recalcitrant leaders. But by June of 1901 about half the people of Luzon were living under military rule and about half under civil government.

A particularly refractory Insurgent captured at this time was Major Manuel L. Quezon. This twenty-three year old youth had been a law student at the University of Santo Tomas at the outbreak of the insurrection and had forthwith enlisted in Aguinaldo's army as a private. Promotion had been rapid and an almost fanatical belief in the righteousness of the Insurgent cause motivated him to remain hostile to the Americans even after Aguinaldo's proclamation. Following his capture, he was rewarded for his efforts by six months imprisonment. With the establishment of peace he engaged in law practice and then drifted into politics still a passionate, if peaceful, apostle of Philippine Independence. Possessed of a brilliant mind, a pleasing personality, and capable of forensic eloquence, he saw his ideals materialize thirty-five years later in his own inauguration as the first President of the Philippine Commonwealth.

By June the number of American troops in the Philippines had been reduced to some 42,000, and 23,000 Insurgent rifles had been either captured or surrendered. General MacArthur wrote:[36]

"The armed insurrection is almost entirely suppressed. At the present writing there is no embodied rebel force in all Luzon above the Pasig. In the Department of Visayas all is pacified excepting only the Island of Samar; and in the Department of Mindinao and Jolo, the Filipino rebels have all submitted and been disarmed. In the Department of southern Luzon, disorders still continue in several provinces but in such progressively diminishing force as to encourage the hope that all will be pacified at an early date."

On June 20, 1901, by proclamation of the President, the executive authority in the Islands was transferred from the Military Governor to the civil authority. William Howard Taft, chairman of the Philippine Commission, was designated as the Civil Governor, but the legislative power still remained in the commission to whose membership was added three natives. The proclamation contemplated, however, that in provinces which were not sufficiently pacified for the full inauguration of civil rule, the Military Governor would be the executive authority. It will thus be seen there was a sort of dual executive authority installed. Of the seventy-seven provinces in the Archipelago twenty-two were placed under the civil authority and fifty-five under the military. At first glance it may appear that the Archipelago was less than one-third pacified, yet the twenty-two provinces in which the civil government was instituted contained nearly 50% of the population of the Islands. Many of the provinces still under military rule were in wild, sparsely settled areas, which during the Spanish regime had not even been occupied; many of them were peaceful, and the inauguration of civil rule was merely the matter of running down a few local bandits. On July 4, 1901, the day that the new regime became effective, General MacArthur returned to the United States. He was succeeded by Major General Adna Chaffee, who had just returned from China as commanding officer of the American forces sent there as a result of the Boxer Rebellion.

The establishment of Civil Government proceeded apace. Within three months, thirteen more provinces had been placed under civil authorities, and the Insurrection as such was definitely on the wane. American garrisons were kept in many towns, but relations between American soldiers and Filipino natives were friendly and in many respects similar to conditions in the United States. The main duty of the military consisted in running down recalcitrant ladrones and protecting the civilian population of the native villages from wandering isolated bandit bands. Except for the provinces of Batangas, parts of the Islands of Cebu, Bohol and Samar and Mindoro, the situation was relatively quiet. During the summer Cebu and Bohol became so quiet that civil government was instituted there. Then just as peace appeared to be in sight occurred the horrible affair at the town of Balangiga, on the Island of Samar.

Samar was a wild unsettled island. Virtually no roads existed there, and what towns had been settled were scattered along the coast line. During the Spanish regime the island had not been fully occupied and the few garrisons which were maintained along the few coastal barrios were commanded by non--commissioned officers, who were usually directed to "marry a relative of the leading Filipino in the town and secure the protection of the natives." The interior of the Island was inhabited by a mongrel type of native whose blood was mixed with the aboriginal negritos and the Moro pirates who had raided the Island for centuries.

The 9th U. S. Infantry had but recently returned from the China expedition. It had performed signal service there, had taken part in the capture of Tientsin, and had been among the first to rush the walls of the Imperial city at Peking. With the cessation of the Boxer activities in China it had returned to the Philippines and had been scattered in small garrisons throughout the Islands. On August 11, Company C had been sent to Samar and had occupied without opposition the small coastal village of Balangiga. The officials of the town professed friendship for the Americans. The company, whose strength consisted of seventy-four men, was housed in the public buildings. The company commander, Captain Thomas W. O'Connell, was a West Point graduate in the class of 1894. Lieutenant E. C. Bumpus, second in command, had served throughout the Insurrection in Luzon and had accompanied the regiment to China. Major Richard S. Griswold, attached to the company as surgeon, had seen service throughout the Insurrection. The company itself consisted mainly of veterans: a few had gone through the campaign in Cuba, many through the Insurrection in Luzon, and all through the Boxer campaign. One man had been a member of the crew of the *Olympia* during the battle of Manila Bay.

It was known that the die-hard leader, Vincente Lucban, was active throughout the Island of Samar, but since he had confined his activities to the regimentation of the hapless natives in the interior of the Island, or the attack of small patrols of American troops, no particular trouble was expected from him.

Established comfortably in Balangiga, Captain O'Connell set out to clean up the town. He directed the local presidente to assemble the citizens and put them to work sweeping up the years-old accumulation of rubbish and trash scattered throughout the streets and clearing the underbrush which had been permitted to grow unrestricted under houses and in the streets. In response to a complaint from the Presidente that he was unable to get the people to volunteer for work, the company canvassed the town and forced some one hundred able-bodied men to work under guard. A short time later, the town presidente and the chief of police suggested that since several natives in the hills close to the town were supposed to work out their taxes, that it would be a good idea to assemble them in Balangiga to assist in the work. O'Connell assented and a couple of days later eighty natives were brought in and lodged in conical tents in the vicinity of the soldiers' barracks. As was later determined, these men were picked bolomen from the guerrilla force of General Lucban.

In the evening of September 27, Lieutenant Bumpus with a detail of men, returned from the town of Basey, some twenty miles away, with the company mail. Basey was just across the narrow Sanjuanico Straits from the large town of Tacloban on the Island of Leyte. With Tacloban it contained a fairly large garrison. Company C of the 9th Infantry had received no mail for four months and the men were overjoyed at the large sack which Lieutenant Bumpus brought back with him. Also they learned for the first time of the assassination of President McKinley, some three weeks previous.

By 6:30 the following morning the company was up and about, the men anxious to read their mail. The native workmen were lining up near the barracks under the supervision of the civilian chief of police. On guard were three sentries. The remainder of the company was at breakfast at an outdoor kitchen about thirty yards from the barracks. The only time that the soldiers were permitted to move out of their barracks without a loaded rifle was while actually messing.

While everything was apparently quiet and according to routine, the native chief of police walked up to one of the sentries and without warning snatched the rifle from his hands and felled him with the butt. Immediately the bells in the town church rang, conch shells blew from the hills, and the entire male populace of Balangiga, assisted by the bolomen from Lucban's force, rushed Company C.

The few survivors of this massacre were able to give vivid details of what actually happened. The three sentries armed with rifles were dispatched in the twinkling of an eye. A native group hidden in the town church rushed the officers' quarters, which were in the convent across the street from the barracks. Captain O'Connell, caught in his pajamas, jumped from the second story window of his room, started to cross to the barracks, was beset by twenty or thirty bolomen and hacked to death. Lieutenant Bumpus was surprised sitting in a chair in his room, his mail on his lap. A bolo cut on the bridge of the nose severed the entire front part of his head. He was found in this position by the survivors. The Surgeon, Major Griswold, was overwhelmed and stabbed to death without having a Chinaman's chance.

Across the street the majority of the company were seated at mess tables and most of them were killed before they could get on their feet. The first sergeant was caught in the act of washing his mess kit and had his head split in two by a blow from an axe. One sergeant's head was completely severed from his body and fell in his plate. In his hands were grasped a knife and a fork. The company cook, one of the few survivors, had fortunately a few weapons at his disposal. He threw a pot of boiling coffee at the first group of natives who rushed him and then held them off by hurling all the canned goods he could reach. When these were exhausted, he grabbed a meat cleaver and fought his way towards the barracks where the rifles were located. The few men who had gained their feet and survived the first onslaught grabbed any weapon they could lay their hands on and tried to reach the barracks—picks, shovels, baseball bats, clubs, a bolo wrenched from a native's hand. Three men mounted a rock pile and defended themselves with rocks. Sergeant George F. Markley, a man of herculean proportions, though he was wounded, managed to reach the barracks by swinging his arms like a flail and kicking natives in the stomach. He obtained a rifle and began pumping Krag-Jorgeson bullets into the natives surrounding him. One soldier reached the barracks, but was grabbed by three natives, who threw him down under a shower of bolo cuts. His arms reaching out in a last effort touched a pistol thrown on the floor in the melee, and he was able to save his life by shooting his assailants.

Hopelessly outnumbered, the Americans were butchered like hogs. American brains and entrails strewed the plaza and barracks. A few who sought flight in the water nearby were hunted down in boats and boloed to death. Fifteen minutes after the attack started all but five of the seventy-four men in the company had either been killed or wounded. Of those wounded, twelve were able to be on their feet, and under the protection of Sergeant Markley's fire had managed to unite and gain possession of rifles. This small group, despite the disparity in numbers, by firing their rifles until they became too hot to hold, were finally able to drive the bolomen away from the immediate vicinity of the barracks.

A quick check indicated that the small group could not expect to hold the town. So a decision was made to escape by boat to the nearest American garrison. Under fire from the natives who had retired to a respectful distance, the senior survivor, Sergeant Bentron, loaded the group on five barotas which were found in the vicinity, and started towards Basey. The dead, fifty-six rifles and several thousand rounds of ammunition were left at Balangiga. Before leaving, at the cost of two more casualties, the survivors hauled down the American flag which flew over the city hall and took it with them.

The trip of the survivors to Basey was nearly as harrowing as the massacre itself. The barotas, small, narrow, canoe-like craft, whose equilibrium was maintained by outriggers, could be rowed only at a snail's pace. A short distance out, one barota containing four men filled up with water and slowly drifted back to shore. There two wounded men were boloed to death. The other two, by running for their lives and then hiding, finally managed to find another boat and put to sea where they were picked up the following day by a steamer. Another boat containing two men floated away from the rest and drifted into shore where its occupants were butchered to death. The other three boats contained enough unhurt men to row, and gradually worked their way along the coast towards Basey. At noon the water supply became exhausted and drinking salt water only increased the suffering of the wounded. Boats put out from shore, containing natives armed with spears and bolos. They intended to board the barotas but were held off only by the rifle fire of the few who were able to shoot. Several attempts to land were prevented by the appearance of large numbers of natives on the shore armed with spears and a few rifles. A school of sharks, attracted by the blood dripping from the boats, followed the beleaguered fleet. With only one man able to talk, the survivors reached Basey at 3:30 the following morning. Of the twenty-six survivors, twenty-two were wounded. Two had died en route.

Company G of the 9th Infantry, under Captain Edwin V. Bookmiller, was stationed at Basey. Bookmiller obtained the services of the steamer *Pittsburgh,* which was at Tacloban, and with fifty-five men of his company, immediately returned to Balangiga, arriving there at noon the same day. The Insurgents were driven from the town without difficulty, but the sight which met Bookmiller's eyes was not pretty to see. The barracks were on fire, consuming the bodies of the American soldiers there. Other bodies had been thrown down a well. The body of a sergeant and the company dog were found in the kitchen covered with flour. The eyes of the dog had been gouged out and replaced by stones. The body of Lieutenant Bumpus was found with his eyes gouged out and his face smeared with jam to attract ants. The bodies of American soldiers not burned in the barrack's fire were denuded of clothes and mutilated in one way or another. Captain Bookmiller buried the bodies of the three officers and twenty-nine enlisted men in the plaza, burned the town, and returned to Basey. Yet, surprised though they were, the Americans had sold their lives dearly. Some 250 Filipinos had been killed in the massacre. Company C's score was as follows:

Killed during the massacre	36
Wounded, died later	8
Wounded	22
Missing	4
Not wounded ......-..............	4
	—
Total present during massacre	74

Shortly thereafter Lucban issued a congratulatory proclamation to the natives of Balangiga and enjoined the citizens of other towns to follow their example. A similar attempt on Company E of the 9th Infantry in the town of Gandara on October 16, a short time later, using the same methods employed at Balangiga, was frustrated by the watchfulness of the garrison, but not until after ten Americans had been killed and six wounded.

The Balangiga incident, in the face of the growing peaceful conditions throughout the other parts of the Islands, called for strong measures of repression. The number of troops on the island was increased and the job of pacification given to Brigadier General Jacob ("Hell Roaring Jake") Smith. As General Smith was leaving for Samar, General Chaffee said to him:[37]

"We have lost 100 rifles at Balangiga and 25,000 rounds of ammunition. You must get them back. You can have $5000 gold.

Capture the arms if you can, buy them if you must; whichever course you adopt get them back."

As soon as he arrived at his headquarters, General Smith issued a proclamation to the officers of his command in which he said in part: [88]

> "The policy to be pursued in this brigade will be to wage war in the sharpest and most decisive manner possible. . . . . No civilized war however civilized can be carried on on a humanitarian basis. . . . . Every native whether in arms or living in the Pueblos will be regarded and treated as an enemy until he has conclusively shown that he is a friend. . . . . Neutrality must not be tolerated on the part of any native . . . . if not an active friend, he is an open enemy. . . . .

To separate further the sheep from the goats, General Smith established a policy of concentration. He issued notices that all natives living in the interior of the islands would present themselves to certain coastal towns. Those who did not respond would be treated as active enemies and shot without any questions being asked.

A battalion of Marines was sent to garrison the southern Ports of Samar and to assist in cleaning up the Island. The commanding officer of the Marines, Major Littleton W. T. Waller, a capable energetic officer, took his duties most seriously. It appears that General Smith instructed Major Waller in the methods he was to employ: "I want no prisoners. I wish you to burn and kill; the more you burn and kill the better it will please me."[39] Major Waller took the General at his word and undertook a campaign of death and pillage unique in the annals of American warfare. One of Major Waller's reports ran in part as follows:[40]

> "On the 7th (November) a party went out from Balangiga scouting to the northward and discovered an entrenchment with 30 rifles. The Insurgents fell back but the party was too small to follow, being only 20. They got shells and ammunition, all Krags. On the 8th sent a party to Eba to destroy it and kill or capture all men. They destroyed 40 houses, 3 carabaos and about one half ton of hemp, killed 9 men, captured 11. One of the captured men admitted that they were Insurrectos and stated that he had been fighting against us on the 6th.
>
> "On the 9th sent a party across the Cadacan River to follow the trails and destroy all houses. They destroyed 55 houses and killed 2 carabaos. Another party on the 10th destroyed 40 houses and 3 carabaos. Captain Porter took out an expedition and worked around his place for three days. He found strong entrenchments everywhere and many relics of the 9th Infantry. He destroyed 100 shacks, killed one man and captured 7. Resumé of the happenings: 255 houses burned, 39 men killed, 18

men captured, 17 bolos captured, 1 ton of hemp and one half
ton of rice destroyed, 13 carabaos killed, 50 bancas captured
(approximately)."

Late in December occurred another American tragedy on the
Island of Samar, the Marines this time being the principals. During
the last week in December, Major Waller with four officers and fifty
men of the Marine Corps, accompanied by thirty bearers, made a
brave but foolhardy attempt to cross the Island from Lanang on the
east coast directly across to Basey thirty-five miles distant. Incessant
rains, swollen streams, and other natural obstacles made progress
extremely slow. The trail became so faint in places that the small
band lost its way in the dense tropical jungles. Shortly thereafter the
limited rations being carried for what had promised to be a thirty-
five mile march, became exhausted, and men started falling out of
the column from weakness. Leaving the bulk of the company, Major
Waller with fifteen men pushed on ahead and finally reached Basey
on January 9, utterly exhausted. A relief expedition rushed back into
the mountains from Basey, but after searching for ten days returned
without having located the lost marines. Meanwhile on January 11
another officer of the company, Captain David Porter and two men
managed to find their way back to Lanang, arriving there in a starv-
ing and mentally disordered state. They reported that over thirty
men were still lost in the mountains, and Lieutenant Kenneth P.
Williams of the 1st Infantry stationed at Lanang immediately organized another relief expedition from that end. Pushing up the
Lanang River towards the interior in small boats, which were frequently overturned because of the swollen condition of the river
and further delayed by sporadic shots from Insurgents lurking in
the jungle depths, Williams finally located the remnants of the band
on January 18.

The twenty survivors were in a pitiful condition. All were virtually
naked; none had eaten for eighteen days. Eight of the number were
lying helpless on the ground, delirious with fever; the remainder
were on the verge of insanity, could not remember who they were
or where they had been. Lieutenant Williams carried them back to
Lanang where they were given medical treatment. Ten members of
the band were never located and undoubtedly died of starvation or
at the hands of the Insurgents.

Undeterred by this tragedy, American troops continued to push
into the mountains, using rivers as means of entry into the interior
wherever possible. Scores of natives were shot; hundreds of houses
burned.

Two months after he started to clean up Samar, Smith realized that Luckban was receiving assistance from outside the Island. Across the narrow Sanjuanico Straits on the Island of Leyte, civil government had been established. Although ostensibly peaceful and pro-American, the natives of Leyte were assisting Luckban in numerous and diverse ways. The strait between the Islands was so narrow that small boats could cross with ease; and rice, arms and ammunition were supplied to Lucban by sympathizers across the straits. Moreover several British hemp firms, of which the Smith-Bell Company of Manila was an outstanding example, insisted on continuing trading in hemp with the natives on Samar. Smith believed that it was the income derived from this trade which was enabling the Insurgents to continue their resistance.

In order to curb these activities, he issued an order cutting off all marine intercourse between Leyte and Samar. This immediately brought him into conflict with the American Civil Governor of Leyte, Mr. J. H. Grant. Governor Grant felt that Smith's preemptory orders affecting Leyte usurped his authority as civil governor. He pointed out to General Smith that Leyte was under civil jurisdiction and as such not subject to the orders of the military commander of the district. Smith replied to the effect that if Leyte was pacified and fit for civil government, no more troops should be necessary, and ordered the American troops on the Island off, leaving as the only protection a few civil native constabulary troops which Grant was organizing. Realizing that the absence of troops on Leyte was very apt to result in trouble, Grant called on Governor Taft for assistance. The matter was finally ironed out between Mr. Taft and General Chaffee, whose policy it was to bend over backwards in acknowledging the authority of the civil power in the Islands. The troops remained, and a supervised restricted boat trade between the Islands was permitted.

Smith's policy of blood and iron had its effect. Lucban's force was chased from one end of the Island to the other. It became scattered and Lucban became a fugitive. By February of 1902 conditions were such that Smith felt able to issue a proclamation authorizing the natives to return to their homes and relaxing many of the restrictions which had been placed upon them. Five days later Lucban himself was captured. By April the few Insurgents who remained in the field had surrendered, and henceforth peace reigned on the Island.

General Smith's career was not to have such a happy ending. While his stern policy in Samar was at its height, a newspaper man visited the Island and on his return to the United States published the details of the policy in force there. Various "Anti" societies fomented a wave of indignation at the way the poor Filipinos were being treated by the American soldiery and instigated another Congressional investigation. General Smith was brought to trial for conduct to the prejudice of good order of military discipline, found guilty by a military court and sentenced to be admonished. Shortly thereafter he was retired.

6

Whenever stories of the fighting in the Philippines are told around a campfire, the majority seem to center around the Moros. Possibly it is because the Moro is a Mohammedan with a romantic religious difference, or because he was one of the few tribes encountered in the Philippines who would stand up and fight. At any rate, the fighting with the Moros in the Philippines had always seemed to stir patriotic imagination. Actually, the Moros gave little trouble to the Americans. Any trouble which they caused was fear of the Christian Filipinos or simply plain restlessness born of their native customs.

The principal activities of the American garrisons on Mindanao and Jolo were concerned with keeping the Moros from fighting among themselves, or insisting that the age old custom of engaging in piracy be stopped. The political situation in Mindanao and Jolo was ably summed up by Colonel O. J. Sweet, commanding the district, in May 1901. Colonel Sweet reported:[41]

> "Our relations with the Sultans and Chiefs remains friendly. They will promise anything in the shape of reforms but these are never carried out. The best way to look out for No. 1 is their only object in life and every other interest is secondary to it. Nine out of ten of the population of the Islands would gladly renounce allegiance to the Sultans and Datos and swear allegiance to the United States. There can be no progress until the United States takes complete control of the Islands. Neither the Sultan or any Dato who is in line of succession to the Sultanate can make anything out of the country. They are bound up in traditions and to do anything their ancestors did not do would be wrong. In many things they are inferior to the American Indians and I know of no trait in which they are superior. The Sultan stands on his dignity and quotes erroneously from the Koran as to his duties of Sultan toward his people. So far I can find no case where he lives up to his model."

The principal duty of the American officers in the Moro countries was to prevent hot-headed Moro datos from taking the law into their own hands. On one occasion a dato shot a trader because he had sold some oranges to another man cheaper than he had to himself.

The correspondence between the American officers and Moro datos sometimes assumed a humorous aspect, as is indicated in the correspondence between Colonel Sweet and the Sultan of Jolo concerning the theft of the cemetery gates of the American garrison. The correspondence is in part as follows:[42]

> To his Highness the Sultan of Jolo, from his brother the Governor of Tiange, Greetings:
> Three nights ago the iron gates of the cemetery were stolen. Indications point to the Moros living in your territory as thieves. I desire you to make a thorough search for said gates and have them returned and the thieves punished. . . . . I do not know who committed this theft; if I did I would not call on you but would act myself. The thief was a Moro; this being the case it is your duty to act. The graves of our dead are respected. This act was worse than any of the acts so far reported and it was to a certain extent a desecration of our dead and will not be tolerated.
> Very Respectfully,
> O. J. Sweet
> Major 23rd Infantry, Military Governor

The Sultan's reply was as follows:

> This letter comes from your son the Sultan Hadji Mohammed Jamalul, Kiram to my father the Governor of Tiange:
> Your letter of the 23rd instant received and I understand its contents. I am very sorry indeed that the gates to the cemetery were stolen. It would have been better if the thief had robbed the property belonging to the living, because they have a chance to earn more but the dead have not. Therefore aid me to think how to get rid of stealing in this country. Let us inquire at all places where there are blacksmiths. There are no blacksmiths in Maibun. Above all you must closely examine the blacksmiths in the Buz Buz and Moubu as these gates were too heavy to be carried a long distance. Very likely they are in these two places. I will have a search made in all places where there are blacksmiths. If we find the thief let us bury him alive. I did not tell the thief to steal nor did he do it with my knowledge. You are an old man . . . . and perhaps you have pity on me. As for me I detest thieves. . . . . . .

The trouble between the Americans and Moros of Mindanao came primarily from two causes—the attempt of the Americans to stop the constant raiding and stealing going on between the various Moro tribes; and the exploration by American troops into the interior of Mindanao.

About sixteen miles from the north coast of Mindanao lay the large Lake Lanao, some twenty-two miles long. The shores were dotted with villages which contained a total population of some 100,000 Moros who maintained few contacts with the outside world and resented the intrusion of foreigners, particularly Christians. In 1891 the Spanish, using a force of 4000 men, had penetrated to the lake and undertaken the pacification of the surrounding area. Materials for constructing boats had been packed to the interior and several gunboats erected which cruised along the shore. When the Americans took over the Philippines, the area was by no means pacified and the disgruntled Spanish sunk all their boats in the lake before they left. As long as the Moros had attended to their own business the Americans had adopted a hands-off policy as far as the Lake Lanao Moros were concerned. Then during 1900 raiding parties began to appear from the lake, carried off friendly coastal Moros, and stole American owned horses. On several occasions they boloed American soldiers unfortunate enough to be caught out in small groups.

Brigadier General George W. Davis, commanding the department, sent messengers to all Datos in the neighborhood demanding that the stolen property be returned and that the murderers of American soldiers be turned over. Since the response from the representatives of the Lake Moros was decidedly hostile, an expedition to Lake Lanao was decided upon. The 27th Infantry, under the command of Colonel Frank Baldwin, with a battery of mountain artillery attached, forced its way twenty-five miles into the interior after having been forced virtually to construct a trail the entire distance. Near Lake Lanao in the territory of the Sultan of Bayang and the Dato of Bindayan, the Americans ran up against two Moro cottas, or forts, a relatively medieval type of defense but under the circumstances a distinct obstacle. Around the outside of the cotta was a line of trenches. The walls, ten feet high and several feet thick, were covered by a thick thorny growth so sharp that a ladder provided the only means of crossing. In embrasures around the fort the Moros had erected several brass cannon and had garrisoned the fort with several hundred men armed with rifles. The expedition fought its way up to the walls, but were stopped because they could not be scaled. Baldwin had to content himself with surrounding the fort and waiting until scaling ladders could be constructed during the night. The American soldiers were not particularly comfortable as is indicated in Colonel Baldwin's report:[43]

> "We had met with very serious losses having had one officer and nine enlisted men killed and three officers and thirty-seven enlisted men wounded, few of whom could be brought to the rear in daylight as the moment they showed themselves the bearers would be shot down. When night came it was intensely dark and it was found impracticable to move them until the following morning at daylight. . . . . Medical officers were on the field attending to the wounded as best they could. Added to the misery of the situation both for wounded and men on the line, a heavy rain set in which lasted all night long. The suffering of these wounded men, having to lie on the battlefield as they did, could not be alleviated and would have been made more aggravated had an effort been made to move them to the rear during the darkness, as the country to be traversed was filled with pitfalls, sharpened stakes, and ditches covered with grass."

The American force was much relieved to find white flags flying over the cotta at daybreak, and after short negotiations the Moros surrendered.

After this lesson the Lake Datos came in and established friendly relations. A few remained recalcitrant, however, and continued the practice of annoyance and attack. Between May and September American garrisons were attacked twelve times with a loss of four killed and twelve wounded.

In September, 1903, an expedition under the command of Captain John J. Pershing made a tour of the area, severely punishing the Maciu Moros, and in 1905 Captain Frank R. McCoy led a punitive expedition into the Cottabatto Valley destroying many of their cottas. The Moros were comparatively quiet for the next year, but sporadic uprisings took place in 1906 at Bud Dojo on the Island of Jolo. Even today the Philippine Constabulary has to attack a Moro cotta occasionally to punish law-breaking.

7

To all intents and purposes the Islands were virtually in a state of pacification when shocking conditions were found to exist in the provinces of Batangas, Laguna and Tayabas, a short distance south of Manila. Under the influence of General Miguel Malvar, the natives of this area were found carrying on a dual government even worse than that at the height of the guerilla warfare. The only explanation for this state of affairs is the fact the Americans had been completely hoodwinked. True, it was known that Malvar controlled isolated bodies of guerrillas who occasionally harassed the American garrisons, but it was generally believed that the people living in the towns were heart and soul behind the American administration. The facts came to light in a rather unusual manner. Colonel Cornelius Gardner of the 30th Infantry, in command of the American garrison at Tiaong in Tayabas, had instituted a policy of extreme leniency towards the natives. The province having been placed under civil rule and the natives had elected as the governor of the province their friend and protector, Colonel Gardner. In the exercise of his duties as civil governor, Colonel Gardner arrived at the conclusion that the natives under his jurisdiction were being mistreated by the American soldiery and complained directly to Governor Taft. The report got to Washington, and coming from an army officer as it did, caused another uproar and investigation. Placed somewhat on the defensive by Colonel Gardner's accusations, the military, through secret service and other means, unearthed the shocking state of affairs.

It was found that in May of 1901, the Insurgents had held a junta and had sent word to the American authorities that they wanted to organize Tiong under civil government. All appointive offices in the town were allotted to guerrilla leaders.[44] To an Insurgent colonel was allotted the organization of the police force, whose principal duty was to notify the Insurgents of American movements. One half the profits of supplies sold to American troops was to go to the Ingents. No natives of military age were permitted to be married except upon the contribution of thirty pesos or a rifle. One tenth of all argricultural produce was exacted from the farmers. Nothing could be carried to market without the farmer paying a highway tax to armed guerrillas who patrolled the road. Brass bands had to give half of their earnings to the insurrection. All natives who drew a salary from the American government were forced to contribute a large portion to the Insurgents. The town padre regularly contributed a portion of the church tithes to the Insurrection and natives were secretly licensed to gamble in private houses. In the three provinces of Cavite, Tayabas and Batangas, Malvar was purported to have some 5000 guerrillas off and on in the field.

The duplicity of the Filipinos and the gullibility of the Americans combined to establish this condition of affairs. The record of the Vice Presidente of Tiaong is an indication of the characters with whom the Americans were forced to deal. This man, Isidoro Argao, had surrendered in 1900, lived in the town a while, and then rejoined the Insurgents, accepting a commission as captain. In 1901 he again surrendered and took the oath of allegiance to the United States. He then contributed money to the Insurgents and furnished them information as to the movements of American troops. On one occasion he advised the American commander of the garrison that he could lead the troops to an Insurgent camp. While the garrison was absent, the Insurgents attacked the town; and, needless to say, Argao was "unable to fine the camp." This renegade was finally caught up with and thrown into jail.

The situation as revealed called for drastic action, and it was turned over to Brigadier General James F. Bell, the former Provost Marshal of Manila. General Bell threw aside any idea of a policy of attraction, since he realized that the only way to break Malvar's influence was to make the natives fear American authority more than they did Malvar's. Conseqently the policy of reconcentration was established in the province of Batangas and those portions of the adjoining provinces where it was certain that Malvar's influence was predominant. Around each sizable town which contained an American garrison a boundary line was drawn. The area was extended to permit large numbers of families to live therein. If they desired, the natives were authorized to move their houses within the zone. Areas were set aside for the grazing of cattle. These areas around the towns were carefully patrolled by American troops. All natives were directed to come within the protected areas at once and settle themselves. They were permitted to settle on private property without paying rent. Bell advised that all food supplies found outside the protected zones would be confiscated and that any natives who refused to accept the protection of the Americans would be classed as enemies. Troops then scoured the countrysides and confiscated every bit of food or military supplies that could be found. That which could not be brought into the towns was destroyed. In the protected areas able-bodied men were not permitted to leave the town except in dire emergencies and then only by written pass. In the towns the natives were required to be off the streets by 8:oo p. m. Natives who desired to reap standing crops on their former homes were allowed to work there under protective guard. A proclamation was issued that in the future whenever an American soldier or loyal native was assassinated, an Insurrecto prisoner would be chosen by lot and executed. Rifles were taken from the hands of native municipal police. Whenever army property or telegraph lines were destroyed, native houses in the vicinity were destroyed.

Thousands of natives flocked into the protected areas, many of them impoverished. As a shortage of food became imminent, paupers were permitted to accompany scouting expeditions and, when a cache of food was found, were allowed to take it back to the town. Later the government sold rice to the natives at cost price. Able-bodied men were required to work on provincial roads. The wealthy were excused upon the payment of money, which went for the purchase of rice for the impoverished. The reconcentration policy had a marked effect on the Insurgents. As General Bell reported:[45]

> "People had no sooner entered zones of protection than the Insurgents became greatly alarmed and aroused and the result was felt by increased activity and resentment on their part . . . During December (1901) we had some sharp engagements and a number of unimportant skirmishes but this activity resulted in such vigorous and relentless pursuit that the enemy became thoroughly demoralized and after the 10th of January there was no armed encounter worthy of record here."

The American troops went after Malvar with all the enthusiasm at their command and finally forced his surrender in April of 1902. These last campaigns of the Insurrection taxed the energy and endurance of the troops, who scoured every foot of territory in the area. As General Bell finally reported:[45]

> "We continued to pursue them with relentless persistence. Not waiting for them to come out of hiding we penetrated into the heart of every mountain range, searching every ravine and mountain top. We continually found their barracks and hidden food in the most unexpected and remote hiding places. We burned hundreds of small barracks and shelters as fast as they could construct them. We destroyed their clothing and supplies and pursued them so persistently that they finally ceased to stay more than twenty-four hours in one place. . . . . . .
> "We maintained as many as 4000 troops in the field at once, keeping them supplied in mountains where no roads existed. They camped by companies at strategic points on trails . . . . each sending out detachments radiating from the base. In this way it was rendered unsafe for Insurgents to travel at any time and having no longer a safe retreat in which to hide themselves, they became so scattered and demoralized that they continued to surrender and be captured by wholesale.
> "By this method we succeeded in securing and sending into towns or destroying almost every pound of food which the Insurgents possessed or could obtain and about the first of April it became exceedingly difficult for them to maintain themselves. Their appearance indicated great want and suffering and a number were so sick when captured as to need medical attention.
> "It must not be supposed, however, that we were able to continue such operations so persistently without cost to our own men, many of whom came down with fever, dysentery and other

complaints. Though we had managed to keep them supplied with food, it was impossible to get sufficient clothing to them. Because of the destructive effect of mountain brush and rocks, nearly all became ragged and many almost barefooted . . . ."

General Malvar had time and time again been invited to surrender. His consistent refusal made necessary the rigorous reconcentration policy outlined above. He would have done much better and saved the compatriots, whom he claimed to love so dearly, much suffering had he surrendered at the start instead of forcing the Americans to hunt him down like an animal. With the capture of Malvar, opposition in the affected provinces collapsed and the Insurrection was, in reality, finished.

Later General Bell was thoroughly criticized for the vigorous reconcentration policy he had adopted in Batangas, but was not brought to trial as had been General Smith.

By July of 1902 the number of occupied stations had dropped from the maximum number of 552 to 195. The number of troops in the Philippines had dropped from the maximum of 70,000 to 34,000; peace was in the air.

Although the army had pacified the Islands to the extent that civil government could be inaugurated, the necessity for an armed law enforcement agency still existed. Native bandits could and did organize small bands of *pulajanes* and made travel unsafe particularly in the thickly vegetated mountainous districts. In 1902 there was organized the Philippine Constabulary which was defined as:[46]

"The armed police force of the government of the Philippine Islands, established and administered under the general supervision of the Governor General for the purpose of maintaining order, preventing and detecting crime, and enforcing the laws."

The Constabulary was organized on a military basis and its units distributed throughout the Islands. For officers it drew upon members of the American army or upon civilians in the United States who were graduates of accredited colleges. The various Filipino native tribes furnished its rank and file, outstanding natives being gradually raised to officer rank.

Systematized under the supervision of Major (later Major General) Henry T. Allen, the Constabulary proved its worth countless times. Marching in small groups over narrow mountain trails, through dense tropical jungles, facing death at every turn, occasionally being forced to call on the regular army garrisons for assistance, it rooted out the last vestiges of disorder in the Islands. Several of its officers notably Major Generals, Henry T. Allen, William C. Rivers, Harry H. Bandholtz and James G. Harbord became outstanding military leaders in the American army during the World War. The epic of the Constabulary has been related in several books of recent publication.[47]

On July 4, 1902, President Roosevelt issued a proclamation announcing the establishment of peace, and an amnesty to all who would take the oath of allegiance to the United States, and the establishment of civil government throughout the Christian-inhabited portions of the Islands. Except for ordinary peacetime pursuits the work of the army was at an end, and the military faded into the background of the Philippine picture.

On the same day that the civil power assumed supreme control the President also issued a proclamation of thanks to the Army. The proclamation is such an able synopsis of what the army did in the Philippines that it is published here in part as the closing passage of this book. Said President Roosevelt:[48]

"The President thanks the officers and enlisted men of the army in the Philippines, both regulars and volunteers for the courage and fortitude, the indomitable spirit, and loyal devotion with which they have put down and ended the great Insurrection which has raged throughout the Archipelago against the lawful sovereignty and just authority of the United States. The task was peculiarly difficult and trying. They were required at first to overcome organized resistance of superior numbers, well-equipped with modern arms of precision, entrenched in an unknown country of mountain defiles, jungles and swamps apparently capable of interminable defense. When this resistance had been overcome they were required to crush out a general system of guerrilla warfare conducted among people speaking unknown tongues from whom it was almost impossible to obtain the information necessary for successful pursuit or to guard against surprise or ambush.

The enemies by whom they were surrounded were regardless of all obligations of good faith and of all limitations which humanity has imposed upon civilized warfare. Bound themselves by the laws of war, our soldiers were called upon to meet every device of unscrupulous treachery and to contemplate without reprisal the infliction of barbarous cruelties upon their comrades and friendly natives. They were instructed while punishing armed resistance to conciliate the friendship of the peaceful, yet had to do with a population among whom it was impossible to distinguish friend from foe and who in countless instances used a false appearance of friendship for ambush and assassination. They were obliged to deal with problems

284

of communication and transportation in a country without roads and frequently made impassable by torrential rains. They were weakened by tropical heat and tropical disease. Widely scattered over a large archipelago extending a thousand miles from north to south, the gravest responsibilities involving the life or death of their commands frequently devolved upon young or inexperienced officers beyond the reach of specific orders or advice . . . .

Under all these adverse circumstances, the Army of the Philippines has accomplished its task rapidly and completely. In more than two thousand combats, great and small, within three years it has exhibited unvarying courage and resolution . . . . It has submitted to no discouragement and halted at no obstacle. Its splendid virile energy has been accompanied by self-control, patience and magnanimity . . . . . . .It has added honor to the flag which it defended and has justified increased confidence in the future of the American people, whose soldiers do not shrink from labor or death, yet love liberty and peace.

The President feels that he expresses the sentiments of all the loyal people of the United States in doing honor to the whole army which has joined in the performance and shares in the credit of these honorable services.

Notes on Chapter XI

1 cf Leslies Weekly, June 16, 1900 p. 462
2 cf HD No. 2 Vol. 4 57th 1st p. 74
3 cf HD No. 2 Vol. 6 56th 2nd p. 60
4 cf HD No. 2 Vol. 6 56th 2nd p. 72
5 As told the writer by Major General Herbert J. Brees, then a 1st Lieutenant in the 9th Cavalry.
6 cf HD No. 2 Vol. 7 56th 2nd p. 783 ff
7 cf HD No. 2 Vol. 8 56th 2nd p. 430
8 cf HD No. 2 Vol. 8 56th 2nd p. 425
9 cf LeRoy, James, "The Americans in the Philippines" Vol. II p. 201
10 For full text of Instructions see HD No. 2 Vol. 2 56th 2nd p. 72
11 cf HD No. 2 Vol. 6 56th 2nd p. 61 ff
12 cf For full text see HD No. 2 Vol. 6 56th 2nd p. 65
13 cf HD No. 2 Vol. 6 56th 2nd p. 227
14 cf HD No. 2 Vol. 8 56th 2nd p. 407
15 cf HD No. 2 Vol. 6 57th 1st p. 31
16 Ibid p. 356
17 cf Facts about the Filipinos Vol. 1 No. 10 p. 17
18 cf HD No. 2 Vol. 5 57th 1st p. 98
19 cf Facts about the Filipinos Vol. 1 No. 10 p. 48
20 cf HD No. 2 Vol. 5 57th 1st p. 91
21 cf Ibid p. 93
22 cf Outlook Magazine March 25, 1899 p. 698
23 cf Chamberlain, "The Blow from Behind" p. 74
24 cf LeRoy, op. cit. Vol. ii p. 317
25 cf Nation Magazine, Issue of January 17, 1901, p. 39

26 *cf* Chamberlain, *op. cit.* p. 108
27 For full details see HD No. 2 Vol. 5 57th 1st p. 123
28 *cf* HD No. 2 Vol. 6 57th 1st p. 435
29 *cf* Facts about the Filipinos Vol. 1 No. 10 p. 103
30 *cf* HD No. 2 Vol. 5 57th 1st p. 99
31 *cf* Funston, "Memory of Two Wars" p. 389
32 *cf* Ibid p. 407
33 *cf* Ibid p. 412 ff
34 *cf* For full text see HD No. 2 Vol. 5 57th 1st p. 100
35 *cf* HD No. 2 Vol. 8 57th 1st p. 19 *et. seq.*
36 *cf* HD No. 2 Vol. 5 57th 1st p. 97
37 *cf* HD No. 2 Vol. 12 57th 2nd p. 188
38 Ibid p. 208
39 *cf* Secretary Root's record—a pamphlet published by George H. Ellis Co., Printer's, Boston
40 *cf* HD No. 2 Vol. 12 57th 2nd p. 441
41 *cf* HD No. 2 Vol. 7 57th 1st p. 339
42 *cf* HD No. 2 Vol. 7 57th 1st p. 356 *et. seq.*
43 *cf* HD No. 2 Vol. 12 57th 2nd p. 571
44 *cf* HD No. 2 Vol. 12 57th 2nd p. 229 *et. seq.*
45 *cf* HD No. 2 Vol. 12 57th 2nd p. 271
46 Manual for the Philippine Constabulary, 1915 page 9
47 Particularly *Bullets and Bolos* by John R. White and *Jungle Patrol* by Vic Hurley
48 *cf* HD No. 2 Vol. 4 57th 2nd p. 15

PRIMARY SOURCES, BIBLIOGRAPHY

Documents of the United States Senate

56TH CONGRESS, 1ST SESSION, 1899-1900

Document No. 138, Volumes 44, 45, 46, Report of the 1st (Schurman) Philippine Commission

Documents No. 171 to 208, Volume 12, Miscellaneous

Document No. 221, Volumes 17, 18, 19, 20, 21, 22, 23, 24, Conduct of the War Department in the War with Spain.

57TH CONGRESS, 2ND SESSION, 1901-1902

Document No. 205, Volume 15, Charges of Cruelty in the Philippines

Document No. 280, Volume 21, Gazetteer of the Philippine Islands

Document No. 331, Hearings before the Senate Committee on the Philippines, 3 Vols.

Documents of The House of Representatives

55TH CONGRESS, 3RD SESSION, 1898-1899

Document No. 2, Volume 3, Report of War Department, Major General Commanding the Army

Document No. 2, Volume 10, Report of War Department, Ordnance

Document No. 136 and 268 (bound together), Volume 66, Army and Navy Register, 1899

56TH CONGRESS, 1ST SESSION, 1899-1900

Document No. 1, Volume 1, Presidents Message and Foreign Relations

Document No. 2, Volume 2, Report of War Department, Secretary

Document No. 2, Volume 3, Report of War Department, Chiefs of Bureaus

Document No. 2, Volumes 4, 5, and 6, Report of War Department, Major General Commanding Army

Documents No. 249 and 360 (bound together) Army and Navy Register, 1900

56TH CONGRESS, 2ND SESSION, 1900-1901

Document No. 1, Volume 1, Presidents Message and Foreign Relations

Document No. 2, Volume 2, Report of War Department, Secretary

Document No. 2, Volume 3, Report of War Department, Chiefs of Bureaus

Document No. 2, Volumes 4, 5, 6, 7, 8, 9, 10, and 11, Report of War Department, Lieutenant General Commanding the Army

Document No. 2, Volume 23, Report of War Department, Ordnance

57TH CONGRESS, 1ST SESSION, 1901-1902

Document No. 2, Volume 3, Report of War Department, Chiefs of Bureaus

Document No. 2, Volumes 4, 5, 6, 7, and 8, Report of War Department, Lieutenant General Commanding the Army

57TH CONGRESS, 2ND SESSION, 1902-1903

Document No. 1, Volume 1, Presidents Message and Foreign Relations

Document No. 2, Volume 4, Report of War Department, Secretary and Bureau Chiefs

Document No. 2, Volume 12, Report of War Department, Lieutenant General Commanding the Army

Document No. 2, Volumes, 13, 14, and 15, Report of the War Department, Philippine Commission, 3rd Report

ADJUTANT GENERAL, U. S. ARMY

Correspondence relating to Philippine Islands from May 3, 1898 to July 30, 1902, 2 Volumes, Washington, 1903

American Decorations, Washington, 1927

BIBLIOGRAPHY LIST (Secondary Sources)

ADAMS, CHARLES F. AND OTHERS, *Root's Record in Philippine Warfare*, Boston, 1902

AGUINALDO, EMILIO Y FAMY, *True Version of the Philippine Revolution*, Tarlac (P. I.) 1899

BELLAIRS, EDGAR G., *As it is in the Philippines*, New York, 1902

BLOUNT, JAMES H., *The American Occupation of the Philippines*,
New York, 1912

CHAMBERLAIN, FREDERICK C., *The Blow from Behind*, Boston, 1903

CRAIG, AUSTIN, (Editor), *The Former Philippines Through Foreign
Eyes*, New York, 1917

DAVIS, OSCAR K., *Our Conquests in the Pacific*, New York, 1899

DEWEY, GEORGE, *Autiobiography*, New York, 1913

FREEMAN, N. N., *A Soldier in the Philippines*, New York, 1901

FISKE, BRADLEY A., *Wartime in Manila*, Boston, 1913

FUNSTON, FREDERICK, *Memories of Two Wars*, New York, 1911

GANOE, W. A., *The History of The United States Army*, New York,
1924.

HALSTEAD, MURAT, *The Story of the Philippines*, New York, 1898

HART, ROBERT W., *The Philippines Today*, New York, 1928

LEONARD, JOHN W., (Editor) *Who's Who in America*, Chicago, 1899

LEROY, JAMES A., *The Americans in the Philippines*, Cambridge,
1914, 2 Vols.

MABEY, CHARLES R., *The Utah Batteries*, Salt Lake City, 1900

MILLET, F. D., *The Expedition to the Philippines*, New York, 1899

NEELY, F. T., *Fighting in the Philippines*, New York, 1899

PARKER, JAMES, *The Old Army*, Philadelphia, 1929

PENN, JULIUS A., *A Narrative of the Campaign in Northern Luzon
of the 2nd Battalion, 34th U. S. Volunteer Infantry*, 1933

PHILIPPINE INFORMATION SOCIETY, *Facts About the Filipinos, A series
of Ten Pamphlets*, Boston, 1901

ROBINSON, ALBERT G., *The Philippines, The War and the People*,
New York, 1901

SONNICHSEN, ALBERT, *10 Months a Captive Among Filipinos*, New
York, 1901

SPAULDING, OLIVER L., *The United States Army in War and Peace*,
New York, 1937

STOREY, MOREFIELD AND LICHAUCO, MARCIAL, *The Conquest of the Philippines by the United States*, New York, 1926

TAYLOR, JAMES O., (Editor), *The Massacre of Balangiga*, Joplin, Mo., 1931

VILLAMOR, JUAN, *Unpublished Chronicle of the American Filipino War in Northern Luzon*, Manila, 1924

WORCESTER, DEAN, *The Philippines, Past and Present*, New York, 1914, 2 Vols.

JERNEGAN, PRESCOTT F., *1001 Questions and Answers on Philippine History and Civil Government*, Manila, 1908

FORBES, CAMERON, *The Philippine Islands*, 2 Vols., New York, 1928

MOLINARI, GUSTAVE, *The Society of Tomorrow*, New York, 1904

BROWN, FREDERICK R., *History of the 9th U. S. Infantry*, Chicago, 1909

SORLEY, L. S., *History of the 14th U. S. Infantry*, Chicago, 1909

SMITH, O. M. (and others), *History of the 22nd U. S. Infantry*.

MCALEXANDER, U. G., *History of the 13th Regiment of United States Infantry*, 1905

CEREZO, MARTIN, *Under the Red and Gold*.

MILLIS, JAMES, *The Martial Spirit*.

ACKNOWLEDGMENTS

It is my desire to express my deep gratitude to the number of friends who have in one way or another assisted in the preparation of this book. I shall always be indebted to Major General Upton Birnie, Jr., late Chief of Field Artillery and Major General E. E. Booth, then Commanding the Department of the Philippines, for their encouragement and assistance when the idea was at its inception. I owe thanks to Captain Richard W. Gibson, Air Corps for his patience and assistance in locating the erstwhile battlefields in and around Manila. Profound thanks are due Mr. E. B. Rodriguez, then Assistant Librarian of the National Library of the Philippines for assistance in locating references and acting as interpreter in interviews with ex-Insurgent leaders.

I am indebted to Dr. Walter C. Langsam, of the History Department at Columbia University, for a keen and critical review of the manuscript while in its early stages.

I find it difficult to express my obligation to Captain Thomas M. Watlington of the Department of English at the United States Military Academy, who went over the manuscript in a meticulous and painstaking manner, criticizing it thoroughly as to organization and composition, and offering many helpful suggestions.

I wish to express my appreciation to Lieutenant Colonel Elbert E. Farman, Librarian of the United States Military Academy, and the entire staff of the West Point Library for their cheerful courtesy and great assistance in locating source material.

I also wish to express my deep thanks to Captain T. M. Osborne, Corps of Engineers; and to Corporal Krasnoborski, of the Department of Military Engineering, United States Military Academy, for the execution of the maps.

I wish to thank Captain Gerald F. Lillard and Lieutenant John A. Berry for going over the manuscript and correcting the many errors in diction and punctuation, and Captain John M. Roosma, Infantry, and Captain Clarence Clendenin, Cavalry for critical reviews.

I am deeply indebted to Major General Frank McCoy and Brigadier General Ernest D. Scott for the time which they gave to reading the manuscript and the many helpful suggestions they contributed.

Special thanks are due Major R. Ernest Dupuy, Public Relations Officer at West Point, not only for his critical review of the manuscript but for his wise counsel in the preparation of the final draft.

I wish to express my deep gratitude to Lieutenant Colonel Herman Beukema, the Professor of History at the United States Military Academy, not only for many helpful hints but for the inspiring leadership which motivated me to complete the project.

And finally I wish to thank Ila Gray Packard for her valuable and scrupulous secretarial work, and my wife, Maude Albright Sexton for her assistance and patience throughout the years during which this book was being written.

West Point, New York

May 28, 1939

INDEX *

State volunteer regiments are listed alphabetically by states.
Regular army and U. S. volunteer regiments are listed according to their numerical designations.

INDEX

Taft, William Howard, 246ff, 266ff, 275
Tagalog Scouts, 176ff
Tagudin, Luz., 206ff
Taguig River, Luz., 106
Talavera, Luz., 182ff
Tangadin, Luz., 206ff
Taong River, Luz., 147
Tarlac, Luz., 70, 140, 180, 195ff, 245
Tayabas, Luz., 69, 229
Taytay, Luz., 150ff
Tayug, Luz., 175, 182
Taylor, Lieut. J. D., 260
Tennessee Vols., 95, 162
Teresa, Luz., 151
Third Artillery, 36, 90, 92ff, 109, 113ff, 142ff, 168
Third Cavalry, 176ff
Third Infantry, 103, 108, 130ff, 200
Thirteenth Infantry, 153ff, 159ff, 188ff
Thirtieth Infantry, 228ff
Thirty-eighth Inf., 225ff
Thirty-fourth Inf., 176ff, 206ff
Thirty-ninth Inf., 226ff
Thirty-second Inf., 200
Thirty-seventh Inf., 176ff, 225ff, 249ff
Thirty-sixth Inf., 169ff, 198ff
Thirty-third Inf., 188ff, 189ff
Thomas, Lieut. Bissel, 241
Tila Pass, Luz., 207ff
Tinio, Gen. Manuel, 139, 186ff, 206ff, 265
Tinuba, Luz., 243ff
Tirona, Gen. Daniel, 218ff
Tondo, District of Manila, 101ff
Trembly, W. B., 144ff
Trias, Gen. Manuel, 158, 160, 226, 249, 259
Tubao, Luz., 203ff
Tuguegarao, Luz., 218
Tuliahan River, Luz., 113ff, 131
Twelfth Inf., 153ff, 168ff, 191ff
Twentieth Inf., 103, 105, 224ff
Twenty-eighth Inf., 225ff
Twenty-fifth Inf., 164, 199ff
Twenty-first Inf., 153ff
Twenty-fourth Inf., 164, 176ff, 215ff
Twenty-ninth Inf., 250ff

Twenty-second Inf., 103, 105, 114, 130ff, 168ff, 176ff, 219ff
Twenty-seventh Inf., 278ff
Twenty-third Inf., 24, 104

U

Utah Vols., 24, 38, 90, 108, 142ff, 162

V

Vandvit, P., 137, 213
Van Houton, Capt. C. P., 116
Vicksburg USS., 262ff
Vigan, Luz., 204ff
Villa, Dr. Simeon, 186ff, 203
Villasis, Luz., 185
Virac, Catanduanes, 233

W

Walcott, Capt., C. C., 125ff
Waller, Maj. L. W. T., 274ff
Walton, W., 137, 213
Washington Vols., 90ff, 105, 150ff, 162
Water Cure, 240ff
Wessels, Col. H. W., 184ff, 200
Wheaton, Gen. L. V., 105, 108, 142ff, 153ff, 168ff, 174, 188ff, 225ff, 242
Wheeler, Gen. J. W., 192ff
White, Edward, 144ff
Wholly, Col. James, 150ff
Wilde, Commander, U. S. N., 204ff
Williams, Lieut. K. P., 274
Wise, Maj., 249
Worcester, Dean C., 127, 246
Wright, Luke E., 246
Wyoming Vols., 23, 90ff, 150ff, 162

Y

Young, W. H., 135ff
Young, Gen. S. B. M., 176ff, 200ff, 251
Yorktown USS., 137, 139

Z

Zamboanga, Mind., 236
Zapote River, Luz., 155ff